The Just War Myth

The Just War Myth

The Moral Illusions of War

Andrew Fiala

ROWMAN & LITTLEFIELD PUBLISHERS, INC.
Lanham • Boulder • New York • Toronto • Plymouth, UK

ROWMAN & LITTLEFIELD PUBLISHERS, INC.

Published in the United States of America
by Rowman & Littlefield Publishers, Inc.
A wholly owned subsidiary of The Rowman & Littlefield Publishing Group, Inc.
4501 Forbes Boulevard, Suite 200, Lanham, Maryland 20706
www.rowmanlittlefield.com

Estover Road
Plymouth PL6 7PY
United Kingdom

British Library Cataloguing in Publication Information Available

Library of Congress Cataloging-in-Publication Data:
Fiala, Andrew G. (Andrew Gordon), 1966-
 The just war myth : the moral illusions of war / Andrew Fiala.
  p. cm.
 Includes bibliographical references and index.
 ISBN-13: 978-0-7425-6200-4 (cloth : alk. paper)
 ISBN-10: 0-7425-6200-X (cloth : alk. paper)
 ISBN-13: 978-0-7425-6201-1 (pbk. : alk. paper)
 ISBN-10: 0-7425-6201-8 (pbk. : alk. paper)
 1. Just war doctrine. I. Title.
 B105.W3F53 2008
 172'.42—dc22   2007035796

Printed in the United States of America

⊚™ The paper used in this publication meets the minimum requirements of
American National Standard for Information Sciences—Permanence of Paper
for Printed Library Materials, ANSI/NISO Z39.48-1992

Contents

Preface

My friend, you would not tell with such high zest
To children ardent for some desperate glory
The old Lie: *Dulce et decorum est
Pro patria mori.*

—Wilfred Owen

The purpose of this book is to reduce our zeal for war and our enthusiasm for what I call the just war myth. When we romanticize the idea of the just war, we forget how difficult it is to actually fight one. Just war principles are always applied by finite human beings who are tempted to believe the old lies of war: that war is a noble endeavor and that the wars *we* fight are unequivocally just.

Recent history shows us that those in power can abuse our willingness to believe in the idea of the just war. Our faith in the just war myth is what led us to war in Afghanistan and Iraq. Defenders of these wars—including President George W. Bush—used just war concepts to argue that these wars were necessary and good. And, especially with regard to Iraq, the argument was based on distortion, exaggeration, and deception. An optimistic analysis of the tragedy of the last several years would say that defenders of the Bush Doctrine were high-minded patriots who let their idealism about justice and war get the better of their judgment. A more cynical analysis would call the architects of the Iraq war criminals and rogues who hid their vicious motives behind the mask of the just war theory. In either case, this overzealous employment

vii

of the just war myth shows us the danger. Just war principles are easily misapplied by both idealists and scoundrels. And a credulous population, who wants to believe the mythic idealism of justice in war, is all too willing to accept these sorts of arguments.

We have made progress since Wilfred Owen spoke of the old lies of patriotic war. Western democratic nations have come a long way from the bad old days of aggressive nationalism, racism, and blatant imperialism. We are more closely attuned to moral principles. And we are aware that war needs to be controlled by principles of justice. But we have not come far enough. We continue to ask our children to die—and to kill—for lies.

This is true despite the fact that we are more sensitive to the demands of morality. Most serious moral thinkers generally accept the principles of the just war theory; politicians employ its concepts; and the military academies teach its basic doctrines. Realism—the idea that moral principles simply do not apply in war or in international relations—is not considered as a morally serious alternative. Michael Walzer, the most important current defender of the just war ideal, celebrates this fact by describing what he calls "the triumph" of just war theory.[1] Yes, we are making progress. But to claim that the just war theory is "triumphant" is an exaggeration, since despite our commitment to just war principles, we clearly do fight unjust wars.

The invasion of Iraq shows us this problem. The justification of the war involved extensive use of just war ideas. It is a sign of progress that the American public and the international community demanded just war arguments in support of the war. But where wisdom would have counseled temperance, patience, modesty, and self-criticism, the Bush administration justified war in a spirit of impatience and arrogance. This shows us how just war concepts function in political reality. They are applied by finite persons afflicted by hubris and myopia and motivated by self-interest. The case of Iraq shows us how easy it is to manipulate just war concepts to suit a political agenda.

The Bush administration had decided to invade Iraq soon after 9/11, and they searched for a justification of this war. This search for a justification involved both a manipulation of the empirical evidence and a search among just war concepts. And it included a politicized effort to change our basic principles about justice in war. The war on terrorism has given us, for example, more permissive ideas about preemptive self-defense, humanitarian intervention, torture, and the treatment of prisoners.

This is the reality of war. Politicians use just war concepts to justify wars that are often chosen for other less noble reasons, and they can use war as an excuse for expanding and consolidating power. But even if we do not want to be so cynical about our leaders' motives, we must realize that the just war theory can become a crutch that props up bad decisions. The practical political problem is that it is very difficult to be against a war that is supposed to be "just." And so, just war arguments can become self-fulfilling ideas: if the war is supposed to be just, then it would be wrong to oppose it. But once our children are killing and dying, social and political inertia make it tough to think critically about the justice of war.

In reality, the just war *myth* will be employed as political myths are generally employed. These myths explain and provide rationalizations of political actions that are more complex and sordid than the mythic explanation allows. Most of us do not dare probe too deeply into these myths. Momentous political decisions like war seem to require patriotic solidarity. To question these myths is to undermine the facade of unity and moral purpose that allows public life to go on. Community spirit appears to require us to simply believe these myths.

However, the just war *theory* is most properly understood as a critical theory. Its principles remind us to be critical of war. As I understand it, the just war theory should be used to evaluate war and to show how difficult it is to actually fight a just war. But when we simplistically assume that our leaders and our military forces are making just decisions, the just war theory can be used as a shield to fend off such judgments. This is how the just war *myth* is usually employed: it shelters war from criticism.

Moral theories show us the way through the darkness. They are attempts to see more clearly. But there is a distance between the noble intention of a theory and the reality of its application. Some theories try to account for this problem by talking about the importance of intention. Indeed, the just war theory holds that just wars must be guided by "right intention." This is an important factor. But the difficulty is that intentions can be vague, changeable, and hidden from view. We don't know the true intentions of our leaders (and they may not know their own intentions). Just wars are supposed to be fought by people with noble intentions. But the belief that wars are actually motivated by noble intentions is itself a piece of political mythology. Americans like to believe that the motives guiding the wars we have fought were always pure and just. But this myth proves false. The reality is that self-interested actions are often disguised beneath the language of just intentions.

The just war theory developed out of early Christian pacifism. For Christians, intention is key. Jesus reminded his followers, for example, that it was not enough to avoid adultery or murder. Rather, one's mind must be pure: it was a sin to look at a woman with lust in your heart and it was a sin to be angry with your brother. When Christians, like Augustine, began thinking about the justification of war in the fourth and fifth centuries, they emphasized intention. War was to be a regrettable and dolorous obligation; and just warriors were to fight without hatred or lust. The idea is that to stick to justice, one would have to be motivated only by just intentions. But one wonders in reality whether this is ever the case. This is one of the reasons that some Christian pacifists claim that Jesus's primary commandments are nonresistance of violence and love of enemies. It seems to pacifists as if the justification of war is really an attempt to rationalize immoral action. The worry is that it is practically impossible to fight a war with love and justice as the primary intention.

The just war theory has been described as an effort "to make war morally possible." But the aim of the just war theory should not be to *make* war morally possible but, rather, to *wonder whether* war is morally possible. This difference is crucial. To assume that war must be made morally possible is quite simply to beg the question. Walzer says that the just war theory "made war possible in a world where war was, sometimes, necessary."[2] Daniel Bell echoes Walzer by saying that if we do not find a way to make war morally possible we will "abandon warfare and its victims to the realists."[3] A similar point was made half a century ago by Elizabeth Anscombe, who claimed that since pacifism sets impossibly high standards, people will then feel that there are no limits at all in war: "Seeing no way of avoiding 'wickedness,' they set no limits to it."[4]

But we should be suspicious of this either-or point of view: either pacifism or anything goes; either there are just wars or we must become realists. There is plenty of room for shades of gray here. In all likelihood the truth is somewhere in between the poles of these dichotomies. Some wars are obviously wrong. Some others are less objectionable. But there are very few wars (if any) that live up to the standards of the just war ideal. This does not mean that we should simply scrap the idea and become either pacifists or realists. Rather, it should remind us of the fact, which most people already know, that in the real world it is exceedingly difficult to be good. The truth is that war may not be morally possible, or at least, very few wars are actually just wars. And yet there is no way around the fact that we will still have to fight wars. Global culture has not yet evolved beyond war. This is a tragic conclusion. A tone of tragedy should permeate just war discourse. War is never a triumphant thing to be proud of. Rather, it shows us human finitude, frailty, and failure.

We need the just war idea then to guide us through tragic circumstances, so that we do as little further wrong as possible in a situation that is already wrong. The idea is to be used as a tool of criticism and condemnation. The just war ideal should remind us of our guilt and responsibility. Those who take the just war idea seriously and use it as a guide for thinking about actual wars must admit that the world is a horrible place: wars continue to be fought for no good reason and wars continue to be fought in violation of just war constraints. We should not pretend that we are actually doing right when we are merely doing what is inevitable. The just war theory becomes mythological when it claims that it is right, noble, and good to do what is merely necessary or expedient. In reality, no one is a saint and immoral decisions are routinely made. We should feel outraged and disgusted by the carnage of war: most of it is not justifiable at all. If just war ideals do not leave us feeling guilty and nauseated, then we have succumbed to a mythological interpretation of the theory.

My general thesis, then, is that it is very difficult to say if there is such a thing as a just war. War is morally ambiguous at best. It is brutal, chaotic, and horrific. Yes, there may be good reasons for war. And there can be heroism and nobility in war. But those who claim that some wars are obviously just are deluded. It is a myth to claim that any war is purely good or just. We can tell a simple story of good and evil that is used to rationalize war. But such one-dimensional moral language portrays the world as we want it to be, not as it actually is. The danger is, however, that the more ardently we believe this mythic language, the more likely we are to fight wars that fail to be just. The myth helps us avoid the nausea and makes it possible to do things that are morally repugnant.

The conclusion of this point of view is a sort of pacifism. I think that war is generally wrong; and I think that personal violence is also usually wrong. I can, however, imagine a variety of situations in which I would feel justified in killing in self-defense. And I can also imagine some sorts of war that could be justifiable. But in general, I do not think that most wars are actually just. I think that the principles of the just war theory are good ones insofar as they set a very high standard for good behavior. But I do not believe that it is easy to fulfill the requirements of these principles in practice. I also think that the just war theory can seduce us into thinking that it is a simple matter to wage a just war. For that reason, my position can be called *just war pacifism* or *pacifism in practice*. I have explained this idea in another book, *Practical Pacifism*. I will explain it again here and will expand the ideas presented in that previous book by more closely examining the myths of the just war tradition and by reflecting in more detail on our current war on terrorism. I should note that I also recognize that pacifism has its own mythic quality. This is why I also reject absolute pacifism.

There are no easy answers here. The more one thinks about the justification of war and the ideals of pacifism, the more difficult the whole mess becomes. This is, I think, as it should be. It is too simple to claim as Walzer does that just war theory is "triumphant." We should not be surprised that there are no clear and distinct conclusions about this topic. In fact, all of our most important endeavors suffer from ambiguity: happiness, love, religion, and politics. It would be odd to claim, for example, that one theory of happiness had triumphed over all others, or that it must be possible for human beings to be happy. Certainly there are better or worse theories of happiness; and some ought to be rejected as false. But for the most part, human beings cobble together a variety of theories, and we strive for happiness without fully attaining it. The same is true of thinking about war. We do our best to find a moral language to think about war. But just as no real human being can be described as perfectly happy, no real war can be called perfectly just.

Myths develop around moral topics such as love or war. Myths help explain and give meaning when there is confusion and obscurity. Since Plato, philosophers have criticized myths, rhetoric, and poetry. And yet, as Plato's own work reminds us, philosophers can also succumb to the temptation to mythologize. Philosophers want to know the truth of the matter, and they like to think that it is possible to find one theory that contains this truth. But the problem is that for these difficult issues, truth is not easy to discern and we easily slip into well-worn ruts of tradition and "common sense." Even the best philosopher can succumb to the temptation to tell a simple and compelling story. We should be suspicious of those who claim that the answers are obvious and easy. Perhaps the best we can hope for is ongoing critical evaluation of our myths. This critical (negative or skeptical) approach permeates this book. This is not to say that the myth of the just war theory is completely fanciful and false. Rather, my point is to understand the limits of just war theory by examining some of its mythological assumptions and some of the difficulties we find in trying to apply just war theory in the real world.

This book was written during the course of the Iraq war—a war that is not yet over. The middle chapters of the book were originally published as journal articles. They represent specific attempts to think critically about the problems presented by the Iraq war and the more general war on terrorism. It is important to note that the topics addressed in these middle chapters—preemptive war, the use of torture, casualties in the war in Iraq, the idea of humanitarian intervention, the nature of the Bush Doctrine, etc.—are still evolving. Wars are evolving historical events. So our judgments are always provisional and in need of constant reassessment. Nonetheless, the general conclusion that I draw in light of the current state of affairs is that it is very difficult, if not impossible, for war to actually be just.

ACKNOWLEDGMENTS

A research grant from the College of Arts and Humanities at Fresno State funded preparations for this book. Thanks go out also to my friends and colleagues who helped me think more clearly about the ideas presented here, especially: Derek Jeffreys, Hye-Kyung Kim, Trudy Conway, Lani Roberts, David Chan, David Duquette, Rob Metcalf, and my colleagues in the Philosophy Department at Fresno State.

The middle chapters of this book were originally published as journal articles. Chapter 6 was published as "Citizenship and Preemptive War: The Lesson from Iraq" in *Human Rights Review* 7, no. 4 (July–September 2006): 19–37. Chapter 7 was published as "A Critique of Exceptions: Torture, Terrorism, and the Lesser Evil Argument" in *International Journal of Applied Philosophy* 20, no. 1 (Spring 2006): 127–42. Chapter 8 was published as "The Bush Doctrine, Democratization, and Humanitarian Intervention: A Just War Critique" in *Theoria* (December 2007). And chapter 9 was published as "Practical Pacifism, Jus in bello, and Citizen Responsibility: The Case of Iraq," *Ethical Perspectives* 13, no. 4 (2006): 673–97. And some of the ideas presented in chapter 10 also appear online in my article "Pacifism" in the *Stanford Encyclopedia of Philosophy*.

NOTES

1. This is the title of chapter 1 of Walzer's recent book, *Arguing about War* (New Haven, CT: Yale University Press, 2004).
2. Walzer, *Arguing about War*, 3.
3. Daniel M. Bell Jr., "Just War Engaged: Review Essay of Walzer and O'Donovan," *Modern Theology* 22: 2 (April 2006): 295. Bell claims that this was Paul Ramsey's basic idea. And it seems to be the general approach of many contemporary just war theorists, including: Jean Bethke Elshtain, George Weigel, James Turner Johnson, and Donald O'Donovan.
4. Elizabeth Anscombe, "War and Massacre," in *The Morality of War*, ed. Larry May, Eric Rovie, and Steve Viner (Upper Saddle River, NJ: Prentice Hall, 2006), 209.

Part I

THE JUST WAR MYTH

Chapter One

Introduction: The Just War Myth and the Politics of War

It is naive to suppose that there is a solution to every moral problem with which the world can face us. We have always known that the world is a bad place. It appears that it may be an evil place as well.

—Thomas Nagel, "War and Massacre"[1]

The just war myth is the idea that war is actually just. Many of our highest ideals describe things that do not occur in reality. The theory of true love, for example, sets the standard for loving relationships. But it is false to assume that since we know what true love would be, true love must actually exist. Indeed, to believe this is to court heartache. The just war ideal works in the same way. The just war theory expresses our best moral thinking about war. But it is false to assume that since we know what a just war would be, just wars actually exist. In fact, there are no just wars. Nor is there any good reason to suppose that it is actually possible for there to be just wars. Recognition of this may cause us to despair. But it should also cause us to be more cautious and self-critical. The point of calling the just war theory a myth is to force us to be vigilant against the seductions and heartaches of wishful thinking about war.

Like other myths—the myth of true love or the myths of religion—the just war myth expresses our highest aspirations. We are inclined to take these myths so seriously that we believe that they present a true and attainable thing. While the myth of true love is inspiring, it is delusional to think that romantic love can produce the total satisfaction of "happily

3

ever after." Successful loving relationships must be attuned to the difficulties of love in the real world of finite, changing, human beings. Similarly, uncritical acceptance of the just war myth should not guide our decisions about war. A truly just war—if there were such a thing—would have to be waged with a critical awareness of how difficult it is actually to fight a just war.

This analogy between love and war only hints at the difficulty of the just war myth. War is a complex social event involving masses of people and our deepest political and cultural ideals. If true love is impossible, then a just war must be that much more impossible. Moreover, it is tempting to resort to a form of realism, once one sees through the myth. Thus one might conclude that if there is no true love or just war, then, "all is fair in love and war." But I am not arguing for realism here. Rather, my purpose in showing how hard it would be to wage a just war is to encourage us to take the challenge that much more seriously.

DEFINING WAR

I focus much of my discussion in this book on the temptations and difficulties that we have seen in the war on terrorism. The middle chapters of the book undertake a critique of the Bush Doctrine, the idea of preemptive war, and the use of torture. A discussion of war that is not focused on the concrete reality of war is, for the most part, useless. War is not an abstract thing. So it is too much to say that war in general is wrong or is just. Our judgments must be about particular wars or types of war.

An important problem, then, is defining the term *war*. War is a family resemblance term: there are a variety of related things that can each be called war. War is defined, for example, by Brian Orend as "*actual, intentional* and *widespread* armed conflict between political communities."[2] This definition works well enough. But it needs a lot of clarification, as can be seen if one reflects on the meaning of each of its key words. Philosophers have written shelfloads of books analyzing concepts such as "actual" and "intentional." It seems, at least, that wars are human activities in which groups of people are killed by other groups of people; and this killing has some political meaning, that is, it is about a struggle for power, legitimacy, and/or ideology.

The variety of things that can be called "war" can be organized by the size of the groups involved, by the tactics employed, and by how widespread the conflict is. At one extreme we have total wars in which alliances and countries mobilize en masse against one another. We saw this sort of war during the twentieth century in World Wars I and II. In another sense, the idea of total war could be used to describe the Cold War, although the two main belligerents never attacked each other directly. The goal of a total war is to defeat the whole of the enemy society. Thus these wars use a diverse range of tactics, from trade embargoes to carpet bombing, from infantry invasions to the strategy of nuclear deterrence. The era of total war is, for the most part, over; one hopes that it will remain extinct. At the other end of the spectrum we have a variety of smaller wars: terrorism and counterterrorist war, asymmetric warfare, counterinsurgency warfare, and so-called fourth-generation warfare. The reality of warfare in the twenty-first century is that wars will be more like the war on terrorism than like World War II. There will be no total wars so long as American hegemony and the U.N. system hold together. Rather, there will be civil wars, border conflicts, terrorist attacks, and occasional interventions by American, NATO, or U.N. forces that will seek to keep the peace, provide humanitarian relief, destroy terrorists, and neutralize insurgencies. This book cannot discuss each and every one of these sorts of warfare in detail. Rather, it focuses in its middle chapters on the war on terrorism, especially, the American invasion of Iraq. I hope that more general conclusions can be drawn from this example. But I am aware of the fact that each conflict is unique and that each requires careful judgment.

One of the difficulties to be discussed in this book is that the just war tradition developed in a different era and does not apply well to these new sorts of warfare. The just war ideal works best when there is a clear battlefield and when it is easy to distinguish combatants from noncombatants. But such ideal conditions do not hold in contemporary wars. For example, there is an extreme moral difficulty in a counterinsurgency war, such as we are currently fighting in Iraq. On the one hand, to "win" such a conflict, the easiest thing to do would be to "take off the gloves" and employ the tactics used by the Romans, the Nazis, and everyone else who has effectively suppressed insurgency. The easiest solution is to kill or imprison as many of the male population as possible and to severely punish villages and neighborhoods that support insurgent operations, including punishing the women and children of insurgents and sympathizers. But the problem of this imperial approach is that it is obviously immoral. It requires a sort of brutality that we should rightly condemn. The experts who think about morally acceptable strategies for counterinsurgency warfare claim that the only morally acceptable strategy in such a struggle is to take the moral high ground and employ political, economic, and social tactics in addition to the tactics of (morally restrained) hard power. The difficulty of this approach is that the local insurgents have much more political power: the insurgents are locals who are related by kin, clan, and culture; the counterinsurgency forces are foreigners. And, as we've seen in Iraq, the insurgents are willing to employ immoral brutality—terror bombing and the use of torture and dismemberment on the bodies of their enemies—that is effective at coercing the population into cooperation. The difficulty is that forces that are constrained by just war morality cannot compete with the coercive power of the insurgents and thus cannot gain the support of the population that is needed to defeat the insurgency.

ON WINNING A WAR

This points us to a difficult general conclusion: in order to *win* a war, injustice may be necessary. There is an irresolvable tension between the demands of morality and the need to win. The paradigm for the just war myth in the twentieth century is World War II. But this war was won by employing immoral means: carpet bombing, fire bombing, and atomic bombing that killed civilians on a massive scale. World War II was not a just war: the cause may have been just but the means employed to obtain victory were not. Robert McNamara—the former secretary of defense—has admitted this in the recent documentary *The Fog of War*. McNamara concluded that American forces—including the officers like him and Curtis LeMay who devised the bombing strategy—would have been considered "war criminals" if we had lost the war in Japan.

The victors have the power to shape the moral discourse about war: the wars we win appear as just wars, even if injustices are committed as a means to victory. Moral forces that want to win (and forces motivated by moral ideals should want to win) are sorely tempted to go beyond morality. And the myth of the just war can be used to justify this sort of immorality. I believe that this explains what happened in the notorious use of torture in the war on terrorism. There was the temptation to "take off the gloves" and circumvent morality in order to win. If the cause is perceived as being just, then it becomes easy to justify atrocity in pursuit of this cause.

One solution to resolving the current insurgency problem in Iraq would be to take the gloves back off again and drain the swamp (to use a metaphor borrowed from former secretary of defense Donald Rumsfeld). The Roman or imperial version of this idea would claim that in the real world, victory requires that we sacrifice morality. This idea is known as "realism." The ancient Greek historian Thucydides described realism as follows: "The strong do what they have the power to do and the weak accept what they have to accept." But realism is not morally acceptable. It may be "effective" to torture women and mutilate children as a way of ensuring compliance; but this is not just. The just war theory explains why this is so: noncombatants have a kind of sacred immunity, since they pose no direct threat.

This points us toward a tragic conclusion. It may be possible for a fully just war to also be successful. But wars that are fought within just war limits may fail to achieve total victory. The idea that war must be made morally possible—as expressed by just war theorists like Walzer—seems to imply that it must be possible for moral forces to win. But there is no reason to believe that this is true. In the real world, sometimes the good guys lose. Defenders of the just war idea must show that war is the best solution to social conflict while also showing that we can achieve morally legitimate war aims by fighting justly. A mythological approach to just war thinking will maintain that just wars do result in victory for the good guys. But there is no reason to believe this myth. And in fact, victory is often achieved by scrapping just war niceties and retreating to some version of realism.

PACIFISM AND MILITARY SERVICE

The skepticism expressed here does end up in a kind of pacifism: what I call skeptical, practical, or prima facie pacifism. There are more forceful and affirmative sorts of pacifism. Absolute pacifism claims that war is always wrong. One version of this claims that since killing is always wrong, and war always involves killing, war is always wrong. This idea cannot be right. Sometimes there are people who must be killed. Just as I must kill a mountain lion that is attacking my child, I must kill a human being who is doing the same. To advocate complete nonresistance to evil—as Tolstoy claims Jesus did—is morally suspect and extremely unpractical. Even if one does not accept Tolstoyan nonresistance, I'm not sure how a human being could know that war is *always* wrong— exceptions could be imagined. Absolute pacifism is often tied to religious belief, and so it can be criticized for its mythological aspects. Practical or skeptical pacifism attempts to avoid the mythic quality of absolute pacifism just as it attempts to defuse the mythic force of the just war ideal.

Some pacifists claim that military service is immoral—Tolstoy, for example, pointed in this direction. But this does not necessarily follow from the skeptical position of practical pacifism. This book is not, then, intended to condemn military service. I realize that there can be a kind of nobility in military service: soldiers are willing to sacrifice their lives in defense of those they love. I do not aim to criticize those who serve honorably. Indeed, I hope that those who serve might agree with many of my conclusions. Most soldiers recognize that war ought to be constrained within ethical limits. Since writing *Practical Pacifism*, I have had many conversations with soldiers, veterans, and those who love them. Some people are defensive. But most are quite reflective and take the task of justifying war quite seriously. Soldiers know the moral weight of their service. I admire these men and women for their moral seriousness. The real focal point of my critique of the just war myth is not the soldier but, rather, those who command him. In a democracy such as ours, which prides itself on civilian control of the military, this ultimately directs our attention to elected officials. But these officials are elected by us: thus the real focus is "we, the people." We elect the officials who make decisions about war, we pay the taxes that support the military, and we support war and the military in a variety of other passive and active ways.

The just war myth is grounded on the assumption that the political leaders who declare, organize, and pay for war are wise and just men and women who take seriously the sacrifices of war and who understand the principles of the just war theory. I fear that there is no good reason to have this sort of faith in authority. This does not mean that those who believe the just war myth are simply dupes. Rather, our entire culture promotes this sort of faith in authority through a variety of mythological constructs. While this makes belief in the myth understandable, it does not make it any less mythological.

My criticism of the just war myth is thus offered in solidarity with those who serve. I know many people who are rightly proud of their service: they serve because they truly believe in the values of their country and in the ideals of the just war theory. We've seen that in the war in Iraq, the good faith and loyal obedience of military personnel were misused. It is clear to me that in the real world, nations must have a ready military force. Just as I am glad that there are cops in my city, I am glad that there is an army ready to defend my country. But the myths of military power encourage us to place too much faith in the leaders and the causes for which our military is asked to fight. Moreover, the myth cannot adequately account for the fact that, in addition to citizen soldiers, private security contractors such as Blackwater USA support the military in current wars and work outside of the ordinary structure of military command and control.

THE JUST WAR TRADITION

The just war idea is that war can be used, within limits, to defend and promote the common good. This idea is a good one in theory: if we take our values seriously, then they are worth fighting, killing, and dying for. Indeed, this line of reasoning has been used to argue against pacifism: pacifists are supposed to contradict themselves insofar as they are unwilling to fight to defend their values.[3] But pacifists can respond by claiming that some values are more important than life. Christian pacifists will claim that gaining entrance to the kingdom of heaven is infinitely more important than defending any earthly kingdom. Pacifists are willing to die for their ideals; but they are not willing to kill to defend them.

Philosophers and theologians have developed the just war theory in order to clarify what sorts of causes are worth killing for. This theory developed in response to Christian pacifism. And the just war theory reflects the sorts of deontological principles that motivate pacifism. The just war tradition maintains, for example, that there are some things that just warriors cannot do in defense of such causes. Rape, for example, is excluded as a means of warfare according to the principles of what is called *jus in bello* (justice within war), even if rape would be a useful tool of warfare. The reason for this is that rape—unlike killing—is viewed as *mala in se*, or evil in itself.

It is not accidental that the very language of justice in war (*"jus in bello," "mala in se"*) is articulated using Latin terms that developed during the medieval period. The just war theory still reflects the interests and concerns of medieval religion. Just war theorists talk about the *jus ad bellum* question of going to war in response to a *casus belli*. In the midst of war they focus on questions of *jus in bello*, which includes prohibitions on actions such as rape, which are *mala in se*, or wrong in themselves. Just war thinkers such as Brian Orend have renewed our attention to conditions for ending a war justly: *jus post bellum*.[4] And George Lucas of the U.S. Naval Academy has recently added new Latin terms to discuss the use of military force in the context of humanitarian intervention: *jus ad pacem* or *jus ad interventionem*.[5] I will explain some of these ideas in more detail in the next chapter. But I want to note here that the pervasive use of Latin in just war discourse should remind us that the just war theory is steeped in Christian theology. The just war theory was developed by theologians and monks such as Ambrose, Augustine, Aquinas, Vitoria, and Suarez. This fact is often celebrated by just war defenders who attach importance to the idea that there is a just war "tradition" that is over one thousand years old. But this is one of the main reasons to be skeptical of the just war tradition. It developed in a different time, when wars were fought differently. And more importantly, it developed around a medieval view of politics that held that the sovereign was empowered by God. The Latin language of the just war tradition should remind us of an era in which the Church and its authority were tied to ideas about the divine right of kings.

Just war ideas were also inspired by more secular concerns, although the secular basis for the just war theory is itself imbued with a mythic quality. The noble imagery of Horace's lines, "*dolce et decorum est pro patria mori*"—those lines quoted with scorn in Wilfred Owen's World War I poem that is cited in the preface—remind us of the Roman emphasis on patriotic sacrifice for the good of the fatherland: "It is sweet and proper to die for the fatherland." We see the same sort of imagery in the Marine Corps motto: "*Semper fidelis.*" We celebrate the faithfulness of the Marine Corps along with other martial virtues such as courage, obedience, and sacrifice. The idealism that praises these virtues is part of the just war myth that remains tied to an outmoded way of thinking about politics in terms of "fatherlands."

Liberal-democratic governments have less admiration for obedience and fidelity—although certainly even liberal democracies can demand limited forms of obedience and fidelity. But history reminds us that such virtues can be misused. A courageous and obedient Nazi is not worthy of our praise. But the just war myth allows us to imagine that a soldier can do right even by fighting nobly in an unjust war. A fully developed idea of justice in war should allow for dissenting soldiers to disobey immoral orders. But this is a complicated idea that runs counter to the tradition of obedience. Consider, for example, the case of Lt. Ehren

Watada, who has refused to be deployed to Iraq because he claims that the war there is illegal. Watada is now being court-martialed for his disobedience. The presumption is that soldiers should obey orders, even in a questionable war such as the war in Iraq.

Democratic thinkers have long argued against this sort of blind obedience and conformity. As American troops marched off to the unjust war in Mexico, Thoreau observed: "The mass of men serve the State, thus, not as men mainly, but as machines, with their bodies. . . . In most cases there is no free exercise whatever of the judgment or of the moral sense; but they put themselves on a level with wood and earth and stones; and wooden men can perhaps be manufactured that will serve the purpose as well."[6] Thoreau concludes that the individual soldier has a duty to refuse to serve in an unjust war, and he argues that we all have an obligation to refuse to support unjust governments that lead us into unjust wars. More and better democracy would undoubtedly make it more difficult to fight wars. There is a developing consensus about this found in the so-called democratic peace theory. This theory, which finds its philosophical roots in some ideas developed by Kant, holds that as democracy spreads the people will be empowered to resist the war efforts of their governments. And moreover, if democratic values were to spread, there would be fewer things for nations to fight about. This idea will be discussed in detail in chapter 11.

Ironically, a version of this idea drives current American foreign policy. The Bush Doctrine aims at a version of the democratic peace. The difficulty is that the Bush Doctrine holds that aggressive democratizing wars can be fought in order to spread democracy and bring about the democratic peace. This shows us the pernicious influence of the just war myth. The just war myth, along with other mythological elements in political life and in our military traditions, encourages us to think that wars are noble adventures that produce good outcomes. But in reality, wars are horrible and morally ambiguous at best.

CONCLUSION

This book will argue that the just war theory should be used as a critical tool with which we can examine the morality of actual wars. There is no reason to believe that any real war is actually just. Thus we should be reluctant to affirm wars that are fought in our names.

This argument will include the following basic claims about the just war theory, presented here in outline form, focused on the basic problems for the just war theory that will be discussed in what follows. This outline reflects the basic structure of the just war theory, which will be discussed in more detail in chapter 3. And these problems are focused on issues that have come up in the war on terrorism and especially in the war on Iraq. These claims will be discussed in further detail in subsequent chapters.

- *The problem of just cause.* Just wars are supposed to have just causes, and self-defense is the most obvious sort of just cause. But we have seen that wars are fought for causes that do not live up to this standard. The war in Iraq is one obvious example. Iraq posed no direct threat to the United States despite exaggerated claims about weapons of mass destruction (WMD) and hints about Iraq's connection to the al-Qaeda terrorist network. The war could have been justified by ideas about preemptive war, humanitarian intervention, or the big idea of spreading democracy. But these sorts of causes are even more difficult, if not impossible, to justify. A mythic interpretation of the just war idea holds that our cause must be just. But in reality, even a nation committed to just war principles may end up fighting wars that are not based on just cause.
- *The problem of right intention.* The just war theory requires that wars should be fought for moral intentions. But the controversy over the war in Iraq reminds us that our intentions are not always clear. Decisions about war are politically charged and complex. It is not clear that noble intention motivates these decisions. The just war myth holds that our intentions are always obviously pure and noble. But in reality, political decisions rarely exhibit such purity of intention.
- *The problem of legitimate/proper authority.* The just war theory requires that those who lead us into war have the authority to do so. Traditionally this authority came from something like the divine right of kings: leaders were ordained by God to defend the nation or to execute divine justice. But in a democracy, legitimacy is not so clearly tied to divine justice. And in the evolving system of international politics, things are even more complicated. The myth holds that our nation or our president has the legitimate authority to wage war. But in reality, this creates the problem of unilateral action and double-standards, and the prerogatives of executive power seem to run counter to democratic ideals.

- *The problem of last resort.* The just war theory holds that war should be a reasonable last resort, undertaken after nonviolent means have been given a chance to succeed. But the war in Iraq shows us that there can be substantial variation among our judgments about what is a reasonable last resort. Critics of the war held out for more inspections of Iraq's WMD sites. But proponents claimed that it would be dangerous to give Iraq more time. The myth holds that our leaders are wise enough to discern the right time for war. But in reality, our leaders are fallible humans who must make such decisions in a context of uncertainty.

- *The problem of probable success.* The just war theory holds that war should have a chance to succeed, and this is usually meant to include the idea that war should produce conditions of peace and stability after war. But the wars in Iraq and Afghanistan continue without any prospect for stability or success. The myth holds that it is easy to win a just war. But in reality, war breeds instability, retaliatory violence, and escalation.

- *The problem of proportionality.* The just war theory demands that the harms of war should be proportional to the benefits that are supposed to be obtained. But the destruction and instability in Iraq and Afghanistan give us reason to suspect that the benefits of these wars do not outweigh the harms. The myth claims that wars produce goods that cannot be obtained otherwise. But in reality, it is not clear that wars ever live up to the proportionality requirement. Nor is it clear that a private security contractor such as Blackwater will be willing to take the sorts of risks that the principle of discrimination requires.

- *The problem of discrimination.* The just war theory requires just warriors to avoid deliberately killing noncombatants. Some noncombatant death can be justified by the principle of double effect (which holds that such deaths are acceptable if they are not directly intended). But civilian casualties continue to mount in Iraq and Afghanistan. The Iraq Body Count project puts civilian casualties at over eighty thousand (as of October 2007). And some estimates push the number upward of five hundred thousand. The myth holds that these deaths are justified by double effect or that we are not responsible for the majority of these deaths, which were caused by the insurgency. But in reality, regardless of who is directly responsible for these deaths, it is not clear that tens or hundreds of thousands of noncombatant deaths are ever justifiable or proportional to the benefit that was supposed to be obtained in the first place.

- *The problem of intrinsically evil means.* The just war theory makes it clear that some methods of war fighting are immoral: rape, torture, maltreatment of prisoners, the use of poison. But in Iraq we've seen some of this occur. It is true that the soldiers who raped and tortured prisoners have been prosecuted as criminals. But torture has been legitimized as part of the war on terrorism. The myth holds that military commanders will be able to control the bad behavior of our soldiers and that they will themselves understand the importance of fighting within moral limits. But in reality, one wonders whether it is ever so easy to control the dogs of war once we've set them loose.

All of this taken together gives us reason to be suspicious of the morality of the war in Iraq and the war on terrorism. And it gives us a reason to suspect that war cannot generally be constrained by just war principles. The myth holds that there are just wars. But in reality, wars fail to live up to just war standards.

NOTES

1. Thomas Nagel, "War and Massacre," in *The Morality of War*, ed. Larry May, Eric Rovie, and Steve Viner (Upper Saddle River, NJ: Prentice Hall, 2006), 233.

2. Brian Orend, "War," *Stanford Encyclopedia of Philosophy*, at plato.stanford.edu/entries/war.

3. This is the gist of Jan Narveson's critique of pacifism as articulated in various articles: "Pacifism: A Philosophical Analysis," *Ethics* 75, no. 4 (1965): 259–71; "Is Pacifism Consistent?" *Ethics*, 78, no. 2 (1968): 148–50; and "Terrorism and Pacifism: Why We Should Condemn Both," *International Journal of Applied Ethics* 17, no. 2 (2003): 157–72.

4. Brian Orend, "Jus Post Bellum," *Journal of Social Philosophy* 31, no. 1 (Spring 2000): 117–37; also see Orend's article "War" in the *Stanford Encyclopedia of Philosophy*; or Gary J. Bass, "Jus Post Bellum," *Philosophy and Public Affairs* 32, no. 4 (October 2004): 384–412.

5. George Lucas, "From Jus ad Bellum to Jus ad Pacem," in May, Rovie, and Viner, *Morality of War*.

6. Thoreau, "On the Duty of Civil Disobedience," in May, Rovie, and Viner, *Morality of War*, 124.

Chapter Two

The Myths and
Memes of Political Life

The history of power politics is nothing but the history of international crime and mass murder. . . . This history is taught in schools, and some of the greatest criminals are extolled as its heroes.

—Karl Popper, *The Open Society and Its Enemies*[1]

Political life is organized around mythic stories that color our perception of reality. The just war myth—the idea that wars are actually just—is often tied to a political myth that claims we have justice on our side. Mythologized history makes it appear that there have been just wars in the past; this convinces us that present and future wars can also be just.

This chapter will offer a more detailed definition of the idea of myth. And it will offer a preliminary account of the myths of political life, especially the myths of American politics, which will be completed in more detail in chapter 5. One of my main purposes here is to suggest reasons why we find it so easy to believe the myths of political life including the myth of the just war.

MYTHS AND MEMES

When I use the word *myth* in these pages I mean something like an unproved collective belief that is accepted uncritically. Myths are complexes of shared ideas. These ideas reinforce one another. They provide support for social institutions. And these social institutions themselves help to perpetuate these myths. In this way, the just war myth supports military institutions, and military institutions propagate the myth of the just war. In the same way, an unduly idealistic conception of American power helps legitimize the American system; and the American system works to foster belief in the myths of American history.

A useful idea that helps explain what I am talking about in these pages is the idea of the *meme* that has been employed by biologists and anthropologists. Richard Dawkins coined the term *meme*, which means a replicating unit of cultural inheritance. Myths (or memes) are passed down and believed by uncritical members of culture, not because they are true but because they have the power to propagate themselves. As each generation passes these myths on to the next, they gain a sort of credibility that comes from the inertia of tradition. We believe them because we have always believed them. Dawkins and others (Boyer and Dennett, for example) have applied the theory of memes to religious belief, wondering why it is that obviously false beliefs continue to be widely held. The answer is that religious beliefs work together in what Dawkins calls a "memeplex." These memeplexes, or cultural constructs, are readily accepted by creatures like us because of certain features of our cognitive, emotional, and social machinery. The theory of natural selection holds that memes "compete" with one another in a struggle to replicate themselves. Cultural ideas tend to succeed when they satisfy our cognitive, emotional, and social needs. Success is defined by persistence over time and not by truth.

This approach reminds us that if we are going to understand why the just war myth persists, we must look both to the larger culture in which it occurs and to the cognitive, biological, and social needs that it fulfills. One way of pursuing this line of thought would emphasize biology. The "demonic male" thesis represents one biological approach to violence and war.[2] This idea holds that an inherent tendency toward violence is passed down through structures of male dominance. Violent males dominate the females and thus pass on their tendency toward violence. The thesis is supported by examining other species closely related to Homo sapiens. It turns out that other apes—especially the chimpanzees, our closest relatives—exhibit patterns of group violence and male dominance. There are some difficulties of this cross-species analysis: most notably, the fact that humans are not chimps! I have discussed this in more detail in *Practical Pacifism*. Here my effort is to look more closely at the cognitive and social needs that the just war myth fulfills.

The just war myth is closely related to our political and religious myths. The various components of this memeplex mutually reinforce one another. Faith in certain religious and political ideas is linked to faith in the just war myth. Dawkins hints at this in *The Selfish Gene*, where he writes the following:

> Blind faith can justify anything. If a man believes in a different god, or even if he uses a different ritual for worshipping the same god, blind faith can decree that he should die. . . . Memes for blind faith have their own ruthless ways of propagating themselves. This is true of patriotic and political as well as religious blind faith.[3]

Religious and political myths succeed when they satisfy our need to enjoy solidarity with others and when they fulfill our desire for a coherent story that provides life with meaning. The just war myth gives meaning to war and it allows us to believe that war fits within our religious and moral horizons. But the fact that we want to believe that war is just does not make it true that war is actually just. Nor does the fact that we want to believe that the United States has always been a positive moral force in world history make it true. Despite this clash between myth and reality, it is easy to acquiesce to prevailing myths precisely because they are so satisfying.

The connection between religious fervor, political ideology, and violence can be seen most clearly in the idea of holy war, the crusade, or jihad. The human mind is oddly receptive to the idea that killing and dying for religion or for the fatherland is acceptable. Perhaps there is some Darwinian explanation for this: human groups in which the members were more willing to die for the group's ideology were more successful. But this does not make aggressive ideological wars just.

The just war ideal developed out of the holy war ideal. This development occurred within religious culture—as I will show in more detail in the next chapter. The most important residue of the holy war idea is the just war tradition's idea of "legitimate authority." The holy war myth holds that there is a prophet-king who has special knowledge that authorizes him to wage war with religious justification. It also maintains that those who follow the prophet-king into battle and death will be rewarded or blessed. The secular just war myth holds that kings, presidents, or generals have specialized knowledge that gives them the ability to know when a war is just. And it strives to find ways to foster the belief that soldiers who die for their countries do not die in vain.

We believe all of this—despite evidence to the contrary—because the prevailing myths of our culture incline us toward faith in authority and toward the idea that sacrifice for the homeland is noble and heroic.

This faith in authority and in the myths of "God and country" is a self-replicating meme. Social structures are set up to reinforce faith in authority through the myths and symbols of political power. These myths reassure us that our dead comrades have served a higher purpose. This faith is reinforced by our religious myths as well. Many of us continue to believe that priests and popes have special access to the divine. So it is not surprising that many of us continue to believe that political and military leaders have special access to knowledge about the justification of war. The ritual of the military funeral casts a religious light on the service of the dead. And the ceremonial deism of public life—the phrase "under God" in the Pledge of Allegiance or the president's benediction "God bless the United States of America"—reassures many of us that there is a divine purpose in our political life.

Faith in authority is linked to ideas about divine Providence. In the American context this is part of what is called *American Exceptionalism*—the idea that God has a special providential plan for American power. Such ideas have deep roots in the American self-image, since before the Revolution. And these ideas can be seen more recently in ideas expressed by President Bush both before and after 9/11. In his first inaugural speech, for example—from before the 9/11 attacks—Bush was talking about Providence and its connection to the national mission:

> We are not this story's author, who fills time and eternity with his purpose. Yet his purpose is achieved in our duty, and our duty is fulfilled in service to one another. Never tiring, never yielding, never finishing, we renew that purpose today, to make our country more just and generous, to affirm the dignity of our lives and every life. This work continues. This story goes on. And an angel still rides in the whirlwind and directs this storm.

It is not surprising that a president would use this sort of rhetoric on inauguration day. But we should be clear that the story of American power and its conjunction with divine Providence is a myth. Bush claims that "we are not this story's author." But the fact is that *we are* the story's author. There is no mythic plan for history. History is what we make it. We *make history* in two senses of the term: we tell each other stories about the meaning and purpose of history, and we then act to fulfill the desire and sense of destiny evoked by these stories. One way that historical destiny is fulfilled is through warfare. Indeed, the idea of destiny or providence is often dusted off and brought out in times of war. The American war on terrorism has been justified by appeal to the larger historical myth of American Exceptionalism, which holds that the United States is the leading power in world history, and its military power should be used to spread democratic values around the globe. This story is linked to the prevailing myth of American power in the twentieth century—a story that celebrates American victories in World War II and the Cold War. And this story creates a mission for the United States in the twenty-first century as the defender of freedom and leader of democratizing wars. It is this larger narrative that continues to inspire the Americans who fight and die in the battles of the war on terrorism, as well as those who love them.

It does not take much reflection to see that the justification of war is often mythological. Most of us do not have an elaborate philosophical theory in mind when we think about the justification of war. Indeed, when we think of war, it is often in terms of mythic images, heroic ideals, and grand historical narratives. We imagine the heroism of some film soldier such as John Wayne or Tom Hanks fighting in a war against the evil forces of Japan or Germany. We might hear the striking cadences of the Marine Corps hymn: "From the halls of Montezuma to the shores of Tripoli." When thinking of war we imagine monuments to fallen soldiers, the symbolism of the flag, the patriotic camaraderie of Memorial Day parades, and the words of the national anthem. We think of war as the "Star-Spangled Banner" describes it as a necessary sacrifice in defense of the land of the free and the home of the brave.

We are easily moved when we see and hear the president utter pronouncements of war. He stands behind the presidential seal. He is surrounded by flags. He embodies the will of the nation. His speech is infused with religious fervor and concludes with a phrase such as "God bless America." We believe what he says about the justification of war because our social system encourages us to do so. And we believe that the wars we fight are justified because we want to believe that our cause is just, that our leaders are wise, and that our faith in our national identity is well founded. This reassures us that our loyalty and obedience are in fact justified. This idealism fits with the historical narrative that we have been taught in schools; and it is easier to continue to believe this story than to think critically about it. Socially and emotionally, we want to belong to the power and majesty of the nation; we want to believe that our sacrifices are noble; and we do not want to admit that we have been manipulated or misled.

War is rarely justified in a philosophical way that dispassionately considers the claims that are made by all the parties who are involved in a conflict. Rather, the justification of war is guided by political authorities who make one-sided arguments. Nations justify war *to* themselves in light of their own emotional, social, or cognitive interests. Such justification is rarely neutral or disinterested. The myths of patriotism guide such discussions more than the dispassionate reasoning of the just war theory.

MYTHS AND ILLUSIONS

Related to the idea of myth is the Freudian idea of illusion. According to Freud, our illusions fulfill our wishes. For example, the idea of romantic love is an illusion in Freud's sense. This illusion explains and justifies our behavior while also setting up criteria for the ideal of "true love" and providing us with an odd sort of satisfaction. With regard to love, we want to believe that we can find our true soul mate, that we can find "happily ever after" with that person. For some, the illusion provides what is wished for. Abused spouses, for example, can remain in abusive relationships because they believe the myth of love. Illusions satisfy our basic narcissism and the erotic drive, even when reality proves unsatisfactory. And social conventions often support these illusions as they control and direct us in socially acceptable ways.

The illusion of the just war satisfies our basic urge toward violence—what Freud calls the "death drive"—while also helping us fulfill the obligations of morality. Freud argues, in chapter 5 of *Civilization and Its Discontents*, that group narcissism was organized around the construction of an "us versus them" identity. People unite in love while directing aggression outward toward foreigners and enemies. Political myths facilitate this process. The just war myth satisfies two seemingly disparate forces: the urge to destroy and the urge to achieve justice. It creates the illusion of morality that allows us to satisfy destructive urges and pursue self-interest. And sociobiologists might add that groups that do a good job of utilizing urges that help the group survive tend to be successful and pass on their myths. This is not to say that the urge toward justice is wrong. Rather, my point is that narcissism can make us think that we are just even when we are not.

Freud reminds us that myths and illusions create the "discontent" or "unease" of civilization. We cannot live up to our ideals and so feel always insufficient. This discontent creates all sorts of confusions, self-deception, and self-mutilations along the way. The romanticized myth of the just war suffers from this problem. Wars are fought for a variety of reasons that have very little to do with justice. Wars are fought for economic and political reasons. And wars can happen without any clearly good reason whatsoever, as the result of political inertia or the accumulated pressure of history. It is rare that war is fought for an entirely pure moral reason. But when thinking about war we prefer to dwell on the illusion of morality in war. This covers the brutality, absurdity, and self-interest of war in morally acceptable garb. We don't want to admit that war often has more to do with greed and bloodlust than with justice. And we do not want to admit that wars result from historical forces over which we have little control. The idea that justice governs war is mythological.

But there is discontent in this mythic construct. We find it hard to reconcile the brutality of war with our other moral commitments. And so soldiers return home with post-traumatic stress disorder and we find it hard to reintegrate them into polite society. We find it difficult to admit that our nation can be bloodthirsty, greedy, and self-interested. So we deceive ourselves about our motives and we're happy to believe the transparently shallow rhetorical ploys that are used to justify our actions.

So we continue to prepare for war and continue to have faith in its justification, despite the evidence that it cannot be justified in the way we would like. There is a typically recalcitrant reaction to the process of disillusionment. Sometimes when religious myths are shown to be false, religious people become even more dogmatically faithful, following the motto "*Credo quia absurdum*" (I believe it because it is absurd). Sometimes when love is failing, a spurned lover may retreat to an irrational fidelity to the loved one. And sometimes, those who begin to see that war is not just become more adamant in their claim that it is. If we were to admit that the wars we fight do not live up to the just war ideal, it would seem that we would betray the memories of all of those soldiers who died for the idea. Therefore, for many who have fought, for many who love those who fight, and for the rest of us who indirectly support the war effort, war simply *must* be just. It is impossible to imagine that we could be sacrificing our lives, our treasure, and our values for a false ideal.

Political life is based on myths and illusions. Nations are "imagined communities."[4] They are constituted by shared ways of imagining the world. This includes shared ways of remembering and forgetting: we emphasize some facts and ignore others. The shared myth is kept alive by our faith in it. National identity is constructed by the stories we tell and by our inclination to believe these stories. A government's legitimacy is grounded in the people's convictions about its legitimacy.

Reality does not often live up to the idealized image we find in our imaginations. Myths are powerfully "real" in their ability to impact our lives. But despite their emotional power and social effectiveness, myths are not true descriptions of the world. Indeed, myths often contain internal contradictions that make them susceptible to criticism. But myths are kept alive by the use of ad hoc hypotheses—such as claims about magical powers or divine Providence—which explain these contradictions away. To be effective, myths must have some basis in fact. But myths give facts their moral and political significance. Myths usually do this by locating facts within a larger story. The mythic narrative is believed because of its aesthetic appeal, moral value, and political usefulness.

For a myth to be powerful and useful it must simplify the facts and emphasize a point of view. Myths thus usually focus on the positive while ignoring the negative. In the United States, for example, the prevailing myth of American history includes stories about the noble sacrifice of the Founding Fathers who wanted to create a "city on a hill" that could be a bastion of liberty. It includes further stories about the noble motives of the Union in the war against slavery. And the story continues to extol the American role in the global struggle for liberty, culminating in American victories in World War II and the Cold War. This myth continues to be employed in the war on terrorism, which is conceived of as a war against tyrants and terrorists in which the United States has morality and even God on its side.

THE MYTH OF MAKING WAR MORALLY POSSIBLE

This is the same as it ever was. In Thucydides' history of the Peloponnesian War, the Athenian statesman Pericles delivers his famous Funeral Oration to an audience of Athenians who are mourning their war dead. Pericles evokes a mythic image of Athens that he uses to explain what the Athenians are fighting and dying for. This speech extolls Athenian virtues and praises Athenian democracy. It also ignores the injustice of Athenian imperial power and the question of whether Athens is justified in its fight. This speech is for domestic consumption, designed to console the people for their losses, and to inspire them to continue to fight. This is the way the justification of war works in the real world. It is rhetorical, political, and mythological. We continue to hear the mythological rhetoric of war and military power today. On July 4, 2006, President Bush addressed the military at Fort Bragg in a speech that would have made Pericles proud. Here is part of his speech:

> Without the courage of the soldiers of our Continental Army, the words of the Declaration would have been forgotten by history, dismissed as the radical musings of a failed revolution. We celebrate Independence Day each year because that ragtag group of citizen soldiers challenged the world's most powerful military, secured our liberty and planted a standard of freedom to which the entire world has aspired. Since that first 4th of July, some 43 million Americans have defended our freedom in times of war. These brave men and women crossed oceans and continents to defeat murderous ideologies and to secure the peace for generations that followed. We live in liberty because of the courage they displayed—from Bunker Hill to Baghdad, from Concord to Kabul—on this Independence Day we honor their achievements and we thank them for their service in freedom's cause.

This speech invokes the grand American myth. American power is glorified in a narrative that extends from the Revolution to the war in Iraq. American wars are assumed to be good wars, justified by the ideals of freedom and democracy. But the story of American power excludes much. It forgets that American military force was used in the nineteenth century to eliminate Native American cultures and to expropriate land from Spain and Mexico. Indeed, the line about the "halls of Montezuma" that shows up in the Marine Corps hymn is a reference to the American invasion of Mexico in the 1840s during which the United States effectively stole the western part of the continent: the same military adventure that provoked condemnation by Thoreau. The myth ignores the injustices of American wars and proxy wars in Southeast Asia and Central America. It fails to see the morally problematic use of carpet bombing in Europe and Asia in World War II. It overlooks the fact that the United States is the only nation on earth ever to have used nuclear weapons in war: in the atomic attacks on Hiroshima and Nagasaki. And, of course, President Bush simply assumes that the wars in Baghdad and Kabul are just wars.

This shows us the way that ideas about justice in war are actually employed. Speeches like Pericles' Funeral Oration and Bush's Fourth of July address serve a self-interested function. They aim to assure the nation that the sacrifices of war are justifiable and that military service is noble and righteous. Discussions about the justification of war occur in a politically charged context that can never attain the level of disinterested neutrality that philosophers and theologians aspire to.

Recent scholarly debates about the justification of the war in Iraq remind us that just war theorists disagree among themselves.[5] This disagreement shows us that war is ambiguous. The just war theory is subject to multiple interpretations that are influenced by the political views of the interpreters. Some scholars derive quite militant outcomes from the theory, while others derive something close to pacifism from it. I am not neutral in this debate: my sympathies lie with the pacifist side. But the larger point is that this shows us that the fact that there is a just war theory does not prove that there actually are just wars. The just war theory is a guide for argument, not a trump card that proves that wars are actually just. Unfortunately, in the "real" world of political life the concepts of just war thinking are often used as rhetorical trumps. Wars are marketed and sold by using ideas such as "justice" or "freedom" in a one-sided and politically charged way.[6]

Philosophical proponents of the just war theory view it as establishing criteria or principles that help to guide what George Weigel calls "statecraft." As Oliver O'Donovan explains, the just war theory is supposed to be a guide for "praxis" or "deliberation."[7] Its principles are supposed to guide deliberation both within society and between citizens and their leaders. Such an approach assumes that statecraft is interested primarily in justice and that those who deliberate are both interested in and capable of completing a disinterested inquiry into the question of what is just. The difficulty of this defense of the just war idea is that politicians are not guided by only a concern for justice, and they are not always interested in serious deliberation. Rather, they are often concerned with keeping themselves in power and in promoting their particular party and agenda. As Michael Walzer puts it, politicians inevitably have "dirty hands." This is not to say that all politicians are irredeemably corrupt. This is clearly false. And some politicians are motivated by noble intentions and moral ideals. But just war ideals are easily perverted and manipulated in order to serve politicians' more venal interests.

Defenders of the just war ideal claim that just war ideas should be used within war and within political discourse to help us make better judgments. Since wars must be fought, we need the just war theory to tell us how to fight. I agree with this claim. But Walzer and others go further and condemn the pacifist critique of just war theory as "a doctrine of radical suspicion" because it uses the just war theory to make war impossible. He claims in opposition that the just war theory is a theory of "radical responsibility" that explains to those who expect to fight wars why and how they should fight. He concludes that "fighting itself cannot be morally impermissible. A just war is meant to be, and has to be, a war that it is possible to fight."[8]

In a similar way, Oliver O'Donovan has argued that the just war theory is a method for thinking about war—but that war is too complex to be condemned outright. He puts it this way:

History knows of no just wars, as it knows of no just peoples. Major historical events cannot be justified or criticized in one mouthful; they are concatenations and agglomerations of many separate actions and many varied results. One may justify or criticize acts of statesmen, acts of generals, acts of common soldiers or of civilians, provided that one does so from the point of view of those who performed them, i.e., without moralistic hindsight; but wars as such, like most large-scale historical phenomena, present only a great question mark, a continual invitation to reflect further on which decisions were, and which were not, justified at the time and in the circumstances.[9]

These sorts of defenses of the just war ideal refuse to acknowledge that the just war theory could be so stringent that it would be difficult to live up to. Walzer's insistence on the fact that there must be a way to fight a war within just war constraints is obviously question begging. It makes little sense to simply declare that just wars must be wars "it is possible to fight." Indeed, such an approach is reminiscent of the ontological argument for the existence of God: it is like saying that God must exist because he is a perfect being and according to the theory, perfect beings must exist. The way in which Walzer closes the circle of thinking about the justification of war is a clear sign that there is something mythological going on here.

O'Donovan's defense is even more suspect. O'Donovan's idea that we cannot use the just war idea with "moralistic hindsight" to judge whether past wars have been just is merely another way of saying that the just war ideal is really of little use to us. It shows us that there is no point in applying the just war ideal at all, because complex reality of war cannot be adequately encompassed by it. O'Donovan leaves us with a sort of relativism that is, frankly, useless. It may be true that wars require complex judgment, and it may be true that we should do our best to imagine all of the circumstances of a given war, but this does not mean that we cannot say in the end that a war is just or unjust. And if the just war ideal cannot be employed to make such judgments, then one wonders whether it has any value at all.

The just war theory provides us with a very useful tool for judging whether wars are just or unjust. But this tool is often used to rationalize wars that are not actually just. In opposition to this mythological application of the just war theory, I conclude that we must be honest about the fact that most wars fail to live up to the standards of the just war ideal.

One of the reasons for the disconnect between the myth of the just war and the reality of warfare is that the just war myth assumes that there are reasonable deliberators who employ its principles. But in reality, there is no perfectly just person, leader, or state. This insight has been well known since the time of Plato. In Plato's *Republic* Socrates defines justice by considering an extended analogy that compares the just man to the just city. In both cases Plato hints that the ideal of justice is a myth. For justice to be actualized in a person, that person would need to be ruled by reason. And in the city, justice occurs only when philosopher-kings rule. But in the real world, reason is not in charge and philosophers do not rule. The last half of the *Republic* recounts the variety of ways that the supposedly perfectly just city will eventually degenerate and become unjust. Justice is an ideal that routinely fails to appear in the real world.

This creates a serious problem for the just war idea. If no man or state is perfectly just, then why do we suppose that the wars that are fought by less-than-just states and administered by fallible men with dirty hands are themselves just? We should admit that in our "second-best world" there is no such thing as a just war. Rather, it is better to speak of more or less justified wars. The just war theory gives us an ideal toward which we can aspire. But we must be careful to avoid the seductive belief that the wars we fight are automatically just. Indeed, the nature of warfare in the real world makes it likely that wars will be unjust. Wars are fought for ignoble and selfish reasons. Innocent civilians are killed. And in the real world, even well-trained soldiers occasionally commit atrocities that just warriors should avoid.

CONCLUSION

Myths are seductive. We love a good story and like to believe that compelling stories are true. There are some fairly obvious emotional, cognitive, and social reasons that we tend to believe the myths of political life. For many who fight and for those who love them, the wars we fight simply must be just.

The danger is that belief in myths can lead us to act on them. If we believe that wars can be just—or that the wars we fight are always just—and if we believe the rhetoric of justification that politicians use in advocating war, then we will be more likely to go to war. And once we go to war, our love of country and our concern for our citizen-soldiers makes it that much more difficult to achieve the critical distance that would allow us to evaluate the justice of the war.

The just war tradition's goal is to reduce and limit violence, not to provide an easy argument in favor of war. Reasonable individuals should take the just war ideal seriously as describing circumstances in which war would be just. But reason will also show us that in reality, very few if any actual wars live up to this ideal. The reality of political discourse is that it is easy to be seduced by the mythology of patriotism and the idealized image of justified warfare.

NOTES

1. Karl Popper, *The Open Society and Its Enemies* (Princeton, NJ: Princeton University Press, 1971), 2:270.
2. See Richard Wrangham and Dale Peterson, *Demonic Males: Apes and Origins of Human Violence* (New York: Houghton Mifflin, 1996).
3. Richard Dawkins, *The Selfish Gene* (Oxford: Oxford University Press, 1989), 198.
4. Benedict Anderson, *Imagined Communities* (London: Verso, 1983).
5. I have in mind here the differences between just war scholars who support the war on terrorism and the war in Iraq (such as George Weigel, James Turner Johnson, and Jean Bethke Elshtain) and those scholars who do not (such as Michael Walzer, William Galston, and a long list of others).
6. I have discussed the way that philosophical terms are politicized in *The Philosopher's Voice* (Albany: SUNY Press, 2002).
7. Oliver O'Donovan, *The Just War Revisited* (Cambridge: Cambridge University Press, 2003), chap. 1.
8. Michael Walzer, *Arguing about War* (New Haven, CT: Yale University Press, 2004), 14.
9. O'Donovan, *Just War Revisited*, 13.

Chapter Three

Genealogy of the Just War Tradition

> War is a mass hypnosis, and it is only thanks to mass hypnosis that it is possible.
>
> —Nikolai Berdyaev, *Slavery and Freedom*[1]

There is no reason to believe that there are just wars. There may have been a time when actual war lived up to the ideal—say, in the Middle Ages—although even this is unlikely. But as warfare has evolved and our ideas about justice have developed, it is less likely that any actual war can live up to the just war ideal. The difficulty is that as war has become more destructive, our ideas about justice have become more exacting. Thus it is increasingly difficult for us to believe that modern wars can be just.

This is why the just war ideal is best understood as a myth. It might have made sense at one time. Even though that time is long past, we continue to believe in the ideal. This is true of many of our myths: we believe mythic stories—or pretend to—even though we now know better. The just war myth remains powerful because it is connected to some of our deepest concerns: about religion, politics, and the meaning of life. In a recent book, Chris Hedges explains some of the ways that war is a force that "gives us meaning."[2] The sacrifices and solidarity of war can give meaning to the whole of life. Essential to this process is the belief that the wars we fight are good wars. We believe that this is true despite its apparent falseness, for if we denied its truth we might lose faith in many of the other myths that give meaning to our lives. This chapter will attempt to explain the roots of this sort of compulsion to believe, with a special focus on the religious origin of the just war idea. The just war tradition develops from within the Christian tradition. Thus it has a close connection with the divine command theory of ethics and the idea of holy war. The obvious point to be made here is that our belief in the just war myth is quite similar to religious belief. Although the just war myth is not as absurd or pernicious as the idea of holy war, it still requires a leap of faith to believe that war is just, especially for Christians who must find a way to justify war despite Jesus's command to turn the other cheek. Many agree with Jesus in holding that violence in our personal lives is wrong, but these same people can end up, oddly enough, supporting war. For Christians, especially, there is a significant religious and moral risk in believing that war can be justified. The Christian tradition reflects this tension: Christian pacifists and just war theorists have long argued over the question of whether pacifism or the just war idea is heretical.

My method in this chapter and the next one is genealogical. I aim to look at the source and development of just war ideas. This method reflects that of social critics like Nietzsche and Foucault who have constructed genealogical critiques of other social formations. Foucault once argued that history is "Jupiterian," by which he meant that history is the history of sovereign power.[3] Foucault's analysis of British and French history fills in the details of the general idea that history is written by the victors; and the victors' history somehow convinces us that the victors were justified. For Foucault, the historical discourse of power makes the triumph of sovereign power seem inevitable and beneficial by retrospectively affirming the victorious cause. This idea has an obvious connection to a religious view of history: we like to believe that there is a guiding hand in history—the angel that rides the whirlwind, as President Bush once put it—who gives victory to the righteous. The problem is that victory is not necessarily connected with justice: the just do not always win. In fact there are good reasons to think that forces constrained by justice will have a tough time defeating unjust opponents.

This difficulty is, of course, resolved by invoking a God who rewards the just in the long run anyway. But invoking God as the author of victory does not actually prove that a war was just. To prove that a war actually is just we need clear criteria and a dispassionate view of war. The problem is that Jupiterian history often obscures the truth by making it look as if political authorities are ordained and justified by God. One of the main critical points of this chapter is that the religious justification of war is linked to a view of sovereignty that holds that political power comes from God—a view that modern liberals should reject.

THE CHRISTIAN JUST WAR TRADITION

This genealogical procedure is not foreign to the material we are considering. Most of the thinkers in the Christian just war tradition look back on the tradition to find the justification of war. Calvin puts it this way: "The reason for waging war which existed in ancient times is equally valid in the present age."[4] Calvin makes this remark in response to Christian pacifists who claim that Jesus's pacific message somehow overturned the ancient tradition of holy war. Such claims are common among Christians who would justify war. This requires substantial interpretive effort that has to reconcile the martial values of the Old Testament with the pacific values of Jesus.[5] One focus of this interpretation is to place enormous emphasis on chapter 13 of Paul's letter to the Romans. The other focus is to turn to the Old Testament and to defend the idea of holy war that is commanded by God.

We see this approach in the work of Augustine, the first and most important defender of the Christian just war idea. In his *Reply to Faustus the Manichaean*, Augustine rejects the Manichaean tendency to find fault with the biblical stories of God's wrathful use of war. Augustine says of Moses that he gave the Egyptians what they deserved. And he goes on to say that Moses's virtue was that he waged war when God wanted him to. The real fault would have been "in not doing it when God commanded him."[6] Augustine's basic argument is about the importance of waging war in obedience to the will of God. But he also clarifies that such obedience is located in obedience to the monarch who is authorized to make such decisions:

A great deal depends on the causes for which men undertake wars, and on the authority they have for doing so; for the natural order which seeks the peace of mankind, ordains that the monarch should have the power of undertaking war if he thinks it advisable, and that the soldiers should perform their military duties in behalf of the peace and safety of the community. When war is undertaken in obedience to God, who would rebuke, or humble, or crush the pride of man, it must be allowed to be a righteous war.[7]

When Augustine, Calvin, and other Christian defenders of the just war ideal direct our attention back to the ancient justification of war, they give us good reasons to think that the justification of war is absurdly mythological. In the Old Testament, war is based entirely on God's command; God commands horrible atrocities—massive slaughters and immoral sacrifices—that are carried out by prophet-kings such as Moses, Joshua, Jephtha, Saul, David, and so on. It is important to recognize that the political structure that provides the basis of the Old Testament doctrine of war is one in which the sovereign is empowered by God—indeed commanded by God—to carry out such slaughter. In fact, God's direct intervention is often said to have facilitated holy war massacres, as when God stops the sun in the sky so that Joshua could complete his slaughter of the Amorites. It is not accidental that Calvin and other Christian apologists for the just war idea routinely list the names and adventures of these prophet-kings as evidence that God commands war and rewards holy warriors with victory.

Most of us no longer believe in a God who would stop the sun in order to facilitate a massacre. Thankfully, most of us have evolved beyond faith in holy war. One reason for this is that we reject the Christian view of sovereignty and its emphasis on the divine command theory of ethics. Liberal democratic societies do not believe that political power is ordained by God or that the sovereign executes God's wrath on wrongdoers. But some Christian just war defenders continue to believe that the state does have a religious mandate to use military force. For example, in the conservative Christian journal *First Things* in a recent discussion of the just war tradition, Darrell Cole quotes Calvin with approval and then concludes: "The soldier is thus as much an agent of God's love as he is of God's wrath, for the two characteristics are harmonious in God."[8] Indeed, the title of Cole's book on just war theory shows us the importance of the divine command approach to just war thinking. The title of his book is *When God Says War Is Right*.

The idea that the soldier is an agent of both God's love and God's wrath is based on the theological belief that violence and love can be reconciled in God. The tradition also includes some other ideas that should be rejected by those of us committed to liberal secular values. For example, the tradition holds that war is justified by God's express commandments (as Cole hints in his title, *When God Says*). Also, there is an underlying faith in the idea that immortality and cosmic justice will provide punishment for wrongdoers as well as compensation for those who are wrongly killed. Indeed, this idea is also part of the Christian justification of the death penalty, which looks back—as the Christian justification of war does—to the Old Testament and to Paul's letter to the Romans. Supreme Court Justice Antonin Scalia puts the Christian approach to killing this way, also in an article in *First Things*: "For the believing Christian, death is no big deal. Intentionally killing an innocent person is a big deal: it is a grave sin, which causes one to lose his soul. But losing this life, in exchange for the next? . . . For the nonbeliever, on the other hand, to deprive a man of his life is to end his existence. What a horrible act!"[9] We have an obligation to avoid killing the innocent. But if you are innocent and you are inadvertently killed in a war (or by the misapplication of the death penalty), your unjust suffering will be redeemed by God's final justice.

This idea has deep roots in the Christian tradition. Augustine says something to the same effect in his *Reply to Faustus*: "What is the evil in war? Is it the death of some who will soon die in any case, that others may live in peaceful subjection? This is mere cowardly dislike, not any religious feeling." The danger is not the risk of death that occurs in war—since death comes soon enough to everyone. Instead, for Augustine, the real danger is the injustice of living in subjection and cowardice.

Perhaps the most important feature of Christian just war theory is the idea that state power is sanctified by divine justice. On the first page of his book Cole indicates that the question of sovereignty and legitimate authority is the key: "Wars are called 'just' whenever true governing authorities (proper authority) have both a just cause and a rightful intent in taking violent actions."[10] What is odd, however, is that no one seriously believes anymore that the modern state is empowered by God. The liberal tradition in American politics grounds political power in the will of the people. And it is this liberal faith in democracy that leads many conservative critics of contemporary politics to worry that the state has strayed from its God-serving function. So it is impossible to say that a modern soldier is actually a servant of God, just as it is false to claim that democratic government has anything in common with divine command ethics.[11] In fact, Christian pacifists such as Stanley Hauerwas and John Howard Yoder point out that faith in the sovereign power of the state can become a kind of idolatry.[12] Yoder calls this a "Constantinian" compromise with the state, in which politics trumps religion.[13] The problem, according to Yoder, is that Augustinian Christianity was too willing to accommodate political reality and allow for dual citizenship in the City of Man and the City of God. On the other hand, Christian just war defenders emphasize the importance of the tension of this dual-citizenship approach, claiming that living in this tension between the real and the ideal is the central problem of Christian life.[14] We should keep this tension in mind as we continue our discussion of the origins of the Christian just war tradition.

Most scholars trace the basic outlines of the Christian just war ideal back to Augustine. It is significant that Augustine bases his doctrine of justified killing in warfare on explicit appeal to divine authority and a view of sovereignty that most of us would reject today. When we examine the details of the Augustinian basis of the just war idea we should have reason to be skeptical of the tradition that develops in Augustine's wake.

In book 1 (chapter 22) of *City of God*, Augustine says that killing can be commanded by God or by a person who represents God's will. This idea has obvious roots in Paul's claim in *Romans* chapter 13 that the sovereign uses the sword to execute God's wrath against wrongdoers. Augustine says that a person who kills out of obedience to divine authority does not himself kill; rather, such a killer is an instrument of God's will. And he reiterates this in his *Reply to Faustus* where he claims that war is a form of "righteous retribution" that God can order (chapter 74). Obviously, a key question here is just how we are supposed to know what God's will is. Augustine is not claiming that soldiers should obey moral monsters. But he does assume, as Paul does in *Romans*, that some political authorities are executors of God's will. Modern liberal thinkers are justified in asking, however, why should we believe than any human being or even any state embodies the will of God?

Leaving this vexing question aside, it is interesting that Augustine's view of God is one that allows for all sorts of killing that we would view as barbaric. Augustine turns to the Old Testament to find examples of justified killing. He cites three telling examples in this discussion: Abraham intending to kill Isaac, Jephtha killing his daughter, and Samson killing the Philistines. The Abraham story finds Abraham obeying God's command and planning to use his son as a blood sacrifice. Augustine claims in *Reply to Faustus* (chapter 73) that this story must be read not as an act of "shocking madness" but as a proof that Abraham is "faithful and submissive." But most of us would admit that there are obvious problems with this sort of fanatical faith and submission to authority. Moreover, this story shows us a world in which God commands infanticide (even if only in jest). If God could command such a horrific action, then it is no wonder that Christians believe that God could command war.

Even if the Abraham story is read merely as a test of faith, actual infanticide is seen in the story of Jephtha. This tale is more detailed and has more to do with the question of war. In Judges, chapters 11 and 12, Jephtha is called upon to lead a holy war against the Ammonites. He vows that if he wins the battle, he will sacrifice to God a burnt offering of whoever comes out of his own house when he returns home from battle. God ensures his victory "with a very great slaughter." One supposes that Jephtha meant to sacrifice a goat or a slave. But on returning home, his daughter is the first person he sees coming out of his house, and so to fulfill his vow he sacrifices her to God. The story of Samson is also one that occurs in the context of warfare. You'll remember that Samson leads a fight against the Philistines. Delilah betrays him and he is captured, tortured, and put on display at a Philistine festival. But Samson is again empowered by God, and he pulls the walls of the Philistine building down on himself and his captors in what is clearly an act of suicidal/homicidal fury.

Augustine admits that these examples are extreme. But such examples provide the background to the idea that violence can be justified by God's direct command. And the risk is that when we believe that some human sovereign has divine authority for violence, it can make atrocity appear to be the will of God.

It is easy to imagine how the idea of God's will would be used by a culture to guide decisions about war. The tribal leader would rally his forces by speaking of the divine command. And the community would follow authority in awe of the authority's religious power. Such a religiously oriented social system is assumed as the background for the discussion of justifiable violence that we find in Paul and Augustine: the "legitimate authority" is supposed to enact God's will. It is important, then, to remember that the just war tradition develops alongside the idea that there are religious authorities who authentically interpret God's will and the idea that God would sanction war.

There is thus a continuum between the holy war ideal and the just war ideal. The biblical tradition shows us a long history of wars of domination fought by the Hebrews in pursuit of religious and ethnic superiority. In Deuteronomy (7:2) Moses tells his people that when they fight for the Promised Land, "You must utterly destroy them; you shall make no covenant with them, and show no mercy to them." Joshua carries out this policy of ethnic cleansing after the Hebrews arrive in Canaan. The idea fueling this policy is that God wants ethnic and religious purity. This idea eventually evolved into the medieval European Crusades.

Implicit in the idea of a holy war is a kind of religious, ethnic, and racial essentialism that holds that certain people and ideas are pleasing to God, while others should be slaughtered and eradicated. This racist approach to violence leads to the justification of atrocity throughout the Old Testament. The violent fear and hatred of one's enemies was so extreme that it was viewed as better to be dead than to fall into the hands of one's enemies. We see this in the suicidal vengeance of Samson. And we find it in the story of Saul. When it becomes apparent that the Philistines are going to capture him, Saul asks to be killed by a compatriot: "Draw your sword and thrust me through with it lest these uncircumcised come and thrust me through and make sport of me" (2 Samuel 31:4). His companion is afraid to do as Saul asked, so Saul falls on his own sword. Saul is probably right that he would have been tortured, for when the Philistines find his body, they decapitate him and hang his body on a wall. It should be noted, of course, that this is the same sort of treatment that the Hebrew hero Joshua uses against the enemies he defeats: their dead bodies are put on display as trophies and warnings to others.

These excesses of violence do not easily fade away. The Crusades show us other examples of wars that were justified in the name of God. And the Crusades also involved the same sort of racial essentialism and excessive violence. When he called for the First Crusade in 1095, Pope Urban II condemned the Turks as an accursed race, and he called for Christians to "exterminate this vile race from our lands."[15] Crusaders believed that God would facilitate such slaughter and reward those who took up the call of holy war. Indeed, holy war was a path to redemption. In his call for the Second Crusade, Bernard of Clairvaux claimed that the holy warrior would be rewarded "with pardon for your sins and everlasting glory."[16] We see similar ideas in the Islamic tradition of jihad. Averroes claims that it is appropriate to kill or enslave the enemies of Islam, especially polytheists.[17] More recently Osama bin Laden (in his fatwa of 1998) claimed that a Muslim's duty is to kill Americans—both civilian and military—wherever they are found. And jihadists believe that they will attain a divine reward for dying in defense of Islam.

EARLY MODERN JUST WAR THINKING

This idea of a holy war that requires the indiscriminate slaughter of all enemies and infidels was eventually criticized by proponents of the just war tradition. One focus of this critique was the question of whether innocents should be killed, even if they belong to a rival religious community. One way of approaching this question is to consider whether God would explicitly command the killing of innocents. Like Augustine, Aquinas considers the example of Abraham and Isaac. He notes that this case shows us that God apparently sanctions the deliberate killing of innocents. But Aquinas emphasizes the fact that this was an exceptional case. For Aquinas, killing is primarily supposed to be for the common good; and killing the innocent violates the common good.[18]

Vitoria continues this line of thinking. He explicitly considers the scriptural example of Joshua and others who indiscriminately slaughtered their enemies, including children. But Vitoria claims that the basic principle is that the innocent should not be killed—unless there are no other means available for prosecuting a just war. He claims, "Even with the Turks it is not allowable to kill children. This is clear, because they are innocent."[19] Thus the evolving just war tradition prohibits the slaughter that we often associate with crusades.

Vitoria also clarifies the idea of a just cause in such a way as to preclude the use of war for explicitly religious purposes. He claims that "difference of religion is not a cause of just war."[20] And he argues against the use of force against the Indians of North America. For Vitoria, "the single and only just cause for commencing a war" is a "wrong received."[21] Vitoria's protestations were obviously unheeded by Christian conquistadors. But his ideas were further developed by other modern just war thinkers. In the twentieth century the basic idea that just wars are primarily defensive wars would be developed by Walzer into the idea that just wars are fought primarily against the crime of aggression. But Vitoria also acknowledges that most of the principles of justice in war only really apply to wars among Christians; and he seems to keep a door open to the possibility of crusade. Vitoria notes, "There are times when security can not be got save by destroying all one's enemies: and this is especially the case against unbelievers, from whom it is useless ever to hope for a just peace on any terms."[22]

Vitoria and other early modern thinkers such as Suarez, Gentili, and Grotius sought to find ways to limit war according to principles of justice in war. Essential to this attempt to limit war was an idealized story of the way wars were fought. Just wars are not "total wars" of the sort fought in the last couple of centuries. Rather, just wars were supposed to be fought by soldiers on a field of battle. The field of battle was supposed to be isolated somewhere so that the war would have little direct impact on noncombatants. The soldiers who fought these battles were supposed to fight with a sense of honor and mutual respect. And the wars that were fought by these chivalrous soldiers were thought to be based on a just cause and to aim at establishing a just peace after war.

Just war ideas were thought to be based on proper theology. Suarez argues that an absolute commitment to nonviolence was a kind of heresy. And he traces this heresy back to the Manichaean beliefs that were combated by Augustine. Suarez's conclusion is that "war, absolutely speaking, is not intrinsically evil, nor is it forbidden to Christians."[23] Grotius would make similar sorts of arguments. And like others in the tradition, Grotius looks back to Hebrew and Christian sources for his ideas about the justification of war. He also looks to pagan (Greek and Roman) sources, indicating the growing development of humanism in European thought. Grotius is most interesting because of his attempt to clarify just causes for war. The basic principle is that wars can be justified as a response to an injury received. And Grotius goes on to enumerate a variety of just causes including defense of life and even defense of chastity. Moreover, in a discussion that resonates with contemporary issues, Grotius indicates conditions that make preemptive war acceptable: when the danger is "immediate and imminent in point of time."[24]

The just war theory itself came to be codified by focusing on two main sets of principles: the principles of *jus ad bellum* (principles of the justice pertaining to going to war) and principles of *jus in bello* (the principles of justice in war). Here, in outline, is a summary of the generally agreed-on principles of just war theory, with a brief gloss intended to illuminate how these ideas are currently understood.

Jus ad bellum

a. *Just cause.* A war must have a just cause. Just causes can include: to resist aggression, to defend sovereignty, or to protect human rights.

b. *Right intention.* Just wars should be fought for just intentions. They should not be fought in order to expand power or expropriate land or booty.
c. *Proper or legitimate authority.* Wars can be waged only by a legitimate governing power.
d. *Last resort.* War is to be used only after making reasonable attempts to use nonviolent means to resolve conflict.
e. *Probable success.* Wars should be engaged only when there is some probability of success; futile wars should not be waged.
f. *Proportionality.* The total benefits of the war must outweigh the harms.

Jus in bello

a. *Discrimination.* A good-faith effort must be made to avoiding harming noncombatants. This is the idea of *noncombatant immunity.* Some noncombatant deaths can be justified by the *principle of double effect* (i.e., these deaths cannot be directly intended).
b. *Proportionality.* The means employed within a war must be proportional to legitimate strategic and tactical goals.
c. *No intrinsically bad means.* Certain actions are always wrong, for example, rapes, torture, poisoning of water, and so on.

Each of these ideas is connected to the others. And each would require a book of its own to fully develop. But the general idea is as follows. When deciding whether a nation is justified in going to war one must ask whether the nation has a just cause, as well as whether it has the right intention and the proper authority to engage the war. One must also consider whether all other reasonable methods of negotiation have failed, what the probable success of the war might be, and whether the possible benefits of the proposed violence are proportional to the harms that will be caused. Within the conduct of war, just war theory emphasizes noncombatant immunity and the principle of proportionality with regard to means and ends. And just war theory condemns certain actions (such as rape, enslavement, and genocide) as *mala in se*—evil in themselves—and always to be avoided. The principles of the just war tradition can be used as a decision procedure for deciding when to go to war (this is especially true of the principles of *jus ad bellum*). And they can also be used to critically evaluate current or past wars.

I suggested earlier that it is not accidental that almost all defenders of the just war ideal—even contemporary just war theorists—continue to use the Latin names for these categories. This use of Latin reminds us that these ideals have an ancient origin, that they are connected to the medieval Catholic tradition, and that they are consecrated by a sort of reverential nostalgia for a time of chivalry. When we consider the basis of just war thinking in the work of medieval and early modern just war thinkers, this nostalgia extends all the way back to a reverential awe for the holy wars of the Old Testament. Recall that for Augustine, the primary justification of war would be a war that was sanctioned by God and his divine command. The idea that war is primarily justified as a response to the crime of aggression against the international system of nation-states—as Michael Walzer puts it—is a fairly new one that took centuries to develop.

IDEALS AND REALITY

Nostalgia is a longing for an idealized past. But usually, the actual past never lives up to the idealized image we long for. The chivalrous ideal of medieval warfare never occurred in fact. Medieval wars were fought for self-interested motives. Soldiers were sneaky, corrupt, and dishonorable. And innocent civilians were often harmed along the way.

One classic representation of this is found in Shakespeare's *Henry V*, a play that is famous for its rousing battle speeches: "Once more into the breech, dear friends" and "We few, we happy few, we band of brothers." It is significant that these phrases do arouse us and they can still be quoted by warriors seeking to rally the troops. But these phrases occur in the midst of an unjust war that was often fought without concern for justice (or "the disciplines of war" as they are called within the play). The play begins with King Henry looking for an excuse to start a war of self-interest. The play memorializes the siege of Harfleur with the famous "once more into the breech" speech. But it should be noted that sieges are morally suspect because they harm the innocent (when a town is under siege, the innocent are usually the first to be harmed). And Henry admits that he cannot be held responsible for the atrocities that his men will commit if the town refuses to submit. Moreover, at the battle of Agincourt, where the "band of brothers" speech is made, the chivalrous rules of warfare are broken as the French kill the boys and servants who accompany the English forces and as the English retaliate by killing their French prisoners.

The reality of warfare is less than ideal. Wars are usually fought for reasons that have more to do with self-interest than with noble ideals. Wars inevitably harm the innocent bystanders who are unlucky enough to get caught up in the battle. And soldiers are tempted to violate those principles of honor that regulate the treatment of prisoners, the injured, and even the dead bodies of the enemy. This was true in the Middle Ages, and these problems are exacerbated by conditions of modern warfare. Modern politicians are not immune to the temptation to use war as a means of consolidating power. And modern states continue to use war as a means of expanding their spheres of influence and as a way of maximizing the national self-interest. Moreover, in modern mechanized warfare, there are no battlefields. Rather, bombs fall across the whole of enemy territory, resulting in massive civilian casualties. And even the best trained and most moral of armies can end up doing horrible things to enemy combatants.

CONCLUSION

The idea that any actual war is a fully just war is a myth that is fueled both by nostalgia and by a lack of attention to the facts. It is ironic that we continue to believe in the myth of the just war. We have made substantial moral and political progress in the last two centuries. We have outlawed slavery. We have established equality for women. We have eradicated child labor. We have minimized the use of the death penalty. We have institutionalized ideas about human rights and democracy. But we still believe that war is a just and noble thing.

War runs counter to the evolving modern sense of justice. War is inherently disrespectful of individuals. In war, human beings are used as tools or instruments; they are not given the respect that is due to human persons. If the primary commandment of justice is to respect individuals as having dignity or inherent value, then war violates this commandment. In war, the enemy is seen as a "thing" to be destroyed; enemy soldiers are not viewed as persons. We have worked diligently during the last century to avoid treating persons as mere representatives of their race or class or gender. But in war, prejudice and stereotyping are unavoidable: the enemy is a deindividuated member of a mass; we care little about the personal identity of those who fight and die on the other side. One reason for this can be found in the genealogy of the just war idea. In religious wars, God's forces are blessed, while the evil enemy is damned. Enemy soldiers are viewed as evil by virtue of their status as enemies.

This points to a structurally similar problem found in the way that the military deindividuates its personnel. Soldiers are used by the nation. It is true that soldiers are paid for their service and that they are given certain honors. But the very life of the soldier is put at the disposal of other people. Soldiers are treated as disposable and exchangeable items and not as persons. This fact is unavoidable in war—especially in modern wars fought by massive armies. No one asks the individual troops for their consent; there is no democracy in the military. Indeed, the virtuous soldier is obedient, compliant, and self-sacrificial. Soldiers are trained to view themselves not as individuals but as members of the unit. There is an unavoidable tension in the fact that liberal-democratic societies encourage and support such an undemocratic and illiberal institution as the military. One way this sort of obedience and sacrifice is justified is through the mythological construction of the nation. And this often has religious overtones as it is easy to meld nationalism and religion and view soldiers—as Cole and other just war defenders seem to—as agents of God.

We need a military. But we should avoid giving military service a quasi-religious mystical aura. We should admit that this aura is, for the most part, a mythological construction. And we should avoid claiming that soldiers are somehow actualizing God's will. This idea might be comforting to the dying soldier and his family. But it tends to make it that much easier to justify the injustices of war.

The truism that there are no atheists in the foxhole reminds us that war is imbued with religious significance. War is often senseless and inhumane. In the midst of such chaos, we deeply long to believe—as President Bush has said—that an angel directs the whirlwind. The danger of this sort of mythology is that it can make it seem that the horrors of war are justified when, in reality, they are not.

NOTES

1. Nikolai Berdyaev, *Slavery and Freedom* (New York: Scribners, 1944), 155.

2. Chris Hedges, *War Is a Force That Gives Us Meaning* (New York: Public Affairs, 2002).

3. Michel Foucault, *Society Must Be Defended: Lectures at the Collège de France, 1975–76* (New York: Picador, 2003).

4. John Calvin, "Civil Authority and the Use of Force," from *Institutes of the Christian Religion* 4:20, in *War and Christian Ethics*, 2nd ed., ed. Arthur F. Holmes (Grand Rapids, MI: Baker Academic, 2005), 168.

5. I discuss this in more detail in *What Would Jesus Really Do?* (Lanham, MD: Rowman & Littlefield, 2007).

6. Augustine, *Reply to Faustus the Manichaean*, chap. 78, at www.ccel.org/ccel/schaff/npnf104.txt.

7. Augustine, *Reply to Faustus*, chap. 75.

8. Darrell Cole, "Good Wars," *First Things* 116 (October 2001): 27–31.

9. Antonin Scalia, "God's Justice and Ours," *First Things* 123 (May 2002): 17–21.

10. Darrell Cole, *When God Says War Is Right: The Christian's Perspective on When and How to Fight* (Colorado Springs, CO: Waterbrook Press, 2002), 5.

11. Cf. Robert Kraynak, *Christian Faith and Modern Democracy* (Notre Dame, IN: Notre Dame University Press, 2001).

12. Stanley Hauerwas, *Performing the Faith: Bonhoeffer and the Practice of Nonviolence* (Grand Rapids, MI: Brazos, 2004), esp. chap. 7; also see Hauerwas, *The Peaceable Kingdom* (Notre Dame, IN: Notre Dame University Press, 1983).

13. John Howard Yoder, *The Original Revolution* (Scottdale, PA: Herald Press, 2003).

14. See esp. J. Daryl Charles, *Between Pacifism and Jihad* (Downer's Grove, IL: Intervarsity, 2005); also Jean Bethke Elshtain, *Just War against Terrorism* (New York: Basic Books, 2003); and George Weigel, *Tranquillitas Ordinis* (Oxford: Oxford University Press, 1989).

15. Quoted in Karen Armstrong, *Holy War* (New York: Anchor Books, 2001), 3.

16. Bernard of Clairvaux, "A Holy War," in Holmes, *War and Christian Ethics*, 89.

17. Averroes, "Jihad," in *The Morality of War*, ed. Larry May, Eric Rovie, and Steve Viner (Upper Saddle River, NJ: Prentice Hall, 2006), 21–22.

18. Thomas Aquinas, *Summa Theologica*, in May, Rovie, and Viner, *Morality of War*, 30–31.

19. Francisco de Vitoria, "On the Law of War," in May, Rovie, and Viner, *Morality of War*, 41.

20. Vitoria, 39.

21. Vitoria, 39.

22. Vitoria, 45.

23. Francisco Suarez, "On War," in May, Rovie, and Viner, *Morality of War*, 59.

24. Hugo Grotius, "The Law of War and Peace," in May, Rovie, and Viner, *Morality of War*, 72.

Chapter Four

Duels and Modern Wars

War is that condition in which the vanity of temporal things and temporal goods takes on a serious significance and it is accordingly the moment in which the ideality of the particular attains its right and becomes actuality.

—Hegel, *Philosophy of Right*[1]

Despite the fact that wars are rarely just, the just war myth continues to guide our thinking about war. The idea of just combat may make sense in some contexts. But it does not work in conditions of modern mechanized warfare. And yet, we continue to believe the myth that modern wars are just. One reason for this is that we are too ready to acquiesce to the power that the state has over us. Indeed, there is something satisfying about giving in to the myths of political life. As discussed in chapter 2, Freud explained this in terms of group narcissism and the way that individuals come to identify themselves with the group. But before Freud, Hegel reminded us that the fleeting life of the individual can find its higher purpose in the more lasting and substantial reality of the state. Hegel's idea of "the vanity of temporal things" means that individuals and their concerns are ephemeral. States are the focal point of history and they remain long after individual citizens, soldiers, or statesmen are forgotten. War is a powerful force because it directs our attention to goods that are more important than the life of the individual.

For the just war theory, the most lasting good is justice. George Weigel's defense of the just war theory looks back to Augustine to remind us of the importance of *tranquillitas ordinis*, a rightly ordered political community. From this point of view, the ideal of justice is far more important than the interests of any single individuals. In fact, individuals ought to sacrifice their own interests and even their own lives in order to actualize this ideal. The difficulty of this idea is that for most of us committed to liberal-democratic ideas, the focal point of justice is also supposed to be the life and liberty of individuals. The just war myth assures us that there are good reasons for individuals to sacrifice their life, liberty, and happiness for the state and its pursuit of justice.

It is obvious that *states* go to war; individuals do not. But we are often confused about these two different levels of analysis and their implications for the justification of violence. It is easy to think that wars are merely like personal duels writ large. If this is so, then the principles of honor in combat that apply to individual combat should also apply to war. But war is completely different from individual combat. Indeed, wars use individuals in a way that is disrespectful of individuality. Thus wars are justified only as actions of states. But, as I will argue in this chapter, there are good reasons to be skeptical of this emphasis on states as opposed to individuals. The basic standpoint to be developed here is a "personalist" one that claims that persons are the primary source of value in the world. States do have value. But their value must be understood as derivative of that of individuals. This standpoint gives us good reason to be skeptical of the myth of the just war.

A HEGELIAN APPROACH TO WAR

The ideal of just combat perhaps works best to describe a duel or, at most, a war that is fought by a small number of people on an isolated battlefield. The image of the duel continues to fuel our imagination of war. The great theorist of war, Carl von Clausewitz, claimed that "war is nothing but a duel on an extensive scale."[2] What he means by this is that "war is an act of violence intended to compel our opponent to fulfill our will."[3] This recalls something like Hegel's understanding of the "master-slave dialectic."[4] Clausewitz and Hegel were contemporaries, living in the era in which the modern idea of "total war" or "absolute war" was first developed. Clausewitz and Hegel were both reacting to the Napoleonic Wars and the full flowering of the international system in Europe. This era represented a development away from the prior system in which wars were fought by a professional class of soldiers or hired mercenaries and in which "nations" were viewed as the property of sovereigns who often had no organic connection to the people they governed. In previous centuries, wars were fought in staged battles and there was often no intention to occupy the territory of the enemy nation, let alone to destroy their entire army. One might recall, for example, the wars of the Renaissance condottiere. But in the nineteenth century there was both a growing commitment to the nation-state and a new approach to war that involved mass mobilizations of citizen-soldiers, the *levée en masse*. The Napoleonic Wars represented an attempt to impose a unified rule across Europe. A similar approach could be found in the American Civil War, which brought total war to the United States. This approach to war eventually fueled the world wars of the twentieth century. Those who talk of a "clash of civilizations" today continue to think of wars as total wars in which entire nations, cultures, and ideologies are fighting a life-or-death battle.

David A. Bell has recently argued that the irony of the Napoleonic Wars was that they were inspired by the effort to create perpetual peace.[5] This was the beginning of the idea of a war to end all wars. Prior to Napoleon, the just war ideal was promulgated by Kant in his book arguing for perpetual peace. Kant thought that peace would come about through a combination of the spread of republican government and the spread of morality, including, especially, the development of a greater sense of the morality of war. Kant aimed at the creation of a federation of nations that would help to resolve international tensions. But Kant was not naive enough to think that war would be abolished immediately. Indeed, Kant made it clear that the key to eradicating war was learning to fight wars that were subject to morality. For example, the ideas of *jus in bello* were to be respected because they made future war more unlikely. Kant puts it this way: "No state at war with another shall permit such acts of hostility as would make mutual confidence impossible during a future time of peace."[6] This led Kant to postulate prohibitions against assassination, the use of spies, and wars of extermination.

But Clausewitz and others saw that the era of total war required a new way of thinking about war as a fight to the death. In a fight to the death, anything goes. Thus we find Sherman's idea that "war is hell" and the scorched-earth policy of the Union's attack on the Confederacy during the American Civil War that culminated in the burning of Atlanta and the devastation of Sherman's March to the Sea. The explicit policy of this campaign was to destroy the civilian infrastructure in order to eradicate support for the Confederate army. Sherman's "war is hell" idea is expressed in his letter to the Confederate commander General

Hood: "War is cruelty and you cannot refine it."⁷ Sherman is credited
with implementing a policy of "total war." But it was primarily in the
twentieth century when total war involved both the mobilization of the
entire economy for war as well as the legitimization of attacks on civilians (since each civilian in a completely mobilized economy is part of
the war effort).

War creates a situation in which the choice is a stark one: kill or be
killed. If that is the reality of war, then anything goes. The idea of a fight
to the death can be found in Hegel's idea of the master-slave dialectic:
this is a conflict in which two individuals confront each other and engage in a struggle to the death. This fight is ultimately about pride: one
must either die or submit and be enslaved. At stake in Hegel's account
are the honor and esteem of individuality: it is worth dying and killing
to assert and defend one's value as an individual. And, in this struggle,
there are no rules, except for force. In fact, the struggle occurs because
there are no rules. In other words, the Hegelian duel is outside, or prior
to, the structure of justice that would regulate the struggle.

This way of understanding the violence of the duel can give rise to an
understanding of war as a duel writ large. One of the problems here is
the question of the source of justice. The modern social contract view
of the state claims that principles of justice develop from the contract.
Hobbes's version of this is quite radical, as he seems to imply that outside the contract, there are no rules and thus that there is nothing but
war. The basic idea of the contract is that individuals join together and
form a state in order to better protect their rights. Locke's version of the
social contract is less radical than Hobbes's. Locke allows that there are
principles of the natural law that regulate behavior in the state of nature
even outside the social contract. But the point is the same: that war
properly speaking is about collective violence authorized through the
transfer of power that occurs through the social contract.

Thus for modern liberals, war is best understood as an act of the general will authorized by the social contract. The difficulty is that once the
contract is established, the state takes on a power of its own. And individuals thus end up being used by the state—even against their own
wills, as happens when there are conscripted armies.

This sort of ambiguity is found in Rousseau's discussion in *The Social Contract*. Rousseau distinguishes war, as a political act, from the
state of personal enmity and ubiquitous violence that Hobbes famously
calls "war" in chapter 13 of the *Leviathan* and chapter 1 of *De Cive*.
Hobbes describes the state of nature as a condition of war that is of all

men against all men (*bellum omnium contra omnes*). But for Rousseau, "War, then, is not a relation between man and man, but a relation between State and State, in which individuals are enemies only by accident, not as men, nor even as citizens, but as soldiers; not as members of the fatherland, but as its defenders. In short, each State can have as enemies only other States and not individual men, inasmuch as it is impossible to fix any true relation between things of different kinds."[8] Rousseau's contractarian perspective leads to the idea of limited warfare. As Rousseau puts it, "War confers no right except what is necessary to its end."[9] Rousseau argues, for example, for noncombatant immunity: a declaration of war does not justify the killing of those who are not employed as soldiers. Declarations of war are warnings given to the citizens of the nation that is declared to be the enemy.[10] The warning says that if citizens of the enemy state take up arms, they may be killed by the soldiers of the state declaring the war. Connected with this is the correlative right to surrender: when enemy soldiers lay down their arms, they are no longer acting as soldiers and thus ought not be killed. For Rousseau, then, there is a difference between citizen and soldier. And this distinction provides the basis for noncombatant immunity.

The difficulty of all of this is that in modern mechanized war, the fighting has little to do with the individual. Or rather, in the era of total war, when whole nations fight against one another, the distinction between citizen and soldier is effaced. When war is organized around the abstract idea of the nation-state, we are left with a Hobbesian war at the level of international affairs. This leads to an approach to war that can violate the rights of individuals. Individuals can thus be sacrificed on the "slaughter-bench of history," in Hegel's infamous phrase, because the real focus of history is nations and not individuals.

Hegel recognized this when he claimed that war was a reminder of the "vanity of temporal things." This way of conceiving war directs our attention to the mystical and mythological nature of warfare. But we should recall that Hegel's ideas about politics and war have implications that seem undemocratic and anti-individualistic. For Hegel, as for many defenders of the just war myth, the state and nation are mystical "totalities" that are more valuable than the lives of individual citizens. And indeed, Hegel rejected the social contract view of the state because it was unable to explain the way that the state was superior to individuality. But this reminds us of the problem of war. War is not a duel in which violence makes sense to individuals. Rather, in war, the state "uses" individuals in the name of its "higher" goods.

Just war defenders appear to recognize this and accept it as a necessary fact of political life: politics and war involve a set of rules that is
different from the morality of ordinary individual life. For Hegel, this
explains how it is possible that soldiers could fight without "personal
enmity." It may seem odd that soldiers can violate the commandment
"Thou shall not kill." But Hegel says: "Courts of law and soldiers have
not only the right but also the duty to kill human beings; but in this case,
there are precise definitions as to what kind of people and what circumstances make this permissible and obligatory."[11] Hegel defines the
duty of the soldier solely in terms of the soldier's duty to the state he
represents; Hegel does not prescribe a universal theory of justice in war
that would be the duty of all soldiers of any nationality.

And yet he does think that modern European states share certain
ideas about justice in war. Hegel writes, for example: "Modern wars are
accordingly waged in a humane manner, and persons do not confront
each other in hatred."[12] Hegel continues: "At most, personal enmities
will arise at military outposts, but in the army as such, hostility is something indeterminate which takes second place to the duty which each re-
spects in the other." Hegel's idea is that the individual, insofar as he is
a soldier, will transcend his particular tastes and inclinations (for example, hatred for the enemy). The soldier, as a representative of the state,
is supposed merely to do his duty. That is, the soldier is supposed to
transcend his individual interests (his passions of hostility and hatred,
for example) and act simply as a functionary of the state. The soldiers
themselves are involved only insofar as they are representatives of the
state.

This impersonal approach to the violence of war is typical of those
who defend the just war myth. And it can be traced back to the Augustinian idea that just warriors fight out of a sort of obligation that is supposed to be purely moral. The just warrior goes to war with a sense of
tragedy and duty, not because he hopes for personal gain or because he
is inspired by hatred. The soldier is a servant of the state, God, and justice; he is not supposed to be motivated by personal desires. Weigel,
Johnson, and Elshtain have recently reemphasized the difference between the just war idea of war as a public or political act and the private
violence of the duel (in their language, the just war tradition is about
bellum and not about *duellum*). This distinction is the basis of Weigel's
argument against pacifism, especially Christian pacifism. Christian
pacifists claim that Jesus prohibited violence and they argue that Jesus
would be opposed to war. But the Christian just war theory claims that

Jesus's pacifism was at best about private violence. In other words, they argue that Jesus's "pacifism" was based solely on a rejection of the violence of the duel (or more broadly, the idea that private individuals should employ violence on their own). They argue that Jesus's ideas about "turning the other cheek" and nonresistance to evil apply only to private individuals. The state, however, is empowered to use violence for the public good. Christian just war defenders argue that war is allowed as a specifically public activity, when it is declared by a legitimate public authority.

This reasoning can be persuasive. And indeed, most of us do not fight private duels. Instead we call the cops, thus showing our faith in public authority. However, as noted before, this places great emphasis on the legitimacy and wisdom of the public authority. Moreover, it appears to invert a commonsensical idea about the justification of violence in terms of self-defense. Violence used in self-defense appears to be easier to justify: for individuals, duels make more sense than wars. Dueling situations are conceived of as a matter of personal self-defense in a fight to the death. When I confront my opponent in single combat, I either kill him or he kills me. In such a context—say when someone invades my home or aggresses against me in the street—I am entitled to fight back in defense of my own life. This entitlement is derived from my right to life. But war is not like this, especially modern wars fought by developed nations. These wars are often based on humanitarian interests, speculative threats, and geopolitical strategies, in which self-defense is not clearly the cause. Even in wars of national self-defense, it is not clear that the safety of my life has anything to do with the safety of the nation. All of this requires a sort of Hegelian faith in the nation as a higher sort of good. It is this that leads Christian pacifists such as Yoder and Hauerwas to complain that just war ideas promote a sort of idolatry.

Christian just war defenders such as Paul Ramsey will also argue that love of the neighbor can be used to justify war. We go to war to defend our neighbors. This sort of reasoning might be used to justify humanitarian interventions. But the difficulty is in knowing whether "the neighbor" wants and deserves our help. In the personal case, when my neighbor is in a fight, I must have some way of knowing what my neighbor wants and deserves. It may be, for example, that my neighbor prefers—as a matter of pride—to fight his own battles and he may resent my interference. Moreover, it may be that my neighbor is a bad man who does not deserve my help. The difficulty is that at the level of politics, all of this becomes quite muddy: how do we know what neighboring peoples want or deserve? Moreover, the reality of war is that interference can provoke escalation and backlash. The intervening power can commit atrocity along the way. And intervenors also often have some strategic or economic interest in their intervention.

A PERSONALIST RESPONSE TO MODERN WAR

The violence of a duel is both more understandable and easier to justify than the violence of war. In a situation of personal self-defense, I "know" my enemy (at least to the extent that I know exactly what he did to threaten me). In other words, I know that he somehow "deserves" to be opposed by me, insofar as he attacked me and forced me to take up arms against him. Moreover, the experience of fighting in self-defense is quite different from the experience of fighting amid the mass violence of war. When I raise my fists or some other weapon against a personal attacker, I can look him in the eye as I fight him and see him as an individual. I can even ask him to surrender or I can communicate with him in some other way. And in a duel, I can control the means I employ and can usually easily avoid harming innocent bystanders. In war, none of this is true.

Another way of putting this is that duels put a *personal* face on violence, in the sense of "personal" that is employed by so-called personalist philosophers. Philosophers who have defended personalist ideas include such diverse thinkers as Immanuel Kant and the late pope, John Paul II. The basic idea of personalism is that persons deserve respect because they have inherent dignity, and they should not be treated as mere means to some other end or as instruments for some larger purpose. This basic idea is what led John Paul II to oppose the American invasion of Iraq. For example, in his speech of January 13, 2003, the pope said, "No to war! War is not always inevitable. It is always a defeat for humanity." Personalists and other individualists have long been opposed to the impersonal idealism of those who overvalue the nation and the state.

John Paul II also reminds us that the very idea of justice, which is so important for defenders of the just war theory, can itself lead us astray. For Christian personalists like John Paul II, justice is not the whole of the moral law. Morality also requires love, charity, and forgiveness. John Paul II put it this way in his speech on World Peace Day in 2004:

Justice and love sometimes appear to be *opposing forces*. In fact they are but *two faces of a single reality*, two dimensions of human life needing to be mutually integrated. Historical experience shows this to be true. It shows how justice is frequently unable to free itself from rancor, hatred and even cruelty. *By itself, justice is not enough.* Indeed, it can even betray itself, unless it is open to that deeper power which is love.[13]

The idea of love should direct us back toward the personal face of war. Love requires us to address individuals as the individuals that they are. But the just war idea can be so obsessed with justice and the demands of *tranquillitas ordinis* that it can fail to see the very real suffering that is caused by the pursuit of justice.

The treatment of individual persons should be based on morally relevant facts about the person: what a person deserves is determined by who he or she is and what he or she has done. It is possible from within an individualistic theory to fight in self-defense and to punish wrongdoers. But even in using violence we should treat criminals and our enemies as persons. This is why, for example, Kant says that we may execute murderers but we should refrain from torturing them. As Derek Jeffreys has recently argued, torture tends to depersonalize individuals, as the basis of torture is to use a person's basic instincts and experience of his own body against him.[14] The Kantian idea is that we should give people what they deserve without abusing them and treating them as objects. But war depersonalizes people and treats persons as objects. Nikolai Berdyaev puts it this way:

Warfare is possible only against an object. You cannot make war on a subject. If in your enemy you recognize a subject, a concrete living being, human personality, war becomes impossible. War means the men have been turned into objects. In warring armies there are no subjects, no personalities.[15]

Thomas Nagel expresses a similar idea as follows: "Hostility or aggression should be directed at its true object. This means both that it should be directed at the person or persons who provoke it and that it should aim more specifically at what is provocative about them."[16] The just war theory does contain the idea that just warriors should avoid harming the innocent, that is, those who have done nothing to incur hostility. This is the basic idea of noncombatant immunity. This is what makes the use of indiscriminate weapons of mass destruction wrong; it is also what makes terrorism wrong. Such weapons and tactics do not respect persons in the sense that they make no effort to give persons what they actually deserve. Unfortunately, modern warfare is conducted by such indiscriminate means.

Collateral damage is justified by using the principle of double effect: if the harm to noncombatants is an unintended accidental effect of a legitimate war aim, then it is allowable. But this idea is flexible enough to permit all kinds of noncombatant death, and it requires a sort of purity of intention that rarely obtains in reality. And wars are usually based on the utilitarian idea that some innocent persons can be killed provided that the greater good is achieved. But again, this postulates a mythological construct—"the greater good"—and allows some individuals to be sacrificed in order to attain it. The principle of double effect is discussed in more detail in chapter 7.

In a duel, it is easy enough to imagine that noncombatants remain unmolested. And it is assumed that the combatants deserve what they get. Of course, even in a duel, this is a questionable assumption. Desert is a moral idea. But victory in a duel usually has very little to do with moral desert. Rather, duels are decided by a combination of superior fighting ability and good luck. But, at least, when a duel is entered into voluntarily, both parties agree to abide by the vicissitudes of might and fortune. In war, things are quite different. In some parts of the world, soldiers are still conscripted. And even in a volunteer army, soldiers have very little say about the battles they fight. Moreover, the methods employed in modern warfare aim at destroying deindividuated enemies who are part of the modern mass army. And finally, modern warfare spills over and harms persons who are not themselves part of the fight.

Despite this, the dueling ideal continues to fuel much of our imagination about warfare. When we imagine a hero, it is usually an individual who fights in single combat, looking his enemy in the eye and killing the enemy in a hand-to-hand battle. But this is far from the reality of modern warfare. Warring parties do not fight as individuals. Rather, soldiers must fight as a unit and the local fighting unit is controlled by those at higher levels of command. While there are some instances of single combat in modern wars, for the most part individuals fight in concert with others and the enemy who is fought is an abstraction consisting of groups of men who are often not even seen directly.

The impersonal nature of modern warfare is seen in recent films such as *Saving Private Ryan* or *Flags of our Fathers*. The battle sequences of these films show us mass confusion and indiscriminate death. Soldiers are flung upon the beach. Some drown; some are shot. Others improbably make it to safety. Any individual who survives the assault on the beach is just lucky. There is no individual skill or strength involved in emerging victorious here. Rather, it is a process based on large numbers and the laws of probability: if enough individuals are thrown into the battle, some will make it to their destination. Around three thousand Allied troops were killed on D-Day in Normandy and at Iwo Jima around five thousand Americans were killed before the island was secured. This reminds us of the nature of modern warfare. There are no individuals in such a war, only masses: squads, platoons, companies, and piles of deindividuated corpses.

It is interesting, however, that as these films develop, we find a different idea expressed, as the military (and the film) turns its focus to a few individuals. In *Saving Private Ryan*, the military wants to save Private Ryan because he is the last living son of a family whose other sons have already been killed in the war. In *Flags of our Fathers*, the military wants to find the individuals responsible for raising the flag on Mount Suribachi, so it can use them to sell the war back home (ironically, still not really caring about the soldiers as individuals). These films return us to the familiar plotlines of ordinary life that focus on individuality. Our stories—our imaginations—dwell on individuality. Perhaps this is why we imagine that wars are like duels: a duel makes sense, but a war is simply chaos.

In a duel, the combatants come together voluntarily and fight alone. We see this ideal in vivid detail at the beginning of the Western tradition. In Homer's *Iliad*, in the midst of war, the great heroes confront one another in single combat. It seems that the narration cannot include the totality of war. Instead our attention focuses on individuals and their private battles. Indeed, Homer makes it seem that when the heroes come together in their duels, the rest of the war stops around them. We thus find a sort of combat that makes sense: "mano a mano," hand to hand and man to man. We see the idealized image of the duel in medieval stories of knights and their jousts; we find it in stories and movies that represent the swordplay of early modern Europe; and we see it in Western movies, where dueling gunfighters shoot it out on deserted streets.

A duel can be described as a just form of combat. In a duel, both parties consent to the combat. And most importantly, only the other dueling party is a target of violence. If one of the dueling parties dies, he "deserved" to die in the sense that he deliberately put himself into the situation, he knew what he was fighting for, and he was willing to accept the consequences of the fight. And the combat itself is supposed to be regulated by a certain code of honor. The dueling fighters are not supposed to accept help from bystanders. And the fighters are supposed to respect some conventions about surrender and about respect for the body of the defeated foe.

Of course, the dueling ideal is often violated. Homer's *Iliad* shows us this in the story of Achilles' duel with Hector. Achilles is unfairly assisted by Athena, who confuses Hector with her divine interference. And then Achilles refuses to honor Hector's body; and instead he vents his rage on Hector's corpse in a way that would have offended the moral sensibility of the ancient Greeks. This story reminds us that honorable duels are rare. In the middle of combat our instincts take over. In a fight to the death, anyone might "cheat" by biting, kicking, scratching, or throwing sand in the opponent's eyes. Dueling fighters can easily become less than human as they are thrown back onto the animal imperative to kill or be killed. This is graphically portrayed by Homer in Achilles' speech before he defeats Hector. Achilles says that he would like to destroy and disrespect Hector's body to such an extent that he would eat Hector's flesh raw if he could. Simone Weil's interpretation of the *Iliad* reminds us that violence strips us of our humanity and turns us into beasts.

This depersonalizing aspect of violence is amplified and exacerbated by modern warfare. In modern warfare, armies of young men are thrown at one another with mechanized weapons. Some of these soldiers have no idea what they are fighting for. They have little choice about whom they fight. Many are killed and kill at a distance in which there is no direct connection to the enemy. Most importantly, modern warfare does not occur on a field of battle that is isolated and free of noncombatants.

The raw emotions and brutal instincts that fuel Achilles' rage continue to influence warfare. We see it again in the much-publicized atrocities that occurred in the Iraq war: one might recall the brutality of the torture at Abu Ghraib, the rape and murder at Mahmoudiya, or the massacre at Haditha. These atrocities were committed by American soldiers, who are well trained and disciplined in just war ideals. It is to the military's credit that it treats these events as war crimes. But gross brutality also occurs as a routine method of modern warfare. Recall, for example, that American forces engaged in a "turkey-shoot" on the so-called Highway of Death during the first Gulf War: as Iraqi troops retreated from Kuwait, American forces slaughtered them from the air. Or recall the bulldozer assault during the first Gulf War in which American forces used bulldozer tanks to overrun the Iraqi trenches, burying both the dead and the living. Or recall the destruction caused by NATO forces in the former Yugoslavia as they used high-altitude bombing and targeted civilian infrastructure as part of their "humanitarian intervention." The slaughter and atrocity is even worse on the other side: terrorists deliberately target the innocent, captured enemies are tortured, and bodies are decapitated and desecrated.

The niceties of the duel have little to do with the brutality of war. A formal duel is a highly stylized combat in which force is regulated by conventions of honor that both parties recognize. In war, there is a breakdown of conventions. Wars occur because the conventions of civility and mutual respect are no longer in effect. The goal of war is victory over the amassed forces of the enemy. And the means to such victory involve the destruction of massive numbers of the enemy. The pursuit of victory thus pushes us beyond moral limits. Some soldiers go over the edge and resort to egregious brutality fueled by rage and raw emotion. Military and civilian leaders are not immune to the temptation of brutality. And sometimes, as in the case of the deliberate bombing of civilians that was used throughout World War II, the most horrifying atrocities become routine policy.

CONCLUSION

This chapter and the last have discussed two sources of the just war myth. In previous chapters, we discussed the genealogy of the just war tradition. We saw that it is easy to think that wars are sanctioned by God and divine justice. In this chapter we have discussed the connection between war and a Hegelian approach to politics that denies the value of individuality. Both of these sources point to the problem of our faith in the nation or state as the embodiment of God's will and the idea that there are higher goods that are worth the sacrifice of individuality. In the next chapter we will look at a more concrete contemporary form of this problem.

NOTES

1. G. W. F. Hegel, *Philosophy of Right* (Cambridge: Cambridge University Press, 1991), sec. 324, remark. For further discussion see Andrew Fiala, "The

Vanity of Temporal Things: Hegel and the Ethics of War," *Studies in the History of Ethics*, February 2006.

2. Carl von Clausewitz, "On the Art of War," in *The Morality of War*, ed. Larry May, Eric Rovie, and Steve Viner (Upper Saddle River, NJ: Prentice Hall, 2006), 115.

3. Clausewitz, "Art of War," 116.

4. Hegel, *Phenomenology of Spirit* (Oxford: Oxford University Press, 1977), sec. 4.

5. David A. Bell, *The First Total War: Napoleon's Europe and the Birth of Warfare as We Know It* (New York: Houghton Mifflin, 2007).

6. Immanuel Kant, *Perpetual Peace*, in May, *Morality of War*, 113.

7. Quoted in Michael Walzer, *Just and Unjust Wars* (New York: Basic Books, 1977), 32.

8. Jean-Jacques Rousseau, *The Social Contract*, in *The Social Contract and Discourse on the Origin of Inequality* (New York: Washington Square Press, 1967), 13–14.

9. Rousseau, *Social Contract*, 15.

10. "Declarations of war are not so much warnings to the powers as to their subjects." Rousseau, *Social Contract*, 14.

11. Hegel, *Philosophy of Right*, sec. 140, remark.

12. Hegel, *Philosophy of Right*, sec. 338, addition, p. 370.

13. Pope John Paul II, "World Peace Day Address," para. 10, January 1, 2004, at www.vatican.va/holy_father/john_paul_ii/messages/peace/documents/hf_jp-ii_mes_20031216_xxxvii-world-day-for-peace_en.html.

14. Derek Jeffreys, "Eliminating All Empathy: Personalism and the 'War on Terror,'" *Logos: A Journal of Catholic Thought and Culture* 9, no. 3 (2006): 16–44.

15. Nikolai Berdyaev, *Slavery and Freedom* (New York: Scribner's, 1944), 162.

16. Thomas Nagel, "War and Massacre" in May, *Morality of War*, 228.

Chapter Five

The Myth of
American Exceptionalism

For we must consider that we shall be as a city upon a hill. The eyes
of all people are upon us.

—John Winthrop

The just war myth holds that war is a national project organized around
the rational decisions of the legitimate authority, fought in pursuit of a
just cause, and executed by morally upright soldiers. This myth assumes
that there is a unity of purpose and moral spirit that permeates a just war
and that this moral spirit guides the actions of the soldiers on the
ground. In the United States, this myth is connected to a way of understanding the United States as a moral power, a city on a hill. This is the
basic idea of *American Exceptionalism*, that America is the moral leader
on earth. This ideal reminds us of our responsibility, and it gives us a
charge to live up to. But it becomes mythic when it causes us to believe
that we actually are in fact a moral power.

American Exceptionalism came into its own in the twentieth century
and continues to affect judgments about war in the United States. For
example, in calling for the United States to enter World War I, Woodrow
Wilson claimed that the United States would fight "without rancor and
without selfish object" and that American forces would "observe with
proud punctilio the principles of right and fair play that we profess to be
fighting for."[1] This idealism has continued to guide our judgments about
the wars we fight from World War II to Iraq.

In reality there is no war that lives up to the ideal. Nations are not
perfectly just. Motives are often less than pure. Soldiers occasionally

misbehave. And leaders make mistakes. President Bush recognized this when he acknowledged in a ceremony dedicating the World War II Memorial that even the soldiers of that war were "flesh and blood, with all of the limits and fears of flesh and blood." Bush rightly admitted that the heroes of World War II were "not exactly angels." Despite its paradigmatic status in the American imagination, even World War II is not a perfectly good war. Civilians were slaughtered and injustices were committed even by the "good guys." The same tragic fact haunts all wars: wars fought for noble ideals are still fought by human beings with feet of clay.

This fact is easily overlooked. The myths of patriotic idealism compel us to ignore the limits and fears of flesh and blood. We want to identify with the community and feel a part of the group, and this identification leads us to believe that the state is justified in its decisions. But the reality of political life is much more complicated than naive patriotism allows. States are not perfect. Political decisions can be wrong. No soldier or president or nation is infallible. It is often difficult to see this, however, because political life is infused with patriotism that shows up in the rituals, ceremonies, and symbols by which we reaffirm our collective identity. Our faith in our nation makes it easy to believe that the nation is above reproach, that it is always and only interested in justice, and that the wars it fights are good ones.

This mythological construction of national values can be found in President Bush's speech at West Point on June 1, 2002. This speech is significant because it is quoted in the introduction to the National Security Strategy of the United States of America (NSS) in 2002, the document that established the policy of preemptive war that was eventually employed in Iraq. Bush said:

> Our Nation's cause has always been larger than our Nation's defense. We fight, as we always fight, for a just peace—a peace that favors liberty. We will defend the peace against the threats from terrorists and tyrants. We will preserve the peace by building good relations among the great powers. And we will extend the peace by encouraging free and open societies on every continent.[2]

We Americans believe that we have always fought for a just peace that favors liberty. This belief is part of the larger story of American Exceptionalism: the idea that the United States is a moral exemplar with a unique historical mission. The Bush Doctrine is part of this mainstream of American thought.³ John Winthrop proposed in 1630 the idea that America was a city on a hill. And since the Revolution, Americans have believed that America's cause is the cause of all mankind. Thomas Paine said it directly, in the introduction to his pamphlet, *Common Sense*: "The cause of America is in a great measure the cause of all mankind." And Benjamin Franklin referred to this idea in a letter to Samuel Cooper (1777): "It is a common observation here (Paris) that our cause is the cause of all mankind, and that we are fighting for their liberty in defending our own." In the twentieth century, this idea developed into the idea that American military power should be used, as Wilson said, to make the world safe for democracy.

THE PEARL HARBOR MOMENT

The model of the American just war myth is World War II, where American heroes prevailed against evil Germans and Japanese. It is true that there was a just cause in World War II. The Nazis *were* evil. They slaughtered six million human beings in gas chambers and concentration camps. They invaded their neighbors and used blitzkrieg warfare and aerial bombing that made no effort to discriminate between combatants and civilians. The Japanese were just as bad. They spread their power throughout Asia, using barbaric techniques of war including torture and gang rape. These techniques were perfected in the Rape of Nanking, where at least two hundred thousand people were killed. And the Japanese did provoke war by deliberately attacking the United States at Pearl Harbor.

Pearl Harbor continues to resound in America's mythic memory as a classic case of unprovoked aggression. And the "Pearl Harbor moment" has become a mythic symbol of that sort of provocation that leads to a just war. Indeed, the attacks of September 11, 2001, were almost immediately described as a new Pearl Harbor. The basic idea is that the United States was a peaceful nation that was attacked, literally, out of the blue. The war against the Japanese and the Germans is often seen as classic case of a justified response to unprovoked aggression, and the response to 9/11 is often modeled on World War II.

But the world is more complex than this and the moral record is more ambiguous than we like to admit. Although there was a just cause in fighting the war against Germany and Japan, American and Allied forces used morally suspect strategies, such as carpet bombing and fire-bombing, that aimed to destroy entire cities: Hamburg, Dresden, and Tokyo. American forces also used atomic weapons to destroy Hiroshima and Nagasaki. Although the causes of World War II seem to clearly indicate the American and Allied forces were the good guys in this war, deeper reflection reminds us of the moral ambiguity of even this claim. Michael Bess has recently concluded: "There can be no excuse, in the end, for the practices of large-scale area bombing and fire-bombing of cities; these were atrocities, pure and simply. They were atrocities because the Anglo-Americans could definitely have won the war without resorting to them."4 This critique of American excesses in World War II has been articulated by many commentators including G. E. M. Anscombe, John Rawls, and Jonathan Glover.5

The easy explanation of the war points to German aggression against Czechoslovakia and Poland; in the Pacific it points to the Japanese expansion throughout Asia culminating in the attack on Pearl Harbor. But history does not consist of simple events. Germany's expansion was the result, in part, of the punitive conditions of the Treaty of Versailles that ended World War I; Germany's expansive nationalism was grounded on claims about linguistic and ethnic affinities that did transcend official borders and that fit—however uncomfortably—within the Wilsonian idea of national self-determination. Japan's ambitions developed as a reaction to European colonialism, including the forced "opening of Japan" that was caused by Admiral Perry and the United States Navy in 1854. The American presence in the Pacific is often left unmentioned when the attack on Pearl Harbor is discussed. But it is important to remember that the United States had been interfering in the Hawaiian Islands since the nineteenth century. And the real focus of the Japanese attack on Pearl Harbor was probably as preparation for invading the Philippines: the day after the Pearl Harbor attacks, the Japanese invaded the Philippines. But the Philippines had been an American colony since American forces had won them (along with Guam, Cuba, and Puerto Rico) in the Spanish-American War of 1898. A glance at the map reminds us that the Philippines are closer to Japan than they are to the United States. This is not to say that the Japanese invasion of the Philippines was morally acceptable. But it reminds us that the war in the Pacific—including the attack on Pearl Harbor—was the result of a long history of colonialism, in which the United States was an active player.

By offering this bit of historical context, I am not excusing German or Japanese aggression. Rather, my point is that war is often the result of historical forces that are much larger than the events that actually precipitate war. The just war myth tends to focus our attention on single moments as the cause of war. We think of Pearl Harbor day— December 7—or September 11 as days of infamy which provoked a passive and uninvolved nation into war. Yes, these days are important. But the ease with which we remember key dates makes us forget that these dates represent a whole complex series of events. Wars are not created in a single day. They are processes that develop through a long period of gestation.

We must also remember that it takes at least two parties to make a war. We like to believe that war occurs when the good guys are attacked by the bad guys. Thus it is easy to believe that wars come out of the blue by sneak attack. But the truth is more complex. Wars result from long sustained interaction. It sometimes makes sense to speak of "good guys" and "bad guys." But it is rare that one side is perfectly just. For example, it is easy to forget that the United States provoked Japan in July 1941 by imposing a trade embargo that cut off up to 90 percent of Japan's oil imports. Pearl Harbor happened five months later. This is not to say that the United States was to blame for the war. Rather, my point is that we must avoid a simplistic myth that holds that American forces merely react to unprovoked evil.

The attacks of 9/11 also did not come out of the blue. Prior to 2001, there was a long and complicated American entanglement in Afghanistan, Iran, and Iraq. Osama bin Laden's grievance prior to 9/11 pointed back to the use of U.S. military force in the first Gulf War, U.S. support for Saudi Arabia, and the sanctions against Iraq of the 1990s. Obviously, a deep and long-standing issue was also American ties to Israel and the problem of the Palestinian uprising. And, another obvious point is that American interests in the Middle East have a lot to do with oil. The aim of bringing all of this up is not to defend bin Laden or the attacks of 9/11. These attacks were immoral because they deliberately targeted innocent noncombatants. But they need to be understood as the result of a complex process involving decades of American action throughout the Middle East.

It is important to remember the moral complexity of war, and it is important to acknowledge that no war—not even World War II—was perfectly just. It is easy to believe the myth that all American wars are like the myth we've been taught about World War II: that it was a just war in which the good guys defeated evil without themselves succumbing to evil. However, World War II remains morally ambiguous. And other

American wars are much more ambiguous—such as Vietnam or the American invasion of Iraq. I am not saying that American power is always unjust or even that these wars were complete moral failures. Rather, my point is that it is a myth to believe that wars are perfectly just or that a nation such as the United States is always perfectly just.

The idealistic view of American Exceptionalism comes from a sort of nostalgia for a time of lost innocence, where moral lines were clear and easy to draw. We long for a mythic past or golden age in which heroes fought nobly for a just cause. This nostalgia crept into Bush's speech at the World War II Memorial:

> The years of World War II were a hard, heroic and gallant time in the life of our country. When it mattered most, an entire generation of Americans showed the finest qualities of our nation and of humanity.

World War II is viewed as "the good war" of "the greatest generation." Michael Bess has concluded of World War II that "rarely in history has a war seemed so just to so many."[6] Bess points out that the moral imperative that guided the war also gave the Allied powers the will to win. We continue to think that the moral high ground is the way to victory. This is one reason that it becomes easy to believe that the wars we fight are just: to admit their ambiguity would make it that much more difficult to fight and thus to win.

This sort of closed circle is found in the thinking of those who question whether it is appropriate to question or critique a war while the war is ongoing. Pat Robertson, for example, recently claimed that "attempts to undermine the commander in chief during time of war amounts to treason."[7] His idea seems to be that it is treason to criticize the troops or their commander because we need moral unity in order to continue and win the fight. One supposes that it would also be wrong to question the myths of American Exceptionalism while the troops are fighting to expand American influence.

But from a different perspective one could argue that it takes quite a leap of faith to believe that our troops and our commander in chief are actually morally competent to execute a just war. And it clearly is important to clarify the historical background of the wars we fight. Wartime criticism is useful for reminding us of the moral demands that we expect our commander and his soldiers to live up to. And if critics help us recognize the ambiguity and complexity of international affairs, this should help us make better judgments about whether war is acceptable to begin with and about what legitimate war aims might be.

THE MYTH OF LEGITIMATE COMPETENT AUTHORITY

One of the key ideas of the just war myth is the idea that just wars are declared and administered by a legitimate and competent authority. For those who adhere to democratic principles, legitimacy is derived from the consent of the people and governance is done for the well-being of the people. One of the duties of a legitimate government is to defend its people against attack.

This duty can be abused, however, when the state engages in more speculative endeavors. President Bush, for example, indicated in the speech quoted above that a nation can have a "cause" that is larger than national self-defense. The difficulty is that as we move away from self-defense, the justification of the cause becomes more tenuous. The people may agree, nearly unanimously, that military force should be used for their defense when they are directly attacked. The state has the legitimate authority to defend the nation. But the legitimacy of its authority becomes questionable when it uses the people's trust for other sorts of military adventures.

There are some deep philosophical questions about what nations or states really are. The idea of "collective agency," for example, is a complicated one that opens many questions: What are collective entities and how do they act? How is it that nations can be said to "act" or "decide" at all, when there are very few, if any, unanimous national decisions? And when there is lack of unanimity in such decisions, how are we to think about the minority opinion, and the very idea of a "nation's cause"? Moreover, in what sense are the people of a nation responsible for the misdeeds of their political leaders and/or armies, when there is lack of consensus or when consensus (or the appearance of consensus) is the result of coercion?

Most of us simply assume that there is a unified "thing" called "the nation," that all citizens share in responsibility, and that the state represents the will of the people. This assumption is obviously mythological. It makes it easier for us to talk about "the Germans" or "the Iraqis" or "the Americans." But the reality is that the individuals who are grouped together as "Germans," "Iraqis," or "Americans" are quite diverse. Indeed, we recognize this when, for example, we deal with dissenting members of the enemy nation. Not all Germans were Nazis, not all Iraqis were Baathists, and not all Americans supported President Bush's war on Iraq. But it is often too difficult to make these sorts of distinctions in the context of warfare. When nations go to war, the entire nation is at war. Indeed, citizens who object to warfare are often coerced into at least a grudging sort of support. If they don't support the war effort, they can be accused of sedition or treason.

If we assume that it makes sense to talk about the agency of a collective entity such as the state or nation, one can still wonder whether states act *rationally* and whether states act *morally*. A crucial assumption of the just war myth is that states fight wars based on *good reasons*. As the just war tradition puts this, war must be based on *right intention*.

When we delve into the intentions and reasons behind war, however, it becomes obvious that the idea of moral leadership is a mythic ideal. In reality states go to war for a variety of reasons and with mixed intentions. Chalmers Johnson has argued that the chief reason for recent wars is what he calls "military Keynesianism": wars are fought as a need of the military-industrial complex.[8] Others have argued that American power is slowly constructing and defending an empire. And still others have claimed that American power is used to defend the interests of big corporations or to facilitate American demand for oil. But we do not have to accept such cynical views of war to admit that states often have mixed intentions.

A further difficulty is whether the people actually know what the real reasons for war are. State officials can exaggerate, lie, and aim to deceive us. And these officials may not themselves know the whole truth about the situation. We saw this quite clearly in the American invasion of Iraq. There was a dispute about the nature of the evidence that was used to justify the war. And the war itself had a variety of justifications. Some cynics claimed that it was all about the oil. Others argued that it was a war to enforce UN resolutions against Iraq. The war was publicly justified as necessary for self-defense: preemptive war against the threat of weapons of mass destruction. Then it was justified as a war of humanitarian intervention against a tyrannical government. And now continued American presence in Iraq is justified by the need for regional stability and an attempt to avoid civil war. The president admitted the shifting nature of the war in his January 2007 State of the Union address: "This is not the fight we entered in Iraq, but it is the fight we're in." This reminds us that war rationales change even within war. Rational moral agents are assumed to have some degree of self-knowledge. In order to make good decisions—indeed, in order to be moral—one must have some degree of clarity both about one's intentions and about the reasons for and consequences of one's actions. Moral agents are supposed to try to understand their own interests and inclinations, and they are supposed to be honest in appraising the harms and benefits of their actions. We have good reason to condemn agents who lie to themselves, who ignore their own base motives, who misunderstand the past, who distort the present, and who ignore the negative consequences of their actions. But at the level of the nation-state, citizens are often much more forgiving of self-deception, ignorance, and distortion. We easily ignore the fact that politics involves a certain amount of lying, self-interest, corruption, nepotism, and plain old-fashioned power. It is quite odd that although many people know that there is propaganda and misinformation in political life, they continue to have faith in the state and state officials as competent legitimate authorities. One of the reasons for this is that we want to believe the myths that are told (i.e., that we tell ourselves) about the nation-state.

To conclude this discussion of the legitimacy and competency of authority, let me clarify a problem that stems from Plato's *Republic*. Plato was suspicious of democratic rule because he thought of democracy as a sort of mob rule. At least, he thought, democracies lack virtues such as wisdom, self-control, and justice. The mob can be whipped into a frenzy by the clever rhetoric of the demagogue. This is why Plato called for the rule of philosopher-kings. But modern political philosophy reminds us that there are no philosopher-kings. Our rulers are not disinterested, virtuous, and wise. Rather, they are flesh and blood just like us: fallible, limited, and occasionally foolish. That is why they need to be restrained by a system of checks and balances that is ultimately based on accountability to the people. But Plato's worry about democracy still holds. There is no guarantee that the judgment of the masses is wise or just. We live in a second-best world (as Plato hinted in *The Statesman*) and in this world there is no guarantee that justice is served. For this reason, we should be reluctant to give the state power over life and death. And we should continue to question the myth that holds that wise rulers have some special power to make competent moral and prudential decisions about war.

If we were governed by philosopher-kings, it might be that the just war ideal would be actualized. But as one of my colleagues recently reminded me, if we were ruled by philosopher-kings, then there would probably be no reason for war to begin with. On the other hand, many of our leaders do care about justice. And they do their best to make wise judgments. But the burden of proof rests on the authorities to prove that they are wise and that they care about justice. The authorities must prove to the people that there is a just cause for war, that war is a necessary last resort, and that war will be fought within the proper limits of proportionality. In general, we must be careful to avoid a mythological construction of authority, and skepticism about the just war myth is warranted.

AMERICAN EXCEPTIONALISM AND THE BUSH DOCTRINE

Americans like to believe that American politicians are motivated by noble intentions and that they have a kind of wisdom and virtue. They also believe that the American nation has a system of values and a history of noble wars that is different from the immorality of other nations. This faith in authority is linked to a historical narrative in which the United States is the moral leader of the world. The basic idea is that when the United States fights wars, it fights for a just cause and it fights according to just war principles. Again Woodrow Wilson's speech before Congress in April 1917 is a useful example of this way of describing the American way of warfare. Wilson claimed, "We have no selfish ends to serve. We desire no conquest, no dominion."

Such noble intentions were supposed to ensure that Americans would fight justly. Similar ideas were expressed in President Bush's National Security Strategy. In the section of the NSS (2001) that defends the idea of preemptive war, the just war language echoes the sentiment of Wilson:

> We will always proceed deliberately, weighing the consequences of our actions. . . . The purpose of our actions will always be to eliminate a specific threat to the United States or our allies and friends. The reasons for our actions will be clear, the force measured, and the cause just.

These statements indicate that just war principles will govern the American use of preemptive force. We will discuss the preemptive war doctrine in more detail in a subsequent chapter. But let us continue to look at examples of the link between American Exceptionalism and the myth of the just war. A further example can be found in President Bush's introductory letter to the revised NSS of 2006:

> The path we have chosen is consistent with the great tradition of American foreign policy. Like the policies of Harry Truman and Ronald Reagan, our approach is idealistic about our national goals, and realistic about the means to achieve them. To follow this path we must maintain and expand our national strength so we can deal with threats and challenges before they can damage our people or our interests. We must maintain a military without peer.

This invocation of Truman and Reagan in conjunction with the idea of a "military without peer" shows us the way that American Exceptionalism is understood. American heroes—especially those who stood firm against communism—are celebrated for their idealism and the way that they built and employed military force to accomplish their ideals. President Bush has claimed Truman as one of his models in a number of documents and speeches. For example, in his commencement address at West Point in May 2006, President Bush devoted one-third of his speech to recounting the way that Truman successfully "set the course" that won the Cold War. Bush looks to Truman as a model because he believes that the war on terrorism is a struggle similar to the Cold War, and he believes that Truman's model of aggressive action against communism is a useful model for the war against what he calls "Islamo-fascism."

What is remarkable about the faith in American Exceptionalism is that it endures despite obvious contradictions. Most notably, although the language of just war infuses this discussion, the wars we have fought in the name of democracy have often not been entirely just. It should be remembered that Truman authorized the use of atomic bombs against Japan. This violation of the idea of noncombatant immunity led Anscombe to call Truman a war criminal and it led Rawls to characterize Truman as a failed statesman. Truman also supervised the Korean War—a war in which American forces were involved in atrocities. But Truman has become a hero for those who, like Bush, accept the just war myth.

Moreover, the "victory" of the Cold War supervised in the end by Ronald Reagan was facilitated by the immoral nuclear war policy of mutually assured destruction. This policy relied on a strategy that deliberately targeted noncombatants: American weapons threatened to destroy Soviet population centers. And the Cold War was often far from cold. Millions were killed in Korea, Vietnam, Central America, and Africa as a result of American Cold War policies.

Americans do not like to dwell on the dark side of the American narrative. Instead we like to believe that American military force is used only for noble purposes. There are a variety of reasons for the endurance of this faith. Faith in American Exceptionalism is self-serving. Our economic success is, at least partly, based on our military power. So as we reap the benefits of military power (some call it imperial power) we pretend that our military power is based on justice and not on self-interest.

But perhaps the most important reason that faith in American Exceptionalism endures is that the American Exceptionalist myth is written into the heart of our understanding of history. And it is closely tied to the prevailing religiosity of the American people. Some Christian fundamentalists apparently believe that American history developed as part of God's providential plan. Some Christians have turned George Washington and others of the Founding Fathers into something like secular saints.[9] Some Christians believe that Bush himself was the providential choice for leadership during these turbulent times. And some Christians believe that God also punishes the United States for failing away from Him, even attributing the 9/11 attacks to God's judgments against anti-Christian values.

Not everyone is so enamored of this Christian version of the American myth. The American faith in the nobility and virtue of the American nation has a more widely accepted secular expression. We learn it in school through history lessons that exaggerate the good and ignore the bad in the American story. And the American myth is repeated in public holidays and ceremonies: the Fourth of July speech, the Memorial Day parade, the Veteran's Day commemoration, or when we sing the "Star-Spangled Banner" at sporting events.

The myth has been repeatedly used to justify American military adventures. It requires great effort to question both the predominant historical narrative and the faith that grounds the service and sacrifice of our fellow citizens who support the military and the current war effort. This closed circle of mutually reinforcing ideas is one of the reasons that the Bush Doctrine has been so successful. It is one of the reasons that the nation fell obediently behind the president during the early years of the war on terrorism. And it is one of the reasons that it is so difficult, even now, to criticize the wars in Iraq and Afghanistan. To mount such a critique requires a wholesale critique of American military power and the idealistic self-image of the American project.

The secular myth of American Exceptionalism is grounded in the idea that the liberal-democratic values of the United States give the United States a mandate to lead the vanguard of history. From this standpoint, American military power has a moral focus that points beyond self-defense and includes the defense of democratic values around the globe. This creates a context that can be used to justify a crusading war for freedom such as we've seen in Iraq.

Even prior to September 11, President Bush articulated the idealism of American Exceptionalism. Indeed, no president is immune from using such rhetoric. It is an accepted and expected part of political discourse. But the idea has serious implications when it is linked to the Bush Doctrine of foreign intervention and regime change. In his first inaugural address, Bush explicitly explained the story of American Exceptionalism:

> We have a place, all of us, in a long story—a story we continue, but whose end we will not see. It is the story of a new world that became a friend and liberator of the old, a story of a slave-holding society that became a servant of freedom, the story of a power that went into the world to protect but not possess, to defend but not to conquer. It is the American story—a story of flawed and fallible people, united across the generations by grand and enduring ideals.

This is inspiring. And much of it rings true, especially the admission of our fallibility. But the acknowledgment of fallibility should give us pause as we go about devising grand strategies and waging wars. A growing number of critics argue that the Bush Doctrine is a disguise that hides imperial ambition.[10] Others have focused on the role of prophetic Christianity in the White House.[11] There are good reasons to take such criticism seriously; but this sort of criticism misses the point that the "Bush Doctrine" is part of the mainstream of American idealism. The Bush Doctrine is widely supported by the American people, in part because Americans do believe that American power can be used for moral purposes. Again, World War II is a paradigm: American boys did die fighting to liberate Europe and Asia from totalitarianism. Moreover, although President Bush does use religious and moral language to describe his foreign policy, his language is more inclusive and reflective

than some critics give him credit for. His second inaugural address
shows this:

> We go forward with complete confidence in the eventual triumph of free-
> dom. Not because history runs on the wheels of inevitability; it is human
> choices that move events. Not because we consider ourselves a chosen na-
> tion; God moves and chooses as He wills. We have confidence because
> freedom is the permanent hope of mankind, the hunger in dark places, the
> longing of the soul. When our Founders declared a new order of the ages;
> when soldiers died in wave upon wave for a union based on liberty; when
> citizens marched in peaceful outrage under the banner "Freedom Now"—
> they were acting on an ancient hope that is meant to be fulfilled. History
> has an ebb and flow of justice, but history also has a visible direction, set
> by liberty and the Author of Liberty.

This sort of language connects the Bush Doctrine with mainstream
American thought and history, and it is this sort of language that inspired the American people to celebrate the fall of Saddam Hussein and
to support the "triumph of freedom" in Iraq.

The explicitly stated goals of the Bush Doctrine are: to spread democracy, defend human rights, and end tyranny. Some of the critics
mentioned above argue that these concepts are vacuous when used by
the Bush administration. This critique holds that "freedom" is an ideological construct that either means nothing or means something like
"whatever is in the interests of American capitalism." I cannot respond
to this criticism in detail here. But it is important to note that the Bush
Doctrine is guided by a fairly specific idea of democracy that includes
several elements: a written constitution, representative legislature, a division of powers, and institutional safeguards that defend human
rights. The revised National Security Strategy of the United States
(March 2006) maintains, for example, that effective democracies do
the following:[12]

- Honor and uphold basic human rights, including freedom of religion,
  conscience, speech, assembly, association, and press
- Are responsive to their citizens, submitting to the will of the people,
  especially when people vote to change their government
- Exercise effective sovereignty and maintain order within their own
  borders, protect independent and impartial systems of justice, punish
  crime, embrace the rule of law, and resist corruption

- Limit the reach of government, protecting the institutions of civil society, including the family, religious communities, voluntary associations, private property, independent business, and a market economy

These are noble ideals shared by liberals in the United States and abroad. Thus the problem of the Bush Doctrine is not these ideals. Rather, these ideals create a problem when they are linked to an idealized approach to aggressive military action that believes that military force is the best means to accomplish the "triumph of freedom."

The further structural problem of American Exceptionalism is that it creates a double standard in which the United States allows itself some uses of power that it would deny to others; this breeds resistance among both friends and enemies.[13] I will discuss exceptions and double standards in more detail in chapter 7.

CONCLUSION

Even in the aftermath of the Iraq war, American Exceptionalism continues to be articulated as explicit policy. The National Security Strategy of March 2006 remains grounded in an interpretation of history that understands American power as the engine of historical change:

> It is the policy of the United States to seek and support democratic movements and institutions in every nation and culture, with *the ultimate goal of ending tyranny in our world*. . . . Achieving this goal is the work of generations. The United States is in the early years of a long struggle, similar to what our country faced in the early years of the Cold War.[14]

I have added emphasis in this passage to the claim that "the ultimate goal" of American foreign policy is "ending tyranny in our world." This is a remarkable claim to find in a policy statement: American foreign policy—and the guiding strategy for national security—states that it is grounded in this world-historical goal. This way of conceiving the world-historical task of the United States creates an imperative for the United States to use its military power in pursuit of democratization. And it creates conditions for crusading wars that aim at historical transformation.

All of this reminds us that the just war myth is actualized in real nations in accord with their own political mythologies. These political myths are infused with nostalgia and they tend to reduce history to a simple story in which we are the good guys. The just war theory maintains that decisions about war are supposed to be made by authorities who are morally serious and reflective. But we no longer believe in prophet-kings who hear the voice of God, and we don't believe that there are philosopher-kings either. Instead our leaders are recognized as fallible human beings. Furthermore, each nation is motivated by its mythic self-image. The problem is that when decisions about war are infused with myths such as the myth of American Exceptionalism, these decisions can be both mistaken and insulated from criticism.

NOTES

1. Woodrow Wilson, "President Woodrow Wilson's War Message," in *War Messages*, 3–8. 65th Cong., 1st sess. Senate Doc. No. 5, Serial No. 7264 (Washington, DC, 1917), at net.lib.byu.edu/~rdh7/wwi/1917/wilswarm.html.
2. President Bush's speeches and policy statements can be found on the White House website: www.whitehouse.gov.
3. See: Francis Fukuyama, *America at the Crossroads: Democracy, Power, and the Neoconservative Legacy* (New Haven, CT: Yale University Press, 2006); Mark Lewis Taylor, *Religion, Politics, and the Christian Right* (Minneapolis: Augsburg Fortress Press, 2005); or Walter Russell Mead, *Power, Terror, Peace, and War: America's Grand Strategy in a World at Risk* (New York: Vintage/Random House, 2005).
4. Michael Bess, *Choices under Fire* (New York: Knopf, 2006), 110.
5. G. E. M. Anscombe, "War and Murder" and "Mr. Truman's Degree," both in, *Ethics, Religion, and Politics* (Minneapolis: University of Minnesota Press, 1981); John Rawls, "Fifty Years after Hiroshima," in *Collected Papers* (Cambridge, MA: Harvard University Press, 1999), 565–72; Jonathan Glover, *Humanity: A Moral History of the 20th Century* (New Haven, CT: Yale University Press, 2000).
6. Bess, *Choices under Fire*, 75.
7. Pat Robertson, *The 700 Club*, December 7, 2005, at http://mediamatters .org/items/200512120002.
8. Chalmers Johnson, "Republic or Empire," *Harper's Magazine*, January 2007. Also see Chalmers Johnson, *The Sorrows of Empire* (New York: Henry Holt, 2004).
9. Jeff Sharlet, "Through a Glass, Darkly: How the Christian Right Is Reimagining American History," *Harper's Magazine*, December 2006.
10. For example: Andrew Bacevich, *American Empire: The Realities and Consequences of U.S. Diplomacy* (Cambridge, MA: Harvard University Press,

2002); Carl Boggs, *Imperial Delusions: American Militarism and Endless War* (Lanham, MD: Rowman & Littlefield, 2005); Noam Chomsky, *Hegemony of Survival: America's Quest for Global Dominance* (New York: Henry Holt, 2004); Robert W. Merry, *Sands of Empire: Missionary Zeal, American Foreign Policy, and the Hazards of Global Ambition* (New York: Simon & Schuster, 2005).

11. See Mark Lewis Taylor, *Religion, Politics, and the Christian Right*; or Michael S. Northcutt, *An Angel Directs the Storm* (London: I. B. Tauris, 2004).

12. National Security Strategy of the United States of America 2006, 4. Hereafter to be cited as NSS.

13. Francis Fukuyama claims that we see this explicitly in the idea of preventive war that is articulated in the NSS of 2002: "The fact that the United States granted itself a right that it would deny to other countries is based, in the NSS, on an implicit judgment that the United States is different from other countries and can be trusted to use its military power justly and wisely in ways that other powers could not." See Fukuyama, *America at the Crossroads*, 101. See also: John L. Hammond, "The Bush Doctrine, Preventive War, and International Law," *Philosophical Forum* 36, no. 1 (March 2005): 97–112; and Andrew Fiala, "Citizenship and Preemptive War: The Lesson from Iraq," *Human Rights Review* 7, no. 4 (July–September 2006): 19–37.

14. NSS 2006, 1 (emphasis added).

Part II

THE MYTHS OF
THE WAR ON TERRORISM

Chapter Six

The Preemptive War Doctrine

Terrorists and terror states do not reveal these threats with fair notice, in formal declarations—and responding to such enemies only after they have struck first is not self-defense, it is suicide.

—President George W. Bush[1]

We are witnessing a general revision of ideas about the preventive use of military force. Although this approach has been articulated under the general rubric of preemptive war, recent policy and its implementation go beyond traditional notions of preemption and articulate a policy of what I call *Reformed Preemption* (RP). These revisions are predicated on the idea that new threats—terrorists with weapons of mass destruction (WMD)—require new methods of prevention. Indeed, the idea of Reformed Preemption is that we should act to prevent threats from becoming imminent in the traditional sense of this term because once they are imminent, it is too late to prevent them. As President Bush said in his ultimatum to Saddam Hussein, quoted above, to wait in such a circumstance would be suicide.

The risk is, however, that a permissive attitude toward prevention will make it easier to justify outright aggression and thus make the world less safe. Reformed Preemption amounts to an effort to expand the idea of *jus ad bellum*: terrorists and rogue states who possess WMD or who intend to acquire them may now be viewed as justified targets. In the present chapter I will argue that citizens of democratic nations should be wary of this policy. This policy may lead to violations of human rights, including the right to national sovereignty and nonintervention.

79

The conventions, treaties, and institutions that form the fragile framework of modern international law were developed in reaction to the two world wars of the twentieth century.[2] The current attempt to revise the concept of preemptive war is dangerous insofar as it threatens the stability of this fragile framework.

Although I acknowledge that new threats create the need for new methods of prevention and response, it is useful to adopt a conservative approach when it comes to thinking about and implementing these new methods. At the very least, wariness on the part of ordinary citizens can act as a brake on overzealous leaders who may abuse the newly evolving permission to use preventive force. Even though we might be sympathetic to the idea of Reformed Preemption in theory, the case of the recent invasion of Iraq gives us good reason to be suspicious of it as a general policy.

TRADITIONAL AND REFORMED PREEMPTION

The idea of aggressive prevention has a long history. It was articulated, for example, in the debate, recorded by Thucydides, about whether Sparta should declare war on Athens. The Corinthians argued that the Spartans should go to war in order to prevent Athens—which had violated treaties and was behaving aggressively—from becoming stronger than she already was. As the Corinthians put it:

> You [Spartans] alone do nothing in the early stages to prevent an enemy's expansion; you wait until the enemy has doubled its strength . . . instead of going out to meet them, you prefer to stand still and wait till you are attacked, thus hazarding everything by fighting with opponents who have grown far stronger than they were originally.[3]

The Corinthians argued that the Spartans' conservative approach would be risky in light of the fact that the Athenians were developing new methods of war and of politics. "New methods must drive out old ones. When a city can live in peace and quiet, no doubt the old-established ways are best; but when one is constantly being faced by new problems, one has also to be capable of approaching them in an original way."[4] This ancient debate is quite similar to the debate surrounding contemporary revisions of security policy in light of the new threat of global terrorism. We should recall that Sparta did decide to wage war, and Sparta won.

The policy of Reformed Preemption war articulated in the 2002 version of the National Security Strategy of the United States of America (NSS) and it was employed in the invasion of Iraq. Some have wondered why this policy was put in place, since it seems to have jeopardized post-9/11 global good will; others have wondered whether this was part of some neoconservative conspiracy or some grand new strategy for global politics.[5] But it is important to note that the idea of what George P. Shultz has called "hot preemption" is not a uniquely American policy.[6] The French Loi de Programmation Militaire 2003–2008 defends a policy of preventive war, and the 2003 British Ministry of Defence "Defence White Paper" states that the British will "be prepared to prevent, deter, coerce, disrupt or destroy international terrorists or the regimes that harbour them and to counter terrorists' efforts to acquire chemical, biological, radiological and nuclear weapons."[7]

The NSS claims that international law has long allowed preemption in light of imminent threat. Indeed, one might justify preemption by appealing to Article 51 of the UN Charter, which allows for an "inherent right" of self-defense. One should note that the UN Charter does not explicitly allow for preemption and that there is ambiguity in the history of interpreting Article 51 and its relation to the idea of preemption.[8] The UN Charter framework was developed out of concern for regulating the behavior of discrete nation-states. Defenders of the NSS would argue that the UN framework needs revision in light of the threat of global terrorism. Just as the Spartans had to evolve beyond their conservative ways, UN member states may have to evolve beyond the conservative limits of the UN framework in order to confront new challenges.

The NSS was written so as to provide a justification for wars to be waged against rogue states and terrorists. Here is one key passage:

> The United States has long maintained the option of preemptive actions to counter a sufficient threat to our national security. The greater the threat, the greater is the risk of inaction—and the more compelling the case for taking anticipatory action to defend ourselves, even if uncertainty remains as to the time and place of the enemy's attack. To forestall or prevent such hostile acts by our adversaries, the United States will, if necessary, act preemptively. The United States will not use force in all cases to preempt emerging threats, nor should nations use preemption as a pretext for aggression. Yet in an age where the enemies of civilization openly and actively seek the world's most destructive technologies, the United States cannot remain idle while dangers gather. We will always proceed deliberately, weighing the consequences of our actions.[9]

One of the focal points of the revised idea of preemption is the traditional idea of imminent threat. Grotius, for example, writes that a war of self-defense is permissible "only when the danger is immediate and certain, not when it is merely assumed." He states: "The danger must be immediate and imminent in point of time."[10] A similar idea, expressed by Secretary of State Daniel Webster in 1837 with regard to the *Caroline* incident, has become an accepted standard for justifying preemption. Webster claimed that anticipatory self-defense was acceptable only when there was "a necessity of self-defense, instant, overwhelming, leaving no choice of means, and no moment of deliberation."[11]

But the NSS explicitly states that the idea of imminent threat must be revised: "We must adapt the concept of imminent threat to the capabilities and objectives of today's adversaries."[12] This idea has been reiterated by several members of the Bush administration. In 2002, Deputy Secretary of Defense Paul Wolfowitz stated: "We cannot wait until the threat is imminent. The notion that we can wait to prepare assumes that we will know when the threat is imminent. . . . Anyone who believes that we can wait until we have certain knowledge that attacks are imminent has failed to connect the dots that led to September 11."[13] Or as the former national security adviser (and current secretary of state) Condoleezza Rice put it: "New technology requires new thinking about when a threat actually becomes imminent."[14]

One of the difficulties of the present analysis is the fact that the language of preemption is being transformed. One could argue that the NSS articulates a policy of *preventive* war that makes use of the language of *preemption*. One of the reasons for appealing to the language of preemption is that the idea of preemptive war has a long-established justification, while preventive war is not so easily justified; the new policy appeals to this traditional justification, including the legal framework of the UN Charter and the criteria of imminent threat articulated by Webster.[15] But the NSS changes the traditional idea by redefining the nature of the threat to be prevented and by being more permissive with regard to our knowledge of this threat. To remain clear in what follows I will distinguish between Traditional Preemption (TP) of the sort described by Webster and Reformed Preemption (RP) of the sort articulated by the NSS.

Traditional Preemption (TP) is anticipatory self-defense when there is an imminent and overwhelming threat; when we are certain of this threat; when there is no alternative to violent means; and when there is no time for further deliberation.

Reformed Preemption (RP) is anticipatory self-defense against a grave threat; when we are uncertain about the exact nature of this threat; when we don't know if there are alternatives to violent means; and when we are uncertain whether time remains for further deliberation. More schematically, TP wars are justified when the following conditions are met:

1. When aggression is imminent
2. When there is no other way to avoid the aggression
3. When waiting for aggression to happen will result in a worse state of affairs than acting to prevent it in advance
4. When the preemptive use of force is proportional to the threat
5. When other just war criteria are applied including: considerations about the likelihood of success, an *in bello* respect for noncombatants, and prohibitions on means *mala in se*

RP would presumably diverge from this only by weakening the first condition about imminent threat, but it also seems to weaken the fourth condition about proportionality (a point I will return to in a moment). RP opens up the possibility that action may be justified to prevent a threat from becoming imminent in the more traditional sense. It is important to note, however, that the idea of imminent threat has always been a slippery one requiring practical judgment. As Taylor puts it, "There is a legal void on the question of imminence."[16] This is so because there are so few generally accepted historical examples of legitimate TP. Moreover, the very idea of imminence will shift depending on changing technologies and means of warfare, a point that was noted by the Corinthians over two millennia ago and that has been reiterated by Wolfowitz and Rice. The NSS aims to respond to these changes by leaving open the possibility of responding preemptively to terrorists who have WMD—a threat that was not previously imagined. In support of this idea, Greenwood has argued that WMD change the very notion of imminence: "When the threat is an attack by weapons of mass destruction, the risk imposed upon a State by waiting until that attack actually takes place compounded by the impossibility for that State to afford its population any effective protection once the attack has been launched, mean that such an attack can reasonably be treated as imminent in circumstances where an attack by conventional means would not be so regarded."[17]

Following Taylor and Greenwood, a revised idea of imminence must consider at least the following criteria:

- The gravity of the threat
- The method employed in delivering the threat
- The intentions of the adversary

The threat posed by terrorists with WMD is especially grave: if terrorists were to launch a chemical, biological, or nuclear attack on a civilian population center, the results could be horrifying. Terrorists can employ nonconventional delivery methods (suicide bombers, suitcase bombs, etc.). Terrorist organizations such as al-Qaeda have the express intention of indiscriminately killing Americans. And they have shown us that they will strike without warning. This makes the threat of terrorism so significant that the imminence criteria established by Grotius or Webster may be irrelevant.

All of this can be quite compelling. But an epistemological problem remains embedded in the very notion of RP: the idea itself admits that it is formulated for conditions of uncertainty. It is the idea that preemptive force can be employed "even if uncertainty remains" (in the words of the NSS) that makes RP problematic. RP appeals to what may be called "speculative" threats. Speculative threats are threats about which doubts remain, and they are threats that have yet to fully materialize in the near present. The difficulty here is that an aggressive response to a speculative threat can look like blatant aggression, and the speculative threat can be seen as a mere pretext for aggression.

The NSS recognizes this problem. It claims that preemption should not be a pretext for aggression. The very care displayed in the articulation of the NSS thus indicates that its authors were aware of the moral and legal difficulty of the idea. This policy states that preemption will be employed to counter "sufficient threat" and that preemptive action will be used "if necessary." But the specifics of sufficient threat remain undefined.

One way to understand the idea of sufficient threat is to consider the idea of the gravity of the threat mentioned above. If the threat is especially grave, preemption is justified. We might imagine a sliding scale for determining the gravity of a threat: the more severe the threat, the more preemption is justified. But we encounter a similar epistemological problem here: what exactly is a grave threat? Obviously, to assess the gravity of the threat we must look beyond the bombastic claims of terrorists to their intentions, history, and actual capacity. Moreover, we would have to consider the sorts of opportunity that terrorists have to attack. One could argue that TP was focused primarily on opportunity: an imminent attack is one in which we can see that the aggressor has the opportunity to attack. Traditionally, troop movements were an obvious indication that an aggressor was preparing the opportunity to attack. But RP acknowledges that with regard to terrorists, it is difficult to know whether they in fact have the opportunity to attack. Terrorists are secretive and their method does not involve troop movements. And, even worse, we may suspect that the conditions of our open society present terrorists with multiple opportunities to attack. In general, all of this is woefully speculative.

The difficulty of understanding the gravity of the threat of terrorism also points us to the problem of proportionality. To allow a terrorist threat to become imminent in the traditional sense is, in President Bush's words (quoted at the outset), "suicide." Condoleezza Rice states, "There has never been a moral or legal requirement that a country wait to be attacked before it can address an existential threat."[18] The gravity of the threat of terrorism is here thought to be such that it involves the question of the continued existence of society. The existential nature of the threat is echoed in the NSS where (as quoted above) terrorists are characterized as "enemies of civilization," implying that their aim is nothing less than the total destruction of Western civilization.

The language used here indicates, however, one of the dangers of the doctrine. If waiting is suicidal, this implies that a proportional response may be quite severe: *existential* threats may be met with significant force. For example, both Walzer and Rawls admit the possibility of a "supreme emergency exemption" to principles of justice in war in order to deal with existential threats.[19] The difficulty is that it is not at all clear that the threat of terrorism is existential in this sense because there are uncertainties about the actual severity of potential attacks. Even though a terrorist or rogue state may have the intention to destroy the United States, the mere intention to kill is not enough to create an existential threat: they must also have the means, the will, and the opportunity to make this threat actionable. We should note, moreover, that the bombastic claims of terrorists need not be based in reality: terror is produced when these hyperbolic claims creep into the public consciousness, despite the fact that terrorists may lack the means or opportunity to actualize them. One of the risks of RP is that speculative threats may be met with unbridled force, especially when they are viewed as *existential* threats. Thus, the permissive idea of RP can lead us to violate the principle of proportionality. Indeed, as I shall argue subsequently, this was part of the problem with the invasion of Iraq.

THE PRACTICAL PROBLEM OF IRAQ

We should consult historical examples of preemptive war in order to discover whether, in practice, there have been justified preemptive wars. Israel's preemptive attack in the 1967 Six Days' War is usually cited as one example. Indeed, the Security Council allowed it. But other examples, such as Israel's bombing of Iraq's Osirak reactor in 1981, are best understood as examples of more broadly construed preventive war of the sort found in the idea of RP. It is significant to note that the Security Council rejected the proposed justification of this attack as a preemptive attack based on Article 51.[20]

Despite the fact that there are some past cases that may be useful, the global scene has been transformed recently in two ways. First, the threat of terrorists with WMD is real. And second, the United States possesses hegemonic power. I've already considered the first of these in examining the justification of RP. I will here consider the second: the issue of U.S. hegemony, especially as applied in Iraq. The case of Iraq presents us with perhaps the most fitting example of how the doctrine of RP will be applied in the next few decades.[21] RP will most likely be applied unilaterally by the sole remaining superpower in an effort to pursue terrorists and rogue states with WMD. But the case of Iraq gives us at least four reasons for skepticism.

First, the fact that the United States possesses hegemonic power indicates that deterrence and the threat of retaliation should make preemption less, rather than more, necessary in the coming decades. Indeed, it was common sense for someone like Montesquieu that a weaker state had more of a right to wage an offensive war than a stronger one did because the weaker state was more vulnerable than the stronger one.[22] Stronger states have a formidable retaliatory capacity that should help to deter attacks, and they have better capacity to thwart attacks using nonmilitary means. And yet, the United States seems more inclined to use preemption as a justification for war, now that it is virtually unopposed in the world. While the justification for this is the new asymmetry of terrorism, it is yet another reason to be skeptical of the doctrine: it runs counter to long-standing thinking about war and power.

Second, there is most likely a double standard underlying the doctrine of RP.[23] The United States views itself as entitled to the policy of RP. But for this policy to work, it cannot be adopted by our enemies. Terrorists and rogue states cannot act preemptively to preempt our preemptive attacks. The danger of establishing permissive preemption is this sort of escalation on all sides. The NSS obviously cannot intend this. So it must appeal to a double standard: the United States is entitled to RP because we are the good guys; the bad guys are not entitled to RP.

Third, the fact that the United States has shown willingness to act unilaterally indicates that it will be difficult to restrain in the future. With a permissive RP in place, the United States will feel entitled to employ unilateral force in the future. But it will be costly to play the role of global peacekeeper, and U.S. unilateralism may lead to destabilization, perhaps by further inspiring terrorists to act against U.S. hegemony.

Fourth, the invasion of Iraq obviously violated the principle of proportionality. RP was applied in this case in a disproportionate manner. If Iraq's weapons were a genuine threat, the proportionate response would have been to destroy these weapons. The Israeli bombing of the Osirak reactor is an example here (even though the international community rejected it as a case of justified preemption). But the United States went well beyond destroying weapons systems and capacity: it invaded and occupied Iraq, changing the constitution of the country, and creating massive dislocation and suffering. Now there may have been other humanitarian reasons for regime change in Iraq. But the main rationale was RP. One indication of this was that Iraq was portrayed as an existential threat and existential threats can be dealt with only by effecting regime change. The risk of RP is that it allows for the disproportionate use of force, in light of hyperbolic claims about existential threats.

If we employ Webster's criteria and traditional ideas about preemption, the war in Iraq could not be justified as a preemptive war: there was no instant and overwhelming threat, and we had other choices with regard to means. And yet, the primary rationale for the war was that a preemptive attack was needed against Iraq because Iraq possessed threatening WMD. President Bush indicated this in his speech of March 17, 2003. He stated: "In 1 year, or 5 years, the power of Iraq to inflict harm on all free nations would be multiplied many times over. . . . We choose to meet that threat now, where it arises, before it can appear suddenly in our skies and cities."[24]

It is true that this was not the only rationale for war. Other justifications of the war included: the failure of Iraq to live up to UN Security
Council resolutions, the need for humanitarian intervention against a
brutal and oppressive regime, and the larger moral and strategic goal of
spreading democracy in the Middle East. But the preemptive justification was the strongest argument in favor of the war. The perception of
threat that forms the basis of any argument for preemption (whether
Traditional or Reformed) is among the most persuasive rationales for a
domestic audience. Citizens may not be motivated to sacrifice their
blood and treasure for humanitarian purposes or to enforce declarations
made by an international body. But citizens will respond more strongly
when they think they are threatened by aggression, whether this threat
is imminent or more speculative. And, after a deliberate attempt to link
Iraq to September 11, it was not surprising that many Americans were
in support of preventive war against Iraq.

As is well known, before the war there was a substantial dispute
about the actual threat posed to the United States and its allies by Saddam Hussein. This dispute has continued through the war, as feared
weapons of mass destruction have not been found either by U.S. arms
inspector David Kay or, more recently, by Charles Duelfer. In other
words, the supposed threat that undergirded the original argument for
preemption has all but disappeared, as several years of postinvasion
weapons inspections have found no evidence of Iraqi weapons of mass
destruction. All of this serves to show that the invasion of Iraq was not
justifiable on preemptive grounds. Even the Bush administration has
backed off from the preemptive war justification in order to emphasize
other justifications for the war.

The Bush administration's recent discussions of Iraqi weapons capacity have admitted that Saddam Hussein may not have posed an imminent threat, but the argument now is that Saddam was a threat because he had the *potential* to develop weapons of mass destruction.
President Bush said the following on October 7, 2004, in response to the
Duelfer report:

> Chief weapons inspector, Charles Duelfer, has now issued a comprehen-
> sive report that confirms the earlier conclusion of David Kay that Iraq did
> not have the weapons that our intelligence believed were there. . . . Based
> on all the information we have today, I believe we were right to take ac-
> tion, and America is safer today with Saddam Hussein in prison. He re-
> tained the knowledge, the materials, the means, and the intent to produce

weapons of mass destruction. And he could have passed that knowledge on to our terrorist enemies. Saddam Hussein was a unique threat, a sworn enemy of our country, a state sponsor of terror, operating in the world's most volatile region. In a world after September the 11th, he was a threat we had to confront. And America and the world are safer for our actions.

The rationale indicated here is one of speculative prevention of a potential threat. It focuses on Saddam's capacity and intent to produce WMD. But capacity and intent do not create an imminent threat. The difficulty of justifying such a speculative war is found in the vagueness of the threat and the multitude of nonviolent actions that could have been taken to prevent the threat from materializing, that is, to prevent Saddam's capacity and intent from becoming actualized as a genuine imminent threat. Of course, one may reply that this is an issue of twenty-twenty hindsight: it is easy to see now that our intelligence was flawed but we had to act despite this. However, Iraq was not an imminent threat before the war, and postwar analysis shows us only more clearly that this was true.

I realize that intelligent people will differ about the nature of the Iraqi threat. I want to look beyond this to the general conclusion we should draw from the problem indicated by the war in Iraq. The general problem indicated here is that in practice politicians will exaggerate threats. And indeed, they may act rightly in doing so: if people are not taking a threat seriously enough a leader may be justified in using some extreme language as a motivator. However, this indicates two problems. First, those in power should not in their own minds be deceived about the nature of the threat, despite the rhetorical excesses they employ when addressing the general public. Our leaders have an obligation to be precise and exact when thinking about these issues. This is a moral obligation to those who will be harmed in war, and it is an obligation that is acknowledged in the NSS. Second, ordinary citizens are left wondering what to believe. If we know that our leaders exaggerate threats in order to motivate action and if we suspect that they don't really understand the difference between potential and actual threats (either in their own minds or in their political rhetoric), we are left confused and suspicious. Thus recent events should serve to make us skeptical about future arguments made for preemption.

The most obvious difficulty of the invasion of Iraq is that it violates the principle of proportionality. This principle holds that the use of violence must result in a good that will outweigh the status quo ante and the choice of not using violence. As Michael Ignatieff puts this idea, "Preemption must not leave things worse than before the action was contemplated."[25] But, there is more violence and suffering now than there were before the war, and it is possible that the war has made terrorism against the United States more likely. Of course, such judgments are quite difficult to make because in a situation where preemption is employed, we do not know the state of affairs that would have resulted if preemption were not employed. Put more extremely, it is almost impossible to know, after preemption has been employed, whether preemption has lived up to the principle of proportionality because the threat that was preempted was, in fact, not allowed to materialize. This is especially difficult when these threats are sold as existential threats which justify unlimited means of response. For example, those who claim that the war is still justified despite the increase in suffering that we have seen in the last few years will claim that the war is justified because it has served to prevent further and worse harms. Indeed, the Bush administration's rhetoric of "fighting the terrorists over there, so we don't have to fight them here" invokes this idea: if we had not preemptively invaded Iraq, we would have been worse off because we would be fighting Iraq-supported terrorists here at home. The idea behind this is that the massive struggle for regime change in Iraq was proportional to the existential threat posed by Iraq.

The difficulty of such a claim is obvious: it would have been possible to disarm and contain Iraq without completely occupying the country. Of course, such arguments are based on counterfactual speculation. But the same logical problems apply to those who would appeal to the principle of proportionality to claim that the war was justifiable. One might argue that it is difficult to know what *would* have happened if other actions had been taken, and thus it is difficult to apply the principle of proportionality in such cases. But the principle of proportionality cannot simply be ignored: proportionality reminds us that violence must be limited in light of the ends we pursue.

The problem of speculating about the proportional employment of RP is worse at the level of the ordinary citizen who does not have relevant information and expertise. There are two problems of logic here. On the one hand, before preemption is employed, we must speculate about the severity of risks and their degree of imminence. Such speculation is based on classified intelligence, and it requires substantial expertise in assessing intelligence data. In retrospect in the case of Iraq, it appears that mistakes were made in assessing intelligence data. This leads one to wonder whether the burden of proof should be much higher than it was in this case. This problem is exacerbated at the level of the ordinary citizen who lacks information and expertise. On the other hand, once preemption has been employed, it is difficult to say, in retrospect, whether it was justified or not due to the fact that such claims are based on counterfactual speculation. There will be dispute after the fact about whether the initial evidence has been altered by the use of violence (WMD may have been hidden or destroyed). And there will be disputes about the intentions of those involved. Saddam Hussein may have been bluffing about his actual military power, he may have actually been contained by the UN sanctions regime, or he may really have had his hopes set on developing nuclear weapons and disseminating other weapons to terrorists. Obviously, it is difficult even for experts to discover the truth of these claims in retrospect, and the problem is worse for ordinary citizens.

All of this indicates the problem of a policy of RP: RP wars must be based on speculation and intelligence assessments that involve a substantial amount of uncertainty. While this serves to make the practical moral task of civilian and military leadership more difficult, it should also undermine citizen support of the doctrine in future concrete cases. And it should lead us to reject the doctrine in general. The war in Iraq shows us the difficulties confronted by our leaders; and it shows us the even worse difficulties encountered by ordinary citizens considering whether to support a war of preemption. It is quite difficult, if not impossible, for ordinary citizens to make rational judgments about the justification of RP war. While it is possible that military and civilian leaders have access to more information than the rest of us, they must keep some of this information secret and they possess relevant expertise in assessing military intelligence that most of us lack. Moreover, the case of Iraq shows us that leaders are either confused or deliberately obtuse when it comes to thinking about preemption and/or prevention. Although the NSS states that we will "proceed deliberately," the case in Iraq shows us either a decided lack of deliberation or deliberate misrepresentation. In either case, citizens are left with skepticism. The dispute over weapons of mass destruction in Iraq thus shows us the problem of making a practical judgment about a potential threat.

PREEMPTIVE WAR AND PRACTICAL PACIFISM

There is, of course, something right about RP. It seems easy enough to justify on consequentialist grounds: if the suffering caused by the preemptive attack were less than the suffering that would occur if the threat of aggression were not preempted, then an act of preemption would be justified. We may be suspicious of this because it risks an escalation of war as nations try to preempt one another. One way around this is to consider the possibility that RP may be justified for the United States but not for everyone else.[26] This double standard is linked to claims about U.S. hegemony and moral superiority. The basic idea is that the United States should have the prerogative to act as a global hegemon because it has both the power and the moral legitimacy to preempt developing threats.

The difficulty for citizens is what to make of both the consequentialist argument and the claims about U.S. moral hegemony. My thesis is that citizens should reject both of these arguments.

The consequentialist argument is difficult to implement in practice because it is based on speculation about risk. This difficulty is noted, for example, by Walzer, who acknowledges that what he calls "preventive" war may be justified on consequentialist grounds: fighting early might lead to less suffering in the long run. However, Walzer recognizes the practical/epistemological problem: "Given the radical uncertainties of power politics, there probably is no practical way of making out that position—deciding when to fight and when not—on utilitarian principles."[27] The traditional basis for restricting anticipatory self-defense was that, without such restriction, we would suffer worse long-term consequences. In Webster's words, a permissive idea about preemption would lead to "bloody and exasperated war."[28] This is so because any country could use speculative threats as a pretext for aggression, thus creating a genuine risk of escalation. Thus, on rule-consequentialist grounds, one could argue that it is better not to accept RP. Both sorts of consequentialist arguments—in favor and against RP—are based on speculative assessment of the long-term consequences of RP. In most cases it is impossible to say one way or another whether a policy of RP will produce better or worse consequences. If we are skeptical, I maintain we should err on the side of conservatism and thus reject RP.

Now one way we could hope to shore up the consequential argument in favor of RP is to adopt the double standard and claim that RP is only for the United States, the de facto moral hegemon. But we have good reason to be skeptical of this claim as well. It is quite difficult to establish the long-term consequences of adopting the double standard. Such a unilateral approach may in fact stimulate further hostility toward the United States and thus inspire more anti-United States terrorism. In the absence of proof that the double standard will produce better long-term consequences, we should be conservative and stay within the more global framework that is found in TP, which admits that all states have an equal right to preempt traditionally understood imminent threats.

These skeptical and conservative conclusions are articulated at the level of the ordinary citizen considering the general adoption of the policy. The NSS admits that the government needs accurate and timely intelligence if it is to adequately justify a preemptive war.[29] The government recognizes the high burden of proof that would have to be met in order to justify a preemptive war. But we have discovered that the government lacked the sort of accurate intelligence that would be needed to justify preemption in the case of Iraq. Thus we have new reason to doubt the judgment of leaders who would apply RP. Citizens should thus be reluctant to assent in practice to preemptive wars and they should also be reluctant to support a policy of RP.

The difficulty for citizens is usually downplayed or overlooked by those who defend preemptive war. But citizens find themselves in what might be called a "fiduciary dilemma" with regard to RP: we need to trust government with regard to national security issues, but we do not know whether we should trust them. A minimal level of trust of governmental authority is both natural and necessary with regard to questions of national security. Democratic governments are understood, following Locke, as fiduciary institutions grounded on trust. One of the government's primary duties is to defend us against attack. Faith in those who have sworn to uphold this duty is normal. It is natural for citizens to give the government the benefit of the doubt, in part because the division of labor is such that those in power have expertise in matters of national defense. The claim that the war in Iraq was necessary from the standpoint of national defense was based on complicated and occasionally classified intelligence assessments, which ordinary citizens do not have access to. Indeed, even when we do have access to relevant intelligence data, we do not possess the expertise to adequately judge its national security implications. For example, we might recall the aluminum tubes that were supposed to be part of an Iraqi nuclear program. Ordinary citizens had no way of knowing if this was true, or whether even if true, this situation actually posed a threat to our security.

But subsequent disclosures show us that the experts generally disagreed with the Bush administration's interpretation of this evidence.[30] Our leaders told us that Iraq posed a threat to our safety and that this threat needed to be preempted. And since they have the expertise and the access to intelligence that ordinary citizens lack, it might seem natural to believe them. But now we discover that the threat was not as acute as we were led to believe.

Rational citizens are thus confronted with the vexing problem of deciding whether to trust military and civilian leadership with regard to issues of national security. The problem of trust is exacerbated by the fact that those who articulate the case for war focus on horrors—for example, terrorist attacks that use weapons of mass destruction—that we all want to avoid. If an expert who is in a position of authority tells us that we should be frightened and that we should act to prevent atrocity, we are likely to believe his or her assessment of the dangers and his or her judgment about what ought to be done. However, history—both recent and not so recent—shows us that our trust and credulity may be taken advantage of by those in power. A rational citizen must realize now—in the aftermath of Iraq—that it is not always reasonable to trust the government's description of the dangers we confront, nor is it rational to trust the government's claims about the risk of pursuing military solutions to these dangers. This claim may be supported with further historical evidence about the manipulation of evidence for war from Vietnam and other wars.

Recent events serve to make the epistemological problem and the fiduciary dilemma more obvious. We have discovered either that the government does not know what it is doing (e.g., that its judgments were based on faulty intelligence) or that it exaggerates its intelligence claims and possibly even deliberately deceives us. Ordinary citizens should thus more vigorously question and resist the idea of Reformed Preemption.

CONCLUSION

It is true that sometimes we must act in conditions of uncertainty: to demand absolute certainty would leave us, in many cases, immobile. But practical pacifism does not require that our hands be immaculately clean. Rather, we should demand as much certainty as possible with as little risk of doing wrong as possible. Thus we should raise the burden of proof with regard to preemption and return to something like TP in order to ensure that we don't continue to fight unjustified wars. While RP may be justified as an exception to our commitment to justice in war, it should be articulated as a regrettable and temporary exception and not as a deliberate long-term strategy. RP should be viewed as a "lesser evil" exception that should be a rare occurrence in extreme emergencies.[31] But the NSS's forward-leaning policy makes it appear that we are actively and aggressively looking for a fight, which may in fact make it easier than it should be for us to justify fighting. Thus, even though we might think that RP is acceptable in theory, we have good reason to be skeptical of it as a matter of policy.

The position I defend here is conservative. It is based on traditional thinking about justice in war. I assume that violence should be a last resort; that it should be employed only for compelling reasons; and that it should be restricted by the principle or proportionality and the other restrictions found in just war thinking. Although the conversation between the Corinthians and the Spartans, as recorded by Thucydides, reminds us of the dangers of conservatism and the need to evolve in light of new threats, Thucydides also reminds us of the horrors that can be unleashed when violence is not properly restrained. The Melian dialogue serves as one reminder. The Athenians famously argued that "the strong do what they have the power to do and the weak accept what they have to accept."[32] This is a clear articulation of the double standard discussed above. And the consequences of this double standard—the slaughter at Melos—is a reminder of the moral danger of this way of thinking. Indeed, this example may be more fitting to our current state of affairs than the Corinthian dialogue with Sparta. The case of Iraq shows us that the United States risks abusing its power by adopting the more aggressive posture that is found in RP and by applying its power in disproportional ways. To prevent such abuses, citizens should be reluctant to affirm the idea of RP and its articulation as policy in the NSS.

NOTES

1. "President Says Saddam Hussein Must Leave Iraq," March 17, 2003, at www.whitehouse.gov/new/releases/2003/03/20030317-7.html.

2. For a recent historical account see Brian Orend, *Human Rights: Concept and Context* (Orchard Park, NY: Broadview Press, 2002).

3. Thucydides, *History of the Peloponnesian War* (New York: Penguin, 1954), 75.

4. Thucydides, *History of the Peloponnesian War*, 77.

5. For skeptical reading of the NSS and the question of why it was published despite the diplomatic damage to the United States' credibility overseas see Paul Berman, *Terror and Liberalism* (New York: Norton, 2003), chap. 7. For a more sympathetic reading of the NSS as part of an aggressive new "grand strategy," see John Lewis Gaddis, "A Grand Strategy of Transformation," *Foreign Policy*, November/December 2002. And for a careful analysis of the new doctrine see Tom Sauer, "The Pre-Emptive and Preventive Use of Force: To Be Legitimized or to Be De-Legitimized?" *Ethical Perspectives* 11, no. 2–3 (2004): 130–43.

6. George P. Shultz, "Hot Preemption," *Hoover Digest*, no. 3 (2002), at www-hoover.stanfor.edu/publications/digest/023/Shultz.html.

7. See the French policy at www.defense.gouv.fr/defense/layout/set/popup/content/view/full/29831; for a discussion see Francois Heisbourg, "A Work in Progress: The Bush Doctrine and Its Consequences," *Washington Quarterly* 26, no. 2 (Spring 2003): 75–88; the British white paper is available at www.mod.uk/NR/rdonlyres/051AF365-0A97-4550-99C0-4D87D7C95DED/0/cm60411whitepaper2003.pdf. The quote is from sec. 1.5, p. 3.

8. For a discussion of this ambiguity see Anthony Clark Arend, "International Law and the Preemptive Use of Military Force," *Washington Quarterly* 26, no. 2 (Spring 2003): 89–103. For a defense of the U.S. invasion of Iraq that appeals to Article 51 see John Yoo, "International Law and the War in Iraq," *American Journal of International Law* 97, no. 3 (July 2003): 563–76.

9. National Security Strategy of the United States of America, September 2002, 15, at www.whitehouse.gov/nsc/nss.pdf. Hereafter to be cited as NSS.

10. Hugo Grotius, *The Law of War and Peace* (Indianapolis: Bobbs-Merrill, 1925), bk. 2, chap. 1, sec. 5, p. 173.

11. Webster to Lord Ashburton, July 27, 1842, at www.danorr.com/webstet/webster_july27_1842.htm.

12. NSS, p. 15.

13. Paul Wolfowitz (speech, International Institute for Strategic Studies, December 2, 2002), at www.iiss.org.

14. "Dr. Condoleezza Rice Discusses President's National Security Strategy," October 1, 2002, at www.whitehouse.gov/newsreleases/2002/10/20021001-6.html.

15. William H. Taft IV, legal adviser to the State Department, states this explicitly in "The Legal Basis for Preemption," a Council on Foreign Relations Roundtable, at www.cfr.org/publication.php?id=5250#. For discussion see Miriam Sapiro, "Iraq: The Shifting Sands of Preemptive Self-Defense," *American Journal of International Law* 97, no. 3 (July 2003): 599–607.

16. Terence Taylor, "The End of Imminence?" *Washington Quarterly* 27, no. 4 (Autumn 2004): 58.

17. Christopher Greenwood, "International Law and the Pre-emptive Use of Force: Afghanistan, Al-Qaeda, and Iraq," *San Diego International Law Journal* 4 (2003): 16.

18. "Dr. Condoleezza Rice Discusses President's National Security Strategy."

19. Michael Walzer, *Just and Unjust Wars* (New York: Basic Books, 1977), chap. 16; John Rawls, *The Law of Peoples* (Cambridge, MA: Harvard University Press, 1999), chap. 14. See my discussion in Andrew Fiala, *Practical Pacifism* (New York: Algora Press, 2004), chap. 6; and "Terrorism and the Philosophy of History," *Essays in Philosophy* 3 (March 2003).

20. Examples of justified preemptive attacks might include Prussia's attack on Saxony in 1756 or Japan's attack on Russia in 1904. See Walzer, *Just and Unjust Wars*, chap. 5; Paul W. Schroeder, "Iraq: The Case Against Preemptive War," *American Conservative*, October 21, 2002; Michael Walzer, "No Strikes," *New Republic*, September 30, 2002; or Michael Ignatieff, *The Lesser Evil* (Princeton, NJ: Princeton University Press, 2004), chap. 6; Arend, "International Law."

21. The invasion of Afghanistan is not an example of preemption because it was an attack in response to aggression.

22. "Among societies, the right of natural defense sometimes carries with it a necessity to attack, when one people sees that a longer peace would put another people in a position to destroy it and that an attack at this moment is the only way to prevent such destruction. Hence small societies more frequently have the right to wage wars than large ones, because they are more frequently in a position to fear being destroyed." See Baron Charles de Montesquieu, *The Spirit of the Laws* (Cambridge: Cambridge University Press, 1989), bk. 10, p. 138.

23. See David Luban, "Preventive War," *Philosophy and Public Affairs* 32, no. 3 (July 2004): 207–48.

24. "President Says Saddam Hussein Must Leave Iraq."

25. Michael Ignatieff, *The Lesser Evil* (Princeton, NJ: Princeton University Press, 2004), 166.

26. The double standard is considered by Luban, "Preventive War."

27. Michael Walzer, *Just and Unjust Wars*, 77.

28. Webster to Lord Ashburton, July 27, 1842. David Luban argues, following Walzer, that as the permission for preventive war becomes broadened, it makes war more likely. See Luban, "Preventive War."

29. In the NSS, the claim is made, for example, that the United States needs to "build better, more integrated intelligence capabilities to provide timely, accurate information on threats, wherever they may emerge." See NSS, 16.

30. "The Nuclear Card: The Aluminum Tube Story," *New York Times*, October 3, 2004.

31. Michael Ignatieff, *The Lesser Evil*, 162–67.

32. Thucydides, *History of the Peloponnesian War*, 402.

Chapter Seven

Torture and Terrorism

Never open the door to a lesser evil, for other and greater ones invariably slink in after it.

—Baltasar Gracian[1]

When we open the door to the lesser evil of terrorism or torture, we may end up sliding down the slippery slope toward further compromises with evil. Of course, not all slopes are slippery. However, there are good reasons to keep a wary eye out for the evil that may slink in with well-intentioned exceptions to principles about the proper limit of violence.[2] One of these reasons has to do with the nature of political power. When political agents make exceptions to moral principles, these exceptions can become precedents that serve to normalize immoral behavior. This aspect of political reality is ignored in contemporary attempts to justify torture and terrorism. The myth we must watch out for is the idea that exceptional uses of violence can be controlled and contained. This myth is closely related to the human tendency to make exceptions and flirt with double standards.

RECENT JUSTIFICATIONS
OF TERRORISM AND TORTURE

Terrorism may appear to be justifiable from the standpoint of consequentialism. More exactly, consequentialist reasoning can lead us to make exceptions to the basic principles of just war theory.[3] This occurs despite the fact that the just war theory would seem to be explicitly opposed to terrorism in its prohibition against deliberately targeting innocent noncombatants. Nonetheless, philosophers such as James Sterba claim that just war theory—even what he calls "just war pacifism"— can lead to a justification of terrorism.[4] Sterba claims, for example, that Palestinian terrorists may be justified because the Palestinian cause is just and because "the Palestinians lack any effective means to try to end the Israeli occupation."[5] In trying to justify such exceptions, Sterba follows Walzer and Rawls, who allow terrorism—at least terror bombing—under what they call "the supreme emergency exemption."[6] Another recent attempt to justify terrorism is found in F. M. Kamm's defense of what he calls "terror-killing": Kamm argues that terrorism is acceptable when there are no other means with which to pursue a just cause.[7] The basic idea common to Sterba, Walzer, Rawls, and Kamm is that in extraordinary circumstances, when the cause is just, and when there are no other means available, terrorism might be justified.

In a similar fashion, some have recently attempted to justify torture as a consequentialist exception to basic principles about restraint of force. The most famous recent discussion is Alan Dershowitz's.[8] Dershowitz acquiesces to the de facto use of torture in police interrogation. The United States, for example, has used torture in the war on terrorism— both at Guantánamo Bay and in Abu Ghraib prison in Iraq—and the United States continues to use the practice of "rendition" by which prisoners are sent to countries that are known to use torture.[9] But Dershowitz goes further and argues that torture can be justified if properly supervised and regulated with "torture warrants." The value of torture is described from a consequentialist analysis of "ticking bomb" scenarios, in which a terrorist has planted a bomb and torture is the only effective means of finding the information needed to defuse the bomb. William Casebeer has argued that there may be certain "tightly constrained circumstances" in which torture could be justified.[10] Casebeer bases this argument on Walzer's supreme emergency exemption. I should note that I agree with much of Casebeer's analysis, especially his conclusion that in practice "it will be practically impossible to justify any particular decision to act on an exception to the prohibition of torture interrogation of terrorists." Along with Casebeer I want to emphasize the difficulty of justifying torture or terrorism in practice. However, my point is broader: I want to indicate the pragmatic and political risks that would occur if we were willing to legitimate the exceptional by making it legal.

My worry is similar to Henry Shue's conclusion of several decades ago.[11] Like Shue, my concern is that attempts to justify torture or terrorism often fail to acknowledge political reality. In order to think about whether terrorism or torture could be justified, we must consider the likelihood that political agents will abuse these exceptional practices— that they will drift toward the exceptional, normalize it, and readjust the moral lines that guide the use of violence. As Shue puts it, hard cases— like ticking-bomb scenarios—make bad law. This is true because extraordinary examples cannot be used as a model for ordinary cases.

Shue argues that justified and controlled uses of torture will be quite rare and that it is more likely that cruelty will run amok if we were to legalize or normalize torture. The force of this claim is obviously limited since it is an inductive and empirical argument based on generalizations about human nature and political reality. Nonetheless, historical and psychological issues must be accounted for. Shue ventures into metaphor in order to make a similar point. He claims that only "angels" could be trusted to have the self-control and moral character to use torture in exceptional cases while laying it aside when the emergency is over. Recent events—at Abu Ghraib, for example—show us the temptation of cruelty and the danger of flirting with the legitimization of torture. Most human beings are not angels, and some are easily tempted by the power of cruelty. Recognition of this fact should make us reluctant to justify torture and terror, even as an exceptional means.

One of my primary concerns here is the human tendency to compromise basic moral principles as we make accommodations for exceptions. Politicians are especially susceptible to this problem, as they feel political pressure to take decisive and dramatic action without regard for moral niceties. Morality always suffers under such pressure: clear moral lines become fuzzy when we are asked to respond to new dangers and emergencies. In political life there is often great pressure to step over a clear moral boundary. And in the life of a nation, a turn to the exceptional can create a precedent for further moves toward immorality.

THE EVIL OF TERRORISM AND TORTURE

Terrorism and torture are closely linked. However, not all torture is terroristic. Thus some distinctions must be made. Terrorism is random and unpredictable violence. In Michael Baur's words, it is "systematically unsystematic."[12] The purpose of terrorism is to create panic and chaos, usually in order to advance a political agenda, although terrorism may be divorced from a political agenda as a sort of nihilistic glee in causing disorder. In the same way, torture may be employed simply for the sake of cruelty and without any further goal. Such cruelty and nihilism are not my focus here, as I assume that such acts can never be morally justifiable. Rather, my focus is terror or torture that aims toward some good consequence, since this is the sort of terror and torture that is thought by some to be morally justifiable.

It is clear that torture can be a means to terrorize. *Terroristic torture* is excessive violence and cruelty that is used to send a message to a population. This sort of torture should be distinguished from *interrogative torture*: torture that is intended to produce information or some other form of compliance. Most defenders of torture—such as Dershowitz and Casebeer—focus primarily on interrogative torture. In the ticking-bomb scenario, the purpose is to defuse the bomb. Once this goal is accomplished, torture is to be terminated. Defenders of interrogative torture imagine that the use of torture in such cases would be limited: pain may be administered but only in the limited amounts that are required to create compliance and extract information. Another sort of torture may be called *punitive torture*: torture employed as a punishment. I will say little here about punitive torture, as this is not the focus of recent discussions and because a full consideration would require further analysis of the nature of punishment.

There are consequentialist objections to the use of interrogative torture that do not focus on a deontological condemnation of the act per se. One of these is the fact—noted long ago by John Locke—that committed individuals can offer great resistance to coercive pressure.[13] Moreover, coercion can produce superficial compliance that is basically insincere—including admissions of guilt and false information that simply tell the interrogator what he wants to hear. The further consequentialist problem, which is my focus here, is that it is hard to prevent the slide down the slippery slope from interrogative torture to outright cruelty and terroristic torture. The events at Abu Ghraib were facilitated by a permissive atmosphere created by the apparent legitimization of torture as a tool of interrogation.

One important difference between terrorism and interrogative torture is the fact that terrorism deliberately targets the innocent (or at least systematically ignores the concept of innocence), while interrogative torture is supposed to be directed only at the guilty. The captured bomber who is to be tortured in order to defuse the bomb is not innocent, even though he is—once in custody—defenseless. Some may argue that the evil of torture is that it is violence used against the defenseless one who is entirely at our mercy. But the further danger is that we may slip from torturing the guilty toward terroristic torture of the innocent. For example, in response to a recalcitrant terrorist who will not break under torture, we could imagine a supporter of torture thinking that it might be justifiable to torture the terrorist's wife, children, or parents in order to get him to comply. Or we could imagine a frantic interrogator rounding up and torturing a variety of innocent members of a given ethnic or religious group in an attempt to discover the guilty or at least to make the guilty party consider surrendering to prevent this terroristic use of torture.

Let me be clear in concluding this section: terrorism is wrong because terrorists deliberately kill innocent human beings. In Kantian language, terrorists use their victims as a mere means to their ends: these victims are used to make a political point. As such terrorism is disrespectful of persons. A prohibition on terrorism can also be supported from the perspective of rule-utilitarianism: more people will be happier if this principle is respected because it will generally reduce harm and create social stability, while avoiding an escalation of violence. Torture also tends to use its victims as means. But interrogative torture—as recently defended—at least attempts to focus only on those who are guilty. There is a qualitative difference between deliberately harming the innocent and deliberately harming the guilty but defenseless. For this reason, terrorism is worse than interrogative torture. However, the risk is that interrogative torture can slide toward terrorism.

DOUBLE STANDARDS,
DIRTY HANDS, AND LESSER EVILS

One need not be an absolutist to recognize that there are good pragmatic reasons for viewing the prohibition on terrorism as, in effect, absolute. One effect of allowing for exceptions to the prohibition on terrorism is that the exceptions can appear to redefine the rule. We see this routinely in daily life in the ways in which individuals compromise their integrity bit by bit by making exceptions to basic moral principles. We also see this in political life: policies that were proposed as temporary exceptions become, through force of inertia, established precedents. Moreover, cruel officials can use the exception as an excuse for their malicious behavior—as happened at Abu Ghraib.

In response to this, my basic contention is that in political life, we are better off erring on the side of a cautious restraint of violence. If it is necessary to stray beyond this limit, we should admit that we are heading toward a region that is beyond the ordinary discourse of justification. Indeed, exceptions are fraught with uncertainty and risk. Said differently, to justify exceptions is to flirt with evil. It may turn out, as Michael Ignatieff has argued, that in reality we may have to choose "the lesser evil."[14] But we should be very clear about the dangers of making such devil's bargains because none of us is a perfect angel.

Political agents who make exceptions view themselves or their situation as exceptional. For example, Americans view America as somehow exceptional, as discussed in chapter 5. Exceptional thinking often leads to a "double standard" in thinking about moral rules: "we" are allowed to make exceptions, but "they" are not. Political power has a tendency toward double standards. This results from the pursuit of self-interest and from a tendency to neglect the impartial standpoint. Political agents can drift toward the exceptional when morality becomes a hindrance to self-interest and when cynical realism appears to allow the use of any means necessary to accomplish our ends. The myths of political life make this drift more likely.

Exceptions are supposed to be temporary and rare suspensions of basic moral principles. But the risk is that the exceptional and temporary will come to be taken as a precedent. Walzer makes it clear that supreme emergencies are quite rare. Walzer says that the supreme emergency exemption to the rules of war kicks in when the threat is "close" and "serious."[15] And he argues that, in the case he examines—Britain during the early years of World War II—there was only a narrow window during which the exemption applied. When Britain was under attack and before the United States had entered the war, it may have been justified to use terror bombing against German cities. The difficulty of this analysis is that it ignores what Jonathan Glover calls "military drift": the tendency of military goals to overshadow moral constraints.[16] Especially in times of crisis, there is an incremental creep toward excessive violence. Once the initial choice to use terror bombing is made (even if this choice is only a temporary and exceptional expedient), subsequent expansions of the use of terror bombing are more easily made.

Walzer's analysis of the supreme emergency exemption requires further consideration. There are some difficulties with the example he examines. It is not clear, for example, that civilian targeting was effective in winning the war against Germany or that this was even a sound use of strategic resources.[17] Allied bombing campaigns were expensive to mount. And it ultimately took a full-scale invasion to end Nazi power. Terror bombing has little to do with the direct strategy of invading and destroying the enemy's armed forces. Moreover, in World War II, the exception became the rule and the Allies bombed civilian targets in both Europe and Japan. This drift toward the exceptional culminated in the firebombings of cities in Germany and Japan and the use of atomic weapons at the end of the war. This in turn made it easier for military planners to target civilian population centers in the MAD-ness (mutually assured destruction) of the Cold War.

Politicians will continue to overreact to threats, since a commitment to military power is a requirement for electoral success. And history shows us that our leaders have often been willing to employ terror tactics in order to exhibit strength before the electorate. The problem of democratic politics is that the momentum of political life pushes leaders to rationalize exceptions to moral principles. This idea can be found in Walzer's idea that most politicians will have dirty hands.[18] This is true, in part, because they must overreact in ways that lead to violations of the basic principles of morality.

We should recognize this fact when thinking about the exceptions that have been made recently with regard to the use of torture. The same sort of exceptional thinking appears in recent revisions of the idea of preemptive war. And it occurs in attempts to revise the United States' commitment to the first use of tactical nuclear weapons. These policies are grounded on the idea that the United States is exceptional in its ability to properly use torture, preemptive war, and nuclear weaponry. But such exceptions reek of the double standard: "we" are allowed to make exceptions to principles that limit the use of force, but other countries are not.

To deal in exceptions is to continue to encourage this sort of slippage. If there are exceptions, they should not be a standard part of our moral vocabulary; nor should they be legalized and regularized as policy. Rather, they should be viewed with fear and trembling as abysses into which the real world pushes us. Indeed, rather than claiming that an exception could be "justified," perhaps it is better to admit that exceptions are not "justified" at all. As exceptions they fall outside the scheme of justification.

This idea is similar to the "lesser evil" approach to moral and political thinking recently articulated by Michael Ignatieff. Ignatieff's idea is that in the real world, what he calls "perfectionism" does not work. The lesser evil approach is supposed to fall somewhere between "cynicism and perfectionism." What is appealing about Ignatieff's approach is his idea that the lesser evil is still an *evil* and that to invoke an evil is to take a *moral risk*.[19] To his credit, Ignatieff rejects terrorism as a "greater evil."[20] And he claims that attempting to justify torture as a lesser evil "seems likely to lead to the greater."[21] But for other "lesser evils"—such as restrictions on civil liberties—he provides guidance for how such exceptions are to be administered. If we make exceptions, Ignatieff argues that these should be temporary responses to emergencies and that they should be regulated by an open and adversarial system.

Unfortunately, our system is not as open and adversarial as we would like it to be. To see the true nature of the danger of exceptional thinking we need a sober analysis of political power. Governments will make more exceptions than are morally acceptable, and the exceptions will not be subjected to the kind of open and adversarial scrutiny that would be required to prevent the drift toward the exceptional. Exceptional thinking encourages self-deception, hubris, and other vices that lead to blatant double standards. In American political life this sort of exceptional thinking is encouraged by the privilege and prerogatives of the executive branch. The danger is that the commander in chief will think himself superior to the people's representatives in government: the scrutiny of the masses and the formalities of congressional oversight will thus be seen as a hindrance and not as a necessary check in an adversarial system. Said differently, to allow for exceptions is to tempt those in power to abuse their power. We saw this most recently in the deception and misinformation that were used to justify the invasion of Iraq. This problem created by the prerogatives of executive power has been with us since Plato defended the use of the noble lie. It remains a problem in democratic republics such as the United States. And it is a worse problem in less representative forms of government. The powerful will continue to think that they are entitled to make exceptions to basic moral principles and they will act to circumvent the adversarial system.

TERRORISM AND THE PRINCIPLE OF DOUBLE EFFECT

Terrorism is wrong because it deliberately harms the innocent for the purpose of advancing a political agenda. Those who defend specific acts of terrorism often claim that the terrorist's agenda is so important that he is entitled to make exceptions to moral rules in order to accomplish his ends. Those who justify terrorism focus almost exclusively on the justness of the cause for which terrorism is employed: national defense or an end to oppression. But the justice of the cause is not the only principle that matters when thinking about the justification of violence. We should also think about the means we employ in pursuit of our ends. The just war tradition speaks of the means of advancing our ends under the general rubric of *jus in bello*. One of the basic principles of *jus in bello* is that innocent victims should not be intentionally targeted. Our moral judgments about such actions should not be changed by questions about the justness of the cause or the structure of political power: these actions are wrong because they deliberately harm the innocent.

We might think that terrorism can be justified by the doctrine of double effect.[22] But double effect cannot justify terrorism. Indeed, where double effect can be employed the act in question would—by definition—not be terrorism. Double effect aims to justify harm to innocents by admitting that sometimes innocents are harmed as an unintended side effect of an action. But terrorism directly intends the harm it creates.

One might respond by claiming that terrorists actually intend some long-term political goal and that the harm created is really incidental to the accomplishment of this end. At issue here is the scope of the intention: how closely is the harm linked to the intended long-term goal? This question aims to distinguish between what an agent actually intends and what he intends incidentally or accidentally. Thus we need to consider the extent of the agent's knowledge as well as questions about an agent's responsibility for obtaining such knowledge. Defenders of terrorism might appeal to the doctrine of double effect by claiming that harm to innocents is not directly intended and that it is not closely linked to the long-term intention. Here, for example, one might consider that a political agent may aim to create fear by exploding a bomb in an empty street in the middle of the night without intending any harm. In such a case, if a human being wandered into the street and was killed by the bomb, the harm was not intended. But it should be clear that such cases are rare and that they do not explain what happens in most actual cases of terrorism. Terrorists explode their bombs in crowded places with the intention of killing people.

Terrorism is wrong because the people killed by terrorists are quite literally viewed as mere means. Terrorists do not care about the particular identities of their victims. Rather, they view the victims as deindividuated members of a "mass." Some may argue that terrorist violence is aimed against members of the mass because of their identity. In Iraq, for example, suicide bombers systematically target police and army recruiting stations; they also target American soldiers. In such cases, we may want to avoid the term "terrorism" and focus on the idea of insurgency. Such attacks aim at groups that are viewed as having some responsibility for fighting. A clearer example of terrorism is found in the September 11 attacks. In these attacks it did not matter who in particular was in the World Trade Towers: anyone there that day was killed, regardless of his or her personal identity. Likewise, in firebombing a city, the identities of those killed are irrelevant (except for the incidental fact that they happen to be in that city on that unfortunate day). The point is that the terrorist has no interest in his victims' personal identities. This shows disrespect for persons and a willingness to consider them as exchangeable objects—as mere things and not as persons.

The random nature of terrorism is both its most frightening aspect and a clear indication of its evil. It leaves everyone feeling vulnerable because anyone could be a victim of an attack. And this is what makes terrorism so morally problematic. In ordinary attempts to justify violence, some claim is made that gives a reason why the victim should be harmed. Such attempts focus on the identity of the recipient of justified violence. In self-defense, one may harm one's assailant because the assailant poses a threat to one's own well-being. In just war thinking there must be a just cause (usually aggression) and violence has to be focused exclusively against the aggressor (the army of the aggressive nation). But terrorism spreads violence in a way that simply ignores the identities of its victims.

Since those who justify terrorism are willing to use violence against the innocent, this gives us reason to be suspicious of their moral character.[23] It is difficult to believe terrorists or their defenders when they make claims in defense of terrorism, since in defending terrorism they display a lack of respect for persons that one suspects will continue once the terrorist has gained power. At the very least those who kill the innocent should feel remorse and view their own acts of terrorism as shameful. But often the presence of a double standard prevents defenders of terrorism from feeling this sort of remorse.

THE INNOCENT

To understand why terrorism is wrong, it is useful to further explain the idea of "innocence" that shows up in the basic principle stated above, that it is wrong to deliberately harm the innocent.[24] What I mean by innocent can be fleshed out in three ways. First, we might focus on causality and insist that innocence means that these individuals did nothing wrong. I will call this *causal innocence*. Second, we might focus on a sense of responsibility and claim that innocence means that these individuals did not intend to do anything wrong. I will call this *intentional innocence*. Third, we might focus on proof of guilt and claim that innocence means that these individuals have not been proven guilty. I will call this *legal innocence*.

Terrorism might be justified when we consider that some civilians are not causally innocent. This is true, for example, when civilians support oppression or a war effort by contributing money or labor to the oppressive or warring regime. Moreover, some civilians are not intentionally innocent. Some civilians do share the violent intentions of the army that fights in their name, and some may explicitly agree with acts of oppression or injustice. When defenders of terrorism claim that "no one is really innocent," they probably mean that many civilians have both a causal role in injustice and that they also have the intention to contribute to and support injustice. The difficulty of this claim is that it is so expansive that every member of the enemy society becomes a legitimate target: no one is innocent, not even children, so everyone can be targeted, even children.

Legal innocence is important as a restraint on this expansive justification of violence. The point of legal innocence is that it is not enough to suspect that someone is not innocent. There must also be proof of guilt. I will leave the criteria for proving guilt open here. But two important limitations should not be overlooked. In legal proceedings in modern Western nations the accused is allowed to respond to the charges against him and the accused is considered innocent until proven guilty. Different degrees of proof are required for different sorts of tribunals. But the idea of being allowed to respond to accusations and the presumption of innocence are deeply entrenched in our legal tradition.

There are strong moral reasons for preserving these conventions about proof of guilt. These limitations require us to deliberate and consider evidence. This is a good thing, since it prevents the innocent from being unjustly punished. But the problem with terrorism is that it does not aim to distinguish the responsible from the innocent. This is why it is inherently unjust. This is not only a legal claim; it is a moral claim. Those who will be harmed by an act of violence have a right to assert their innocence and defend themselves against accusations of guilt. To ignore this is to treat the victim as a mere means. We do things to animals and other "things" without providing them with the opportunity to argue and consent or dissent. But respect for persons demands that we allow the accused to reply to our accusation. Indeed, the idea of respect for persons demands that we present the evidence to the accused so that they may be given the opportunity to acknowledge their misdeeds and make amends.

This discussion of innocence has obvious bearing on considerations of torture. Proponents of interrogative torture claim that it would be justified only when used on the guilty, that is, on those who have a causal and intentional (and presumably legally proven) responsibility for a harm that could be prevented through the use of torture. Terroristic torture is torture that ignores this distinction. Again, in thinking about the justification of torture, we should be careful not to allow exceptional cases to confuse us about ordinary ones. One wonders, for example, how likely it would be in practice for a police force to prove in a court that the suspect in a ticking-bomb scenario is in fact not innocent. In the concrete emergency, the police will be inclined to torture first and ask questions later. But the risk is that the innocent will then be tortured.

THE FAT MAN ANALOGY

Those who would justify terrorism often appeal to something like the "fat man in the cave" analogy. This analogy and others, such as "runaway trolley" arguments, are favored by those who would justify harming innocents to create a greater good.[25] The fat man in the cave analogy comes from Philippa Foot, who uses it in order to call the doctrine of double effect into question.[26] The idea is as follows. There is a fat man stuck in the mouth of a cave. A group of spelunkers are stuck behind the fat man. Floodwaters are rising in the cave and if the party cannot get out of the cave, they will all drown. The doctrine of double effect allows for the spelunkers to use dynamite to blast the fat man out of the cave: the spelunkers' intention is to save the members of the party and they do not directly intend his death.

Sterba uses this story to justify terrorism. His point is stronger than the argument about double effect. He maintains that it may occasionally be justifiable to actually intend the death of someone in order to accomplish a greater good. Sterba goes so far as to claim that the fat man might be morally required to sacrifice his life to save the spelunking party. Sterba focuses on the numbers that can be saved by the sacrifice of the fat man's life. At some point, Sterba argues, we should make an exception to the idea of protecting the innocent fat man, "even if you think it has to be a very unusual case when we can reasonably demand that people thus sacrifice their lives in this way."[27]

The problem with this analysis is that terrorism does not ask its victims to "sacrifice" themselves. The notion of self-sacrifice that Sterba introduces here can deceive us into thinking that the victim has made a choice and consented to death. But in terrorism, this is clearly not the case: victims of terrorism are killed against their wills.

Another important factor in this discussion is the question of whether the fat man is innocent. The fat man clearly has some causal responsibility for the predicament of the spelunkers. But the fat man did not intend the harm they suffer. The fat man is thus causally responsible while intentionally innocent. This introduces a further complexity into the question of what to do in this case. The fat man had no way of knowing that he would get stuck and put his companions at risk. Sterba suggests that what matters is the physical effect and the question of causal responsibility: we need effective means for removing causal obstacles to our ends. But morality may require us to look deeper into intentional responsibility and innocence: we ought not *blame* the fat man for this predicament unless he knew he would get stuck or intentionally wanted to harm his companions. And indeed, it may be immoral to use someone who is innocent in this way as a means to our ends—even to the seemingly moral end of saving other innocent life.

Terrorists often argue that their victims are causally responsible for some of the ills that the terrorists fight against. Osama bin Laden claimed that all Americans shared responsibility for polluting the Muslim holy lands. In his fatwa of 1998 declaring war on Americans, bin Laden claims that all Americans have a sort of causal responsibility for this, which is why all Americans are considered targets for jihad.[28]

There is some truth in this claim about diffused causal responsibility: democracy spreads responsibility across society. But this causal role is not directly intended. No American voter—or very few of them—has ever consciously decided that he or she wanted to pollute Muslim holy lands. In this sense, most Americans are as innocent as the fat man: we may have some causal responsibility for supporting the regime in Saudi Arabia or for propagating policies that are disrespectful of Islam (this fact is of course disputable) but we did not directly intend these harms.

By focusing only on causal responsibility, one might think we could justify the terror bombing campaigns of World War II. The victims of American terror bombing campaigns in World War II were causally responsible for supporting the Nazi and Japanese governments: they worked to support the war effort in this era of total war. And their intentions were probably more explicitly tied to the war effort: whole societies were mobilized around the idea of defending the nation and destroying the enemy. In the era of total war, one might argue that no one is innocent. But this claim obviously goes too far: children share neither causal nor intentional responsibility for the war effort. Terror bombings remain wrong, then, because there are some who are in fact both causally and intentionally innocent, that is, the children.

The fat man example can be applied to the case of torture in the following way. Interrogative torture aims to use torture to produce compliance from those who are causally and intentionally responsible for potential harm. In the ticking-bomb scenario, the bomber is responsible for planting the bomb and presumably has the ability to disarm it. One might think that this is similar to the case of the fat man. In both cases, the potential victim is causally responsible for the potential harm. However, the fat man did not intend to get stuck and cause harm, whereas the bomber does intend this harm. Moreover, the fat man—in the usual scenario—is unable to dislodge himself and is thus unable to comply with the wishes of the spelunkers. To torture him in such a case would have no effect and would simply be an exercise in cruelty. It is easy to see how the spelunkers could succumb to the temptation to torture the fat man as their fear and desperation grows. But in the case where the fat man is truly innocent, such a use of torture would be unjustifiable.

The bomber is, however, supposed to be able to have the ability to comply and disarm the bomb. Defenders of interrogative torture might claim that while it would not be justified to torture an innocent fat man who is unintentionally stuck and unable to dislodge himself, it would be acceptable to torture a fat man who intentionally and willfully obstructs the exit. This is a plausible way to proceed: we can get the fat man to move out of the way (or the terrorist to defuse the bomb) by causing him pain. Consequentialists will have no problem with using torture on intentionally malicious terrorists. In reality there is an open question of how likely it is that a bomber will be persuaded by torture to comply and defuse the bomb. This question depends on many contingent empirical factors including the terrorist's psychological state and the extent of his knowledge and abilities.

But my main point here is that if we dwell on an exceptional case such as the fat man analogy in thinking about torture, we may end up convincing ourselves that torture could be employed in other nonexceptional situations. The reconstructed fat man analogy—in which the fat man is intentionally obstructing the exit and is able to dislodge himself—is an exceptional case. But in reality, most cases in which torture would be contemplated would not have these characteristics. Most likely there would be questions about the innocence or noninnocence of many of the candidates for torture in ticking-bomb scenarios. And it is easy to imagine cases in which the bomber would not be able to help defuse the bomb anyway, even if he has been persuaded by torture to cooperate. In such cases, it is conceivable that some might turn to torture out of a sense of frustration, just as frightened spelunkers might angrily abuse the fat man's body when it becomes apparent that he cannot be budged. While understandable, this would be unjustifiable cruelty. At least we should be aware of the fact that the exceptional case is indeed an exception. If we are to resort to torture, we should do so with fear and trembling in light of the fact that we are flirting with evil.

One last point must be made with regard to the fat man example, as it was originally described: where the fat man is not a terrorist but is innocent. We must do our best to communicate with the fat man about his predicament. The example could be set up so that the rushing water is too loud or the fat man too deaf to have such a conversation. But those who contemplate killing him would at least have the obligation to try to converse with him. At issue here is both an attempt to consider the point of view of the fat man and an attempt to establish legal innocence or responsibility.

Recall that the legal notion of innocence assumes that someone is innocent until proven guilty. The purpose of this procedural constraint is to ensure that only those who are proven to be responsible are to be punished. It is not enough to suspect either causal or intentional responsibility; such responsibility must be demonstrated objectively and rationally.

To prove the fat man's innocence or guilt, we need to talk to him. Moreover, we should ask him what he suggests we do in solving the problem. It is possible, as Sterba suggests, that he may agree to sacrifice himself in order to save the group. This would be expected especially if the fat man had a relation to the spelunkers. We would also want to know if the fat man had any suggestions about alternative possibilities for escape, as well as his insight into potential negative effects of the blast (perhaps he sees that the blast will trigger a cave-in that will kill everyone anyway). At the very least it would be wrong not to attempt to talk to the fat man about his situation and to take his wishes and insights into consideration. Nagel puts it this way: we should be able to justify to the victim what is being done to him.[29] Finally, if, after conversation and deliberation, it is agreed that the fat man must die, we would hope that there would be a sense of grief and tragedy on the part of those who survive the ordeal. This moral identification with the fat man is, in fact, fostered in part by the relationships that were developed through these conversations.

But terrorists do not seek to establish legal guilt or innocence. Either they assume that every member of the enemy group is equally guilty or they simply ignore the question entirely. Terrorists do not enjoin conversations about responsibility or about potential alternatives to violence. And they do not cultivate a sense of shared humanity with their victims. Indeed, they view terror attacks as signs of victory and power and feel no remorse at the suffering of their victims. Likewise, torturers in ticking-bomb scenarios would most likely not have the time to pursue proof of guilt or innocence. And those who employ torture—even in limited interrogatory settings—will be more inclined toward cruelty and more likely to turn to torture as a first rather than last resort when frustration and fury create the conditions for brutality.

CONCLUSION

One objection to my approach is that it is based on inductive generalization about politics and human nature. I freely admit that this is true. But a similar objection could be made against defenders of terrorism or torture. Attempts to justify terrorism often rest on the claim that other effective means for advancing a putatively just cause are lacking. In discussing the supreme emergency exemption that would justify terror tactics, for example, Walzer indicates that this occurs only in a "back-to-the-wall" situation, when there are no other effective means of dealing with the threat. But it is an empirical question as to whether there are other effective means. Likewise, ticking-bomb scenarios are constructed so that there is no way other than torture to defuse the bomb. This is a stipulation in this case—but it would be open to doubt in a real ticking-bomb scenario.

Pacifists have long pointed out that such back-to-the-wall arguments often show a lack of imagination. Pacifists question whether nonviolent or at least less violent means have been employed and also whether they have been tried multiple times. The just war theory requires that one consider whether the means are proportional to the end, whether there is a possibility of success, and whether violence is a reasonable last resort. All of this requires empirical generalization. Defenders of torture and terrorism construct doomsday scenarios and then claim that these may occur in reality, unless exceptions are permitted. My argument locates the danger elsewhere and worries that those who are authorized to torture or to use terrorism will abuse their power.

What is required then is a judgment about history and human nature: are our leaders "angels" who can be trusted to use extraordinary violence judiciously or are they less perfect than this? This does require empirical analysis. But the long history of human cruelty shows us that we have good reason to be suspicious of those who seek to find ways to reintroduce torture and/or terrorism.

It is difficult to do the right thing during troubled times. Discipline and self-criticism are needed in order to resist the temptation of exceptional thinking, double standards, and the rest of the mythic apparatus of political life. This temptation is especially strong for those who have political power, who view themselves as somehow entitled to make exceptions, and who are pressured to take effective measures to establish national security.

My thesis is that to resist the lure of the exceptional we should treat moral rules against terrorism and torture as near absolutes. While exceptions may have to be made in some doomsday situations, to deal in exceptions is to leap into the abyss. The evil of the exception should not be minimized. It may turn out that there is a higher reconciliation, forgiveness, or forgetfulness that can mitigate the evil of the exception. But the discourse of exceptions should not forget that the exception remains an evil—even if it is a "lesser evil." Stephen de Wijze has recently argued that in such situations a new type of emotion may show itself: a sort of "tragic remorse" that "confirms that we live in a world where our moral reality is nuanced and messy."[30] The danger is that without anguish, shame, and remorse, it becomes easier to regularize and even legalize the lesser evils of torture and terrorism. Without such resistance it is easy to claim that the exception is fully justified while thereby creating a new rule that allows for excessive violence. It may turn out that the choice of an exception can be rationalized in retrospect. But for those who choose to follow the exceptional path, there should always be fear and trembling. By resisting the tendency to claim that the exception is fully justified, we can prevent the slide down the slippery slope that would fully legitimate terrorism and torture.

NOTES

1. Baltasar Gracian, *The Art of Worldly Wisdom* (London: Macmillan, 1892), aphorism no. 31.

2. Michael Walzer has criticized certain excuses that aim to justify terrorism. See his "Terrorism: A Critique of Excuses," in *Social Ideals and Policies*, ed. Steven Luper (Toronto: Mayfield Press, 1999). This is a useful source for thinking about a critique of exceptions. However, it is interesting that it is Walzer who opens the door to the supreme emergency exemption, which allows for terrorism.

See, for example, Kai Nielsen, "Against Moral Conservatism," *Ethics* 82 (1972); or Virginia Held, "Violence Terrorism, and Moral Inquiry," *Monist* 67, no. 4 (October 1984). Attempts to justify terrorism and/or torture that are not purely consequentialist can be grounded in something like Ross's idea of prima facie or pro tanto duties. See W. D. Ross, *The Right and the Good* (Oxford: Clarendon Press, 1930). For a recent discussion see Brad Hooker, "Ross-Style Pluralism versus Rule-Consequentialism," *Mind*, n.s., 105, no. 420 (1996): 531–52. I discuss prima facie duties in Andrew Fiala, *Practical Pacifism* (New York: Algora Press, 2004). Such an approach acknowledges that there can be a conflict of goods. Defenders of terrorism invoke consequential reasoning that—in exceptional circumstances—overrides deontological principles against harming the innocent. The possibility of such an override seems to be the gist of Sterba's idea of "morality as compromise." See James Sterba, *The Triumph of Practice over Theory in Ethics* (Oxford: Oxford University Press, 2005), chap. 2. And it is also found in Walzer's idea of the "sliding scale." See Michael Walzer, *Just and Unjust Wars* (New York: Basic Books, 1977), chap. 14.

3. The idea is that we have a prima facie duty to avoid harming the innocent except in rare emergencies when grave consequences follow from avoiding such harm. I will not question here the metaethical idea of prima facie or pro tanto duties that can be overridden in exceptional cases. Rather, my focus is on the practical question of knowing how or when to override such duties.

4. In *The Triumph of Practice over Theory in Ethics*, Sterba argues that what he calls "just war pacifism" can lead to the justification of terrorism. This seems to be an abuse of language as the consensus view is that just war theory proscribes terrorism, despite Walzer's attempts to sneak it in through the back

door of the supreme emergency exemption. Just war pacifism goes further than straightforward just war thinking and leads to a near absolute prohibition against violence. This may be a matter of terminology—Sterba may be employing the idea of "just war pacifism" in a novel way. But we should get clear about the language and concepts employed in such discussions. Just war pacifism should, if anything, be more restrictive than straightforward just war theory. Just war pacifism results from an argument about whether in fact any war can live up to the standards of just war theory: the just war pacifist generally concludes that the standards of the just war theory are so strict as to make war unjustifiable. This position gained adherents in light of the horrors of the total wars and increased killing power of the twentieth century. The use of "weapons of mass destruction" almost by definition makes war impossible to justify. The just war theory prohibits indiscriminate killing of noncombatants, but weapons of mass destruction kill indiscriminately. Terrorism would thus be prohibited according to this way of understanding just war theory.

5. Sterba, *Triumph of Practice*, 138. Sterba has also published the same argument in "Terrorism and International Justice," in *Terrorism and International Justice* (Oxford: Oxford University Press, 2003). Also see Sterba, *Justice for Here and Now* (Cambridge: Cambridge University Press, 1998).

6. Walzer, *Just and Unjust Wars*; John Rawls, *The Law of Peoples* (Cambridge, MA: Harvard University Press, 1999). See my discussion in Andrew Fiala, "Terrorism and the Philosophy of History: Liberalism, Realism and the Supreme Emergency Exemption," special issue, *Essays in Philosophy* 3 (April 2002), at sorrel.humboldt.edu/~essays/v3cline.html.

7. F. M. Kamm, "Failures of Just War Theory: Terror, Harm, and Justice," *Ethics* 114 (2004): 650–92.

8. Alan Dershowitz, *Shouting Fire: Civil Liberties in a Turbulent Age* (New York: Little, Brown, 2002). Also see essays on torture in Timothy Shanahan, ed., *Philosophy 9/11: Thinking about the War on Terrorism* (New York: Open Court, 2005).

9. See Seymour M. Hersh, *Chain of Command: The Road from 9/11 to Abu Ghraib* (New York: HarperCollins, 2004); also see Amnesty International reports on the use of torture in the war on terrorism, at www.amnestyusa.org/stoptorture/reports.do.

10. William Caseebeer, "Torture Interrogation of Terrorists: A Theory of Exceptions (with Notes, Cautions, and Warnings)," in Shanahan, *Philosophy 9/11*, 262. For a similar analysis also see Fritz Allhoff, "Terrorism and Torture," in Shanahan, *Philosophy 9/11*.

11. Henry Shue, "Torture," *Philosophy and Public Affairs* 7, no. 2 (1978).

12. Michael Baur, "What Is Distinctive about Terrorism, and What Are the Philosophical Implications?" in Shanahan, *Philosophy 9/11*.

13. John Locke, *A Letter Concerning Toleration*, in *Classics of Modern Political Theory*, ed. Steven M. Cahn (Oxford: Oxford University Press, 1997).

Also see Jeremy Waldron, "Locke: Toleration and the Rationality of Persecution," in *John Locke: A Letter Concerning Toleration in Focus*, ed. John Horton and Susan Mendus (London: Routledge, 1991).

14. Michael Ignatieff, *The Lesser Evil* (Princeton, NJ: Princeton University Press, 2004).

15. Walzer, *Just and Unjust Wars*, 252.

16. See Jonathan Glover, *Humanity: A Moral History of the 20th Century* (New Haven, CT: Yale University Press, 2000).

17. See Alex J. Bellamy, "Supreme Emergencies and the Protection of Non-Combatants in War," *International Affairs* 80, no. 5 (2004): 829–50.

18. Michael Walzer, "Dirty Hands," *Philosophy and Public Affairs* 2, no. 2 (Winter 1973).

19. Michael Ignatieff, *Lesser Evil*, 18.

20. Ignatieff's rejection of terrorism is found on pp. 110–11 of *Lesser Evil*.

21. Ignatieff, *Lesser Evil*, 140.

22. For discussions of the doctrine of double effect see G. E. M. Anscombe, "War and Morality," in *Nuclear Weapons: A Catholic Response*, ed. Walter Stein (New York: Sheed and Ward, 1961); Philippa Foot, "The Problem of Abortion and the Doctrine of the Double Effect," *Oxford Review* 5 (1967), reprinted in Foot, *Virtues and Vices and Other Essays in Moral Philosophy* (Berkeley: University of California Press, 1978); Warren S. Quinn, "Actions, Intentions, and Consequences: The Doctrine of Double Effect," *Philosophy and Public Affairs* 18 (1989); John Martin Fischer, Mark Ravizza, and David Copp, "Quinn on Double Effect: The Problem of 'Closeness,'" *Ethics* 103, no. 4 (1993); and Alison McIntyre, "Doing Away with Double Effect," *Ethics* 111 (2001).

23. See Norvin Richards, "Double Effect and Moral Character," *Mind*, n.s., 93, no. 371 (1984).

24. See Robert K. Fullinwider, "Terrorism, Innocence, and War," in *War after September 11*, ed. Verna V. Gehring, ed. (Lanham, MD: Rowman & Littlefield, 2003). For a different approach to the question of innocence see Jeff McMahan, "The Ethics of Killing in War," *Ethics* 114 (2004): 693–733.

25. Sterba uses the fat man in the cave example; Kamm uses a runaway trolley example; for further discussion of these sorts of examples see MacIntyre, "Doing Away with Double Effect."

26. Foot, "Problem of Abortion."

27. Sterba, *Triumph of Practice*, 135.

28. Available online at the International Institute for Counter-Terrorism: www.ict.org.il/articles/fatwah.htm.

29. Thomas Nagel, "War and Massacre," in *The Morality of War*, ed. Larry May, Eric Rovie, and Steve Viner (Upper Saddle River, NJ: Prentice Hall, 2006), 229. Richard Brandt reinterprets Nagel's idea along Rawlsian lines: we

should be able to justify such actions impartially and rationally, as it were, under the veil of ignorance. See Brandt, "Utilitarianism and the Rules of War," in *Morality of War.*

30. Stephen de Wijze, "Tragic-Remorse—The Anguish of Dirty Hands," *Ethical Theory and Moral Practice 7* (2004): 465.

Chapter Eight

Humanitarian Intervention and the Crusade for Democracy

> The best hope for peace in our world is the expansion of freedom in all the world. . . . So it is the policy of the United States to seek and support the growth of democratic movements and institutions in every nation and culture, with the ultimate goal of ending tyranny in our world.
>
> — President George W. Bush, Second Inaugural Address

What has come to be known as the "Bush Doctrine" is an idealistic approach to international relations that imagines a world transformed by the promise of democracy and that sees military force as an appropriate means to utilize in pursuit of this goal. The Bush Doctrine has been described in various ways. It has been called "democratic realism," "national security liberalism," "democratic globalism," and "messianic universalism."[1] Another common claim is that this view is "neoconservative."[2] In what follows I will employ the term "neoconservative" as a convenient and commonly accepted name for the ideas that underlie the Bush Doctrine. The Bush Doctrine has been expressed in numerous speeches by President Bush and members of his administration.[3] It is stated in the policy of the National Security Strategy of the United States (NSS).[4] And it was employed in the invasion of Iraq. The hopeful aspiration of the Bush Doctrine is that democratization will result in peace.

This goal is inspiring. The Bush Doctrine intends the end of tyranny and the creation of peace. But the difficulty of this idea is its emphasis on the "hard power" of military force as a means for attaining this end.[5]

121

Some critics argue that the Bush Doctrine is really a form of imperialism that uses the language of democracy to conceal its imperial ambitions.[6] In the present chapter I will ignore such criticisms and instead focus on the connections between the Bush Doctrine and the just war tradition. The Bush Doctrine uses the language of the just war tradition in its defense of an expanded use of warfare as a means for preempting emerging threats and disseminating freedom and democracy. Supporters of this idea argue that the just war tradition was in need of revision, especially as regards the justification of preemptive war. This argument is grounded in claims about the nature of the newly emerging threat of terrorists and rogue states that can use advanced technology and weapons of mass destruction to disrupt a just and tranquil international order. Proponents of the Bush Doctrine claim that the United States is justified in employing both soft and hard power in order to lead the world toward the peace that results from democratization.

In what follows I will use the insights of the just war tradition to argue against the idea that war should be used as a method for advancing freedom and democracy. This idea is misguided and dangerous because it makes war more likely while also having little chance of success. Although I accept the idea that the growth of democracy can lead to peace, I reject the idea that war is an acceptable means to employ in pursuit of democratization.

To make this argument, it is helpful to consider the Bush Doctrine in light of the newly evolving just war idea of humanitarian intervention.[7] This idea is usually constrained by the idea that war can be employed only as a remedy for situations that, in Michael Walzer's memorable phrase, "shock the moral conscience of mankind."[8] But the Bush Doctrine is more permissive. It allows for the use of military force in pursuit of democracy. Although democracy is a good thing, its absence alone is not morally shocking. The absence of democracy is thus not enough to justify war according to Walzer's standard. But others have offered different ideas about the justification of humanitarian intervention. Teson defines humanitarian intervention as follows: "The proportionate international use or threat of military force, undertaken in principle by a liberal government or alliance, aimed at ending tyranny or anarchy, welcomed by the victims, and consistent with the doctrine of double effect."[9] This idea is probably close to what the Bush Doctrine intends: President Bush does talk of ending tyranny, and the National Security Strategy affirms the traditional ideas of *jus in bello*. However, the idea that war may be used to create democracy seems to require more than merely ending tyranny: it requires that military power be used to create democratic institutions. This idea of using war to create democracy is what makes the Bush Doctrine unacceptable from a just war standpoint. The war in Iraq reminds us of one of the problems of the idea of fighting a war in pursuit of democracy: war is so disruptive that it makes it difficult to build democracy in its aftermath. This is especially true in societies that have suffered from a long history of undemocratic government and that lack established institutions of civil society.

FREEDOM, DEMOCRACY, AND THE BUSH DOCTRINE

The word "democracy" is subject to multiple interpretations, as is the related word "freedom." Democracy and freedom might be construed such that their absence is linked to egregious human rights violations that would thus justify intervention on humanitarian grounds. However, my worry is that the rhetoric of the Bush Doctrine lowers the threshold for intervention by allowing intervention to effect regime change even when there are no egregious human rights violations. It may be that the United States would not in practice fight interventionist wars for democratization in the absence of egregious human rights violations, but the language and rhetoric of the Bush Doctrine make it clear that the trigger for war is the absence of democracy. The Bush Doctrine thus represents a revision of Walzer's idea of humanitarian intervention.

We discussed in chapter 5 the idea of democracy that is found in the NSS. The basic ideas of freedom and democracy appear to be linked to a further thesis about modernization: the assumption seems to be that free democracies will have free markets and will be committed to modern secular notions about education and the private nature of religion. It is true that "democracy" and "freedom" occasionally have the ideological function of identifying pro-American nations. While acknowledging the ideological nature of the idea of democratization, I will assume here that the Bush Doctrine is not merely ideological. Rather, it is based on the idea that freedom—as defended in the doctrine of human rights—and representative government are universal goods.

I have no quarrel with these liberal ideas. But I contend that the lack of democracy as understood here is insufficient to justify military intervention. A war cannot be justified simply because a state does not permit freedom of religion or because it does not protect private property.

It may be that states that do not respect such freedoms tend to be outwardly aggressive and inwardly oppressive. But what Walzer and others have in mind when they attempt to justify humanitarian intervention is a state of affairs in which genocide and other atrocities occur. A state that does not permit certain freedoms is not in the same category as a state committed to a policy of ethnic cleansing. It may be that Walzer's standard remains the de facto underlying trigger for intervention for defenders of the Bush Doctrine. If that is the case, then the point of this paper is merely to remind defenders of the doctrine of the nature of this standard. But the larger worry is that the rhetoric of the Bush Doctrine (and of American foreign policy in general) can lead us to think that military intervention in pursuit of regime change (in the absence of egregious human rights violations) is justifiable.

One of the primary tenets of the Bush Doctrine is the idea that democracies are inherently peaceful and that the global spread of democracy is the best way to achieve both international stability and the triumph of human rights.[10] This is a plausible idea; it is one that has been defended in various forms by Kant, Doyle, and Rawls, as we shall see in a moment. But the idea that the best way to achieve international peace is to fight aggressive wars to spread democracy is a dangerous one because it sacrifices short-term peace in pursuit of long-term historical and political transformation and because it requires a substantial military commitment to effect radical regime change. My critique of this idea is grounded in consequential reasoning that emphasizes the following "facts": wars kill people; occupying military forces breed resistance and insurgency; and regime change is best created from within.

Neoconservatives contest these facts. For proponents of the Bush Doctrine, democratizing wars may be justifiable on consequential grounds because forces of liberation will be welcomed by those who are liberated and because it is believed that most people would not resist foreign intervention. Interpretation of such "facts" requires empirical, historical, and political judgment; it also depends on our basic insights into human nature. Neoconservatives generally agree that all human beings are interested in freedom and democracy, and they tend to believe that those who are freed from a tyrannical government will appreciate freedom and cooperate in the construction of a just and stable democratic order.

Variations in neoconservatism have to do with the degree to which the idea of democratization is linked to a forward-leaning foreign policy that engages in unilateral, preemptive, and interventionist wars. There are debates among those who might be broadly construed as neoconservative, for example, about the U.S. invasion of Iraq. Francis Fukuyama, who is sympathetic to neoconservative ideas, agrees with the basic thesis that the spread of democracy is good, but he differs on the prudential question of whether the invasion of Iraq was a wise decision.[11] Moreover, Fukuyama cautions that unilateral action tends to backfire by producing resentment. He is aware of the costs of nation building. And he argues that American attempts at nation building have not been unambiguously successful (as in the Philippines, Nicaragua, Haiti, and more recently in Afghanistan and Iraq). In response to Fukuyama, Charles Krauthammer has argued that the intervention in Iraq has in fact been successful, with democracy taking root despite an ongoing insurgency.[12] And citing Fouad Ajami's claims about a new era in the Middle East—which Ajami calls "the Autumn of the Autocrats"— Krauthammer celebrates the fact that the spirit of democracy appears to be spreading to Lebanon, Egypt, and even Syria.[13] Krauthammer uses this to support the idea that further interventions may be needed in Syria and Iran. Others have argued that the invasion of Iraq has encouraged tyrants to rethink their policies. For example, President Bush argues in his 2004 State of the Union speech that Muammar Qaddafi gave up his weapons of mass destruction after seeing what happened to Saddam Hussein in Iraq.[14]

THE JUST WAR CONTEXT

The Bush Doctrine emerges out of a long-standing debate about U.S. foreign policy. On the one hand, realists and isolationists are wary of idealistic wars of democratization; on the other hand, idealists think that democratization is the primary path to global stability and peace. There are clearly large questions here about the structural dynamics of international affairs, about the new structural asymmetry of American hegemony, and about the relationship between domestic politics and foreign affairs. My focus here is on the morality of the idea that war should be employed as a means for advancing the ideal of democratization. I approach this debate as primarily a question of just war theory. The question is whether, on the one hand, the pursuit of democratization is a justifiable casus belli, and, on the other hand, whether democratization is a requirement of jus post bellum.

The just war tradition has usually held that war was justifiable only as a response to aggression (with preemptive war being justified as an attempt to preempt imminent aggression). A newer idea is that war can be justified in defense of human rights in a foreign land.[15] The Bush Doctrine expands the ordinary understanding of just cause by claiming that military force may be used to transform the domestic political arrangements of nonaggressive sovereign states. This idea is grounded in the idea that undemocratic nations—by definition—pose a threat to democratic nations and global peace. While this view is plausible in some circumstance, it is quite speculative and subject to the objection that undemocratic states can isolate themselves, especially in light of the deterrent effect of the possibility of retaliation. Thus the more plausible argument about the need to intervene to transform undemocratic regimes is grounded in the developing idea of humanitarian intervention. But again, this idea is usually reserved for genocide and other atrocities. Undemocratic states are not necessarily genocidal. And there are a variety of human rights violations that fall short of acts that shock the moral conscience of mankind.

The expansive justification of war in pursuit of democracy is occasionally explained in terms of national interest; the national interest of the United States is quite extensive. This ideal is explained by Irving Kristol: "A larger nation has more extensive interests. And large nations, whose identity is ideological, like the Soviet Union of yesteryear and the United States of today, inevitably have ideological interests in addition to more material concerns."[16] The Bush Doctrine links national interest to an idealistic view of democratic progress that postulates a sort of eschatological idea of history. President Bush postulates the link between national interest and democratic eschatology in his second inaugural address, where he claims that Americans have a moral and even religious obligation to spread democracy.[17] From this perspective, when democratic ideas are challenged anywhere around the globe, American national interests are threatened and war can be justified in order to actualize what Bush calls in his second inaugural "the imperative of self-government." The danger of this point of view is that it can end up both causing more wars and increasing their destructive force. The just war tradition focused primarily on response to overt aggression in order to limit wars to defensive wars. The idea that we might wage war to defend the idea of democracy abroad can easily end up justifying wars in a variety of places. And since democratization requires regime change, these wars will involve invasion, long-term occupation, and large-scale social upheaval.

The idea of fighting wars to spread democracy also runs counter to the just war tradition's attempt to restrain or prevent ideological warfare. It is not sufficient—from within the standpoint of traditional just war theory—to go to war when your *ideas* have been attacked. Rather, the tradition holds that war is justified only as a response to aggression or a tangible threat of aggression. Admittedly, there is a new danger that nondemocratic regimes may employ terrorists who attack with weapons of mass destruction. But the traditional idea of preemption held that the threat of attack had to be imminent and grave. The Bush Doctrine allows for war in the case of ideological differences, even when the threat is not imminent.

One might note, in support of the Bush Doctrine, that the just war tradition developed in the context of nondemocratic government. Augustine, Suarez, Vitoria, and others defended the idea of just war from within monarchical systems of government. Indeed, for Augustine, the idea of just war is based on a domestic analogy in which the sovereign's role is similar to that of the father in a patriarchal family. A defender of the Bush Doctrine might argue that it is time for tyrants to stop hiding behind the idea of sovereignty: the imperative of self-government requires that we oppose nondemocratic government with force if necessary.

The ideal of spreading democracy is a morally defensible idea. But the key question is whether aggressive interventionist and democratizing wars should be fought in pursuit of the long-term goal of opposing tyranny. This is a question both of morality and of prudence. Defenders of aggressive wars of democratization will argue that recent events show us that war is a useful means for advancing democracy and peace: they will cite—as noted above—the "autumn of the autocrats" in the Middle East and Qaddafi's new effort to work with the international community. I have no quarrel with the goal of ending tyranny. My criticism focuses, however, on the question of whether war is the *best and most just* means by which to obtain these results. The Bush Doctrine is too sanguine about the idea that war can be used as a *just* means for advancing the idea of democracy. To be fair, we should admit that President Bush is not as militant as some critics make him out to be. In his second inaugural he states with regard to the goal of democratization: "This is not primarily the task of arms, though we will defend ourselves and our friends by force of arms when necessary."[18] Nonetheless, the war in Iraq reflects a new militancy that forgets the fact that war is too blunt of an instrument with which to perform social surgery.

PRUDENCE AND MORALITY
IN THE LIBERAL TRADITION

Neoconservatism is not all that far out of the mainstream of modern liberal thought. The idea that democratization will lead to international peace has deep roots in the modern liberal tradition: it can be traced back to Kant and it has been defended more recently by Doyle and Rawls.[19] Kant supposed that peace would result from the spread of liberal ideas and by the construction of an international confederation. Rawls recognizes that this is a "utopian" ideal: the limits of this ideal are met in what Rawls calls "nonideal theory," which must consider how to deal with outlaw states and burdened societies. Rawls does allow for the possibility of military intervention in defense of human rights and he generally adheres to the principles of just war tradition as articulated by Walzer. Rawls, for example, has defended the idea that rogue or "outlaw" states who commit "egregious" offenses against human rights can be subjected to forceful intervention.[20] And like Walzer, Rawls admits to the limitations of the ideal of just war theory in his idea of the "supreme emergency exemption" to just war principles.[21]

Rawls also argues that political philosophy can provide little guidance about intervention. He says it requires "political wisdom" and "political judgment" that "depends in part on luck."[22] This assessment is most likely correct. Even if we assume that liberal-democracy is the best political arrangement, it is not clear how best to encourage and support the development of liberal-democracy in a nondemocratic state.

Much of the debate about the invasion of Iraq had to do with the question of prudence. Walzer and others—Michael Ignatieff and Paul Berman, for example—who do not identify themselves as neoconservative often found themselves in an ambiguous position vis-à-vis the war on terrorism and the invasion of Iraq.[23] On the one hand, a liberal interpretation of the just war tradition seems to require humanitarian intervention and preemption of emerging threats; on the other, there are practical and politically charged questions of when and where to intervene as well as how to do it justly. Walzer puts it this way: "America's war [against Iraq] is unjust. Though disarming Iraq is a legitimate goal, morally and politically, it is a goal that we could almost certainly have achieved with measures short of full-scale war."[24] The same could probably be said with regard to the pursuit of democracy in Iraq: it is not clear that war was the best means to create democracy in Iraq. This problem can be focused on the question of the legitimate means for bringing about the ideal of a liberal international peace. Liberals in general (whether progressive or neoconservative) share a long-run ideal that has been described by Rawls as follows: "The long run aim of [decent well-ordered societies] is to bring all societies eventually to honor the Law of Peoples and to become full members in good standing of the society of well-ordered peoples."[25] While sharing this ideal, progressives and neoconservatives part company over the question of whether and when war can be used to achieve this goal.

It should be noted that this liberal ideal is different from the ideal of more traditional conservatives who reject the utopian aspiration of a liberal international order. More traditional conservatives—such as John Kekes—view this ideal as "groundless optimism that substitutes wishes for facts, refuses to face reality, ignores history, and radiates a moralistic fervor."[26] More traditional conservatism is closely linked to foreign policy "realism" of the sort associated with Henry Kissinger, Brent Scowcroft, and the first President Bush. This idea aims for a balance of power aimed at national self-interest, and it is much less sanguine about the possibility of transforming outlaw states and burdened societies. Oddly enough, more traditional, conservative foreign policy realists tended to agree with progressive liberals and just war pacifists in opposition to the war in Iraq. The worry for this ad hoc coalition was that war was not the proper means for containing the Iraqi threat and making Iraq head toward becoming a more democratic society. Neoconservatives believed, however, that war was the best means for attaining this goal.

JUST WAR AND PACIFIST
CRITIQUES OF THE BUSH DOCTRINE

Although Rawls indicates that the question of how best to transform outlaw states is a prudential one requiring political wisdom, a stronger critique would argue on moral grounds that war is not a suitable means for effecting social change. This view has much in common with pacifism, but one need not be an absolute pacifist to reject war as a means for democratic transformation. There is a continuum here of skeptical or critical views: at one extreme absolute pacifists will reject democratizing wars because they reject all violence; at the other end of the spectrum, traditional just war thinking will be wary of interventionist wars because of the risk of escalation and the problem of proportionality; between these two views is the idea of just war pacifism, which rejects war because it holds that modern warfare ends up indiscriminately killing noncombatants. Rawls himself has articulated a version of what he calls "contingent pacifism," which rejects specific wars for failing to live up to the standards of just war theory.[27] A more general conclusion of what I call *practical pacifism* is that since most wars fail to be just, citizens should be reluctant to go to war.

Recent events—in Iraq, for example—give us good reason to adopt a skeptical position toward democratizing wars. Proponents of this war exaggerated and/or lied about the supposedly just cause of the war (i.e., Iraq's links to terrorism and its stockpiles of weapons of mass destruction), and they also encouraged the war by overoptimistically predicting the ease with which victory would be achieved. The war has caused significant numbers of civilian casualties, and it has created instability by encouraging terrorism and insurgency. And the war continues with little hope of a just *post bellum* peace. The example of the war in Iraq should leave us skeptical of the neoconservative faith in military power as an appropriate means for advancing democracy, justice, and peace. In a sense, the war in Iraq was an experiment in which the ideals of the Bush Doctrine were tested. This test shows us the limitations of the ideal. It is true that Saddam Hussein has been deposed. But it is not yet clear that Iraq is on its way to developing a stable constitutional system. And we should not forget the costs of this war, including lives lost on all sides and the risk of regional instability and continued insurgency, as well as the economic costs of reconstruction. War is never easy and it involves long-term investment of blood and treasure. The just war theory reminds us to avoid war except when necessary in defense against aggression. The war in Iraq shows us that it is not clear that foreign intervention is the best way to effect democratic change.

Although the war in Iraq was waged for a variety of reasons (including, initially, preemptive self-defense against weapons of mass destruction), one of the recurrent recent justifications of the war is that its goal is to create democracy. Although we might be required by principles of *jus post bellum* to create democracy to replace a regime we have defeated, the pursuit of democracy is not itself a legitimate initial cause for war. Indeed, it is not clear that democracy is required in the aftermath of war. The most important *post bellum* concern is stability and the administration of justice. While democratization is obviously a valuable long-term goal, the ongoing violence in Iraq reminds us that law and order are the first requirement after war.

The case of Iraq is a complicated one. On the one hand, Saddam Hussein was internally oppressive and externally aggressive. On the other hand, his external aggression was effectively stopped by the first Gulf War. And there were a variety of solutions to the problem of internal oppression short of a full-scale invasion and occupation with the goal of creating radical regime change. The continued violence in Iraq reminds us of the difficulty that an invading army will have in creating a stable democracy.

The Bush Doctrine's emphasis on democratization raises the stakes of this intervention. It is not enough merely to respond to atrocity and deter human rights violations through strategic intervention. Rather, the Bush Doctrine requires radical regime change and thus necessitates long-term occupation. But Iraq shows us that a long-term military occupation breeds resistance and makes democracy that much more difficult to produce.

THE BURDEN OF PROOF

One might reasonably conclude from the case of Iraq that the idea of using war to spread democracy is misguided. This conclusion is based on a comparative judgment that helps us clarify the burden of proof with regard to this issue. The comparative judgment asks us to think about war in comparison with other means for effecting democratic change. The just war theory's idea that war should be used only as a "last resort" reminds us that there are other means that should be employed in pursuit of our goals, and these nonviolent means should be employed creatively and forcefully. In the absence of evidence that war is a better way to spread democracy, the most reasonable conclusion is to reject war. This is true because war produces obvious and significant harms. The war in Iraq shows us these harms. The reasonable conclusion is to place a stronger burden of proof on those who would argue that we should continue to fight wars for democracy. Indeed, depending on how one reads the example of Iraq, this burden may be so high that we should reject the very idea that war can be used to spread democracy.

This argument can be bolstered by more systematic analysis of the nature of democracy and democratic transformation. Liberals such as Dewey have long argued that "democratic ends require democratic methods for their realization."[28] War tends to be undemocratic and seems a quite unsuitable method for creating democracy. Tom Rockmore has gone further in claiming that "democracy, which is imposed by force of other means, is not democracy at all, since it is not a system in which power belongs to the people. Hence, the very idea of imposing democracy from without is self-contradictory."[29] Rockmore appears to agree with John Stuart Mill's claim that cultures need to struggle through history for themselves and develop their own capacity for self-government. When we ignore this basic idea, we can be seduced into the idea that democracy can be imposed from without.

At issue here is a question of history. Neoconservatives might look to the examples of the Cold War and World War II to support the idea that successful democratizing wars can be fought. From the neoconservative perspective, both of these wars show us that military force can be used to set people free. But the war in Iraq reminds us that the project of setting people free is painful and bloody. Indeed, one of the crucial principles for determining whether war in the service of democracy is justified is the idea of proportionality. Although neoconservatives can cite the postwar success stories of Japan and Germany as examples of successful democratization, such an analysis must take into account the horrible destruction that was caused by this war and we must ask ourselves whether this destruction was proportional to the goal. This historical judgment has been colored by an ideological tendency to ignore the excesses of World War II. But we must not forget that Allied forces incinerated whole cities in Germany and Japan and that the "good guys" used atomic weapons that not only killed innocent civilians but also produced birth defects and cancers that plagued the Japanese for decades. Ideology also colors our understanding of the Cold War, which is viewed as a triumph of democracy. But instability remains in the nations that were liberated from the former Soviet Union, and the weapons race that was part of the Cold War now leaves us with the problem of nuclear proliferation and the threat of terrorists who can obtain "loose nukes."

The just war theory clarifies the burden of proof by asking whether the goods obtained by war are proportional to the harms that are caused. With regard to Iraq, neoconservatives can continue to offer the hope that things will stabilize. But others will point to the ongoing instability and long-term costs as an indication of why war is rarely a justifiable solution. We can surely all agree that the removal of Saddam Hussein was an admirable goal. The question is whether in obtaining this goal we also created more harm than good.

The point here is not that the ideal of spreading democracy is wrong. Indeed, the ideal of removing tyrants is compelling. However, the critical perspective offered by the just war theory reminds us of the risks of a permissive attitude about going to war. War is unpredictable and violence is contagious. These are truisms that must be remembered whenever we consider using warfare for noble purposes. The just war tradition recognizes this fact in maintaining that the only justifiable cause for war is to resist aggression. More recent discussions of humanitarian intervention remind us that in fighting humanitarian wars, the burden of proof is quite high and we must be scrupulous about adhering to principles of *jus in bello*. Lucas puts it this way: "In humanitarian intervention, as in domestic law enforcement, we cannot and we do not forsake our laws and moral principles in order to enforce and protect them."[30] This new focus on restraining unjust force reminds us how difficult it is to conduct an intervention that is both effective and morally defensible. When the stakes are raised to include democratic regime change, this difficulty is further exacerbated.

One way to understand the difference between traditional just war ideas and the new idea of the Bush Doctrine is to focus on the difference between moral permission and moral obligation. The neoconservative approach appears to claim that wars in the name of freedom are morally obligatory: it would be wrong, from this point of view, not to fight wars that promote democracy. And because neoconservatism holds to an ideal in which history's purpose is the spread of democracy, the burden of proof is placed on those who oppose the use of warfare to spread democracy. Since history is moving toward democracy, it is up to the opponent of a democratizing war to prove that this war should not be fought: the presumption of the Bush Doctrine is that a war for democracy is always a good thing (within limits imposed by prudential and strategic considerations). But the just war tradition has been reluctant to approve of wars that are fought for such ideological purposes. The presumption of the just war tradition is against war and the burden of proof is placed upon the proponent of war. From this perspective, war is not assumed to be permissible until the proponent of war can establish that it is. One might go further, as so-called just war pacifists do and stipulate an even higher standard of proof.[31] It is not enough that war is morally permissible. Rather, the proponent of war may have to prove that war is indeed a moral necessity, that is, that it would be wrong not to fight, even in light of the horrors of war.

In deciding the question of where our obligations lie, we might return to historical considerations. The war against Hitler is often used as a standard example. The idea is usually not merely that a war against Hitler was permissible but also that it was morally required.[32] To not fight Hitler would be wrong. Examples such as this are used to argue that pacifism is morally wrong. From a standpoint that views a war as morally required, it is wrong to oppose this war.

Crucial for making this judgment is the question of proportionality. It is not enough to claim that Hitler was a genocidal dictator who threatened the world with his aggression. This provides a just cause that would make a war against Hitler permissible. But we must also be able to say that it would be wrong not to fight Hitler. And to make this judgment we would have to take into account a variety of alternative ways for dealing with Hitler including nonviolent resistance and a policy of containment and defensive deterrence. But we would also have to decide whether war would result in a better outcome than some other approach. I am not saying, by the way, that a war against Hitler would not be required. I am suggesting, however, that the case needs to be made not only that such a war is permissible but that to avoid it would be wrong.

The Bush Doctrine seems to claim that wars of democratization are morally necessary—if we do not fight them, we will be wrong, since there is an "imperative of self-government" as Bush states in his second inaugural address. Just war critics and pacifists wonder whether war is really the best means by which to achieve the goal of democratization in pursuit of perpetual peace. From this perspective, the burden of proof rests on the proponent of war to argue clearly and convincingly that such a war is a moral necessity.

The very idea of democracy reminds us of the problem of intervention. Mill and Rockmore are right about the difficulty of justifying interventionist wars. I am not claiming that intervention could not be justified to remedy conditions that shock the moral conscience of mankind. But the important point is that the absence of democracy is not alone enough to justify such intervention. While liberal-democracy is a good thing, its absence is not so repugnant that it requires the extreme remedy of war.

CONCLUSION

The goal of spreading democracy is a noble one. However, we should be reluctant to employ the means of warfare in pursuit of the democratizing goal. I have considered several reasons to reject this goal: (1) The traditional just war theory allows war only in response to aggression. It would not allow war in pursuit of democratization. (2) A more recent development of the just war theory permits wars of humanitarian intervention. But humanitarian aid does not include the goal of spreading democracy; rather, a humanitarian war is a response to conditions that shock our moral consciences. And humanitarian intervention requires a controlled application of force that is regulated by a stringent application of principles of *jus in bello*. This may make it quite difficult to effectively create democratic regime change. (3) Just war theorists and pacifists both remind us that modern wars often exceed the limits imposed by principles of *jus in bello* because they indiscriminately and unjustly kill and disrupt the lives of noncombatants. This is especially true of a war that aims to radically transform a society and its political order.

Even if war does produce good outcomes, in terms of spreading democracy and cowing tyrants, it is not clear that the costs of war are worth this result. The just war tradition asks us to take the question of means seriously, and it asks us to consider whether the goals to be obtained are proportional to the damage inflicted on the way to these ends. There are many ways to bring about social change. Pacifists have long argued that nonviolent means can be used—if employed with sufficient creativity, consistency, and force—to effect positive social change. And liberals have generally agreed that the spread of democracy requires democratic means.

One could object to the Bush Doctrine on prudential grounds. Robert Jervis puts it this way: "Just as the means employed by the Bush Doctrine contradict its ends, so also the latter, by being so ambitious invite failure."[33] Jervis's point is that the ambitious idealism of the Bush Doctrine requires unified domestic and international support that is practically impossible to achieve. War is a brutal means for effecting social change, and even militants are reluctant to support war for long. The creation of a stable democracy is a long-term project that requires substantial trust and goodwill. But war creates enemies and hatred even among those who are supposed to benefit from it, making it difficult for an occupying force to create a stable government that is viewed by its people as legitimate. And as casualties and costs continue to rise, it will be more difficult to inspire the American people to remain committed to the ambitious project of the Bush Doctrine. Indeed, we are seeing support among Americans for the Iraq war wane, which may mean that American forces will withdraw before Iraqi democracy can be stabilized.

We are still waiting to see whether democracy will actually take hold in Iraq, so it is not clear that war is the best means for bringing about the desired result. To fully judge this experiment and the Bush Doctrine we will have to weigh the costs of war—in terms of lives lost and economic costs—against the viability of the incipient Iraqi democracy. And we will have to compare these costs to counterfactual hypotheses about what might have happened if nonviolent means had been employed against Saddam Hussein.

The difficulty is that any judgment about whether the costs of this war were proportional to its aims will be quite speculative: how would we know what would have happened if the United States had not invaded Iraq? Put more generally, how will we know whether the ambitious idealism of the Bush Doctrine will produce a more lasting and just peace in the long run, as compared to other, more restrained approaches to international affairs? To begin to answer this question, we must clarify our basic assumptions about the burden of proof. The war in Iraq shows us the costs of a war that is fought in the name of democracy. This should give us good reason to be skeptical of the Bush Doctrine. One should admit, of course, that such a judgment is contingent. If the war had been a "cakewalk" as it was initially supposed to be, the Bush Doctrine would look more plausible. But the war in Iraq reminds us that war is rarely—if ever—a cakewalk.

I do hope that democracy and a just peace can be created in Iraq. But I also hope that we learn from this experience to be more skeptical of the idea that we are obligated to fight interventionist wars in the name of democracy. War may occasionally be permissible as a response to aggression and as a remedy for egregious human rights violations. But the idea that we are morally required to fight wars to produce democracy around the world is a dangerous one that should be resisted.

NOTES

1. See Robert Jervis, "Understanding the Bush Doctrine," *Political Science Quarterly* 118, no. 3 (2003): 365–88; Robert Jervis,"Why the Bush Doctrine Cannot Be Sustained," *Political Science Quarterly* 120, no. 3 (2005): 351–77; Jonathan Monten, "The Roots of the Bush Doctrine: Power Nationalism, and Democratic Promotion in U.S. Strategy," *International Security* 29, no. 4 (2005): 112–56; Charles Krauthammer, "Democratic Realism: An American Foreign Policy for a Unipolar World" (2004 Irving Kristol Lecture at the American Enterprise Institute).

2. For a concise summary of neoconservative ideas see Irving Kristol, "The Neoconservative Persuasion," *Weekly Standard* 8, no. 47 (August 25, 2003).

3. National Security Strategy of the United States of America (hereafter NSS), at www.whitehouse.gov/nsc/nss.pdf. There are two versions of Bush's National Security Strategy: one from 2002 and one from 2006. They are quite similar, although the more recent document includes an explicit discussion of the rationale for the war in Iraq. President Bush's speeches and policy statements that will be quoted here can be found at www.whitehouse.gov.

4. Here is one crucial passage from the 2006 version of the NSS: "Championing freedom advances our interests because the survival of liberty at home increasingly depends on the success of liberty abroad. Governments that honor their citizens' dignity and desire for freedom tend to uphold responsible conduct toward other nations, while governments that brutalize their people also threaten the peace and stability of other nations. Because democracies are the most responsible members of the international system, promoting democracy is the most effective long-term measure for strengthening international stability; reducing regional conflicts; countering terrorism and terror-supporting extremism; and extending peace and prosperity. To protect our Nation and honor our values, the United States seeks to extend freedom across the globe by leading an international effort to end tyranny and to promote effective democracy." See NSS 2006, 3.

5. For discussion of the difference between hard and soft power see Joseph S. Nye, *The Paradox of American Power: Why the World's Only Superpower Can't Go It Alone* (Oxford: Oxford University Press, 2002); for a more recent discussion, see Walter Russell Mead, *Power, Terror, Peace and War* (New York: Vintage/Random House, 2005).

6. See Andrew Bacevich, *American Empire* (Cambridge, MA: Harvard University Press, 2002); Noam Chomsky, *Hegemony or Survival* (New York: Henry Holt, 2004); Chalmers Johnson, *The Sorrows of Empire* (New York: Henry Holt, 2004).

7. See Duane Cady and Robert Phillips, *Humanitarian Intervention* (Lanham, MD: Rowman & Littlefield, 1996); as well as articles in *The Morality of War*, ed. Larry May, Eric Rovie, and Steve Viner (Upper Saddle River, NJ: Prentice Hall, 2006): David Luban, "The Romance of the Nation-State"; George Lucas, "From Jus ad bellum to Jus ad pacem"; Burleigh Wilkins, "Humanitarian Intervention: Some Doubts"; and Teson, "The Liberal Case for Humanitarian Intervention."

8. Michael Walzer, *Just and Unjust Wars* (New York: Basic Books, 1977), 106–7.

9. Teson, "Liberal Case," 349.

10. See Jervis, "Understanding the Bush Doctrine" and "Why the Bush Doctrine Cannot Be Sustained."

11. Francis Fukuyama, "The Neoconservative Moment," *National Interest*, Summer 2004.

12. Charles Krauthammer, "The Neoconservative Convergence," *Commentary* 120, no. 1 (July–August 2005).

13. Fouad Ajami, "The Autumn of the Autocrats," *Foreign Affairs*, May/June 2005.

14. See also Max Boot, "The Bush Doctrine Lives," *Weekly Standard*, February 16, 2004.

15. This idea is not entirely new. The just war tradition in the Christian West begins with the idea that war can be employed to defend the weak and defenseless, as a sort of love of the neighbor; see Paul Ramsey, *War and the Christian Conscience* (Durham, NC: Duke University Press, 1961). But this idea was effaced by the ideal of nonintervention that was tied to the developing idea of national sovereignty in the last several centuries. See Michael Walzer, "The Politics of Rescue," in *Arguing about War* (New Haven, CT: Yale University Press, 2004).

16. Kristol, "Neoconservative Persuasion."

17. For example: "America's vital interests and our deepest beliefs are now one. From the day of our Founding, we have proclaimed that every man and woman on this earth has rights, and dignity, and matchless value, because they bear the image of the Maker of Heaven and earth. Across the generations we have proclaimed the imperative of self-government, because no one is fit to be a master, and no one deserves to be a slave. Advancing these ideals is the mission that created our Nation. It is the honorable achievement of our fathers. Now it is the urgent requirement of our nation's security, and the calling of our time."

18. More militant defenders of neoconservatism include Charles Krauthammer and especially the members of the Project for the New American Century (including Paul Wolfowitz, Donald Kagan, Robert Kagan, and William Kriston) who authored the report *Rebuilding America's Defenses* in 2000. The PNAC group espouses large increases in defense spending, creating permanent American military bases in Asian spheres of concern, and the militarization of space.

19. See Immanuel Kant, *Perpetual Peace in Kant: Political Writings* (Cambridge: Cambridge University Press, 1991); Michael Doyle, *Ways of War and Peace* (New York: Norton, 1997); John Rawls, *The Law of Peoples* (Cambridge, MA: Harvard University Press, 1999).

20. Rawls, *Law of Peoples*, 94, n. 6.

21. For critical discussion see Daniel A. Dombrowski, "Rawls and War," *International Journal of Applied Philosophy* 16, no. 2 (Fall 2002).

22. Rawls, *Law of Peoples*, 93.

23. See Michael Ignatieff, *The Lesser Evil* (Princeton, NJ: Princeton University Press, 2004) and "The Burden," *New York Times Magazine*, January 5, 2003; Paul Berman, *Terror and Liberalism* (New York: Norton, 2003). For a critique of progressives who supported the war in Iraq see James B. Rule,

"'Above All, Do No Harm': The War in Iraq and Dissent," *Dissent*, Summer 2005.

24. Walzer, *Arguing about War*, 160.

25. Rawls, *Law of Peoples*, 93.

26. John Kekes, *A Case for Conservatism* (Ithaca, NY: Cornell University Press, 1998), 211; also see Kekes, *Against Liberalism* (Ithaca, NY: Cornell University Press, 1997).

27. I borrow the concept of contingent pacifism from John Rawls, *A Theory of Justice* (Cambridge, MA: Harvard University Press, 1971), 381. For discussions of the relation between just war theory and pacifism see the following: Robert Holmes, *On War and Morality* (Princeton, NJ: Princeton University Press, 1989); Richard B. Miller, *Interpretations of Conflict* (Chicago: University of Chicago Press, 1991); Duane L. Cady, *From Warism to Pacifism* (Philadelphia: Temple University Press, 1989); and Stanley Hauerwas, *Should War Be Eliminated?* (Milwaukee, WI: Marquette University Press, 1984). In the background of this discussion is the U.S. Catholic Bishops' pastoral letter of 1983, "The Challenge of Peace: God's Promise and Our Response." Also see Richard Wasserstrom, "On the Morality of War," *Stanford Law Review* 21:1627–56, reprinted in *Moral Problems*, ed. James Rachels (New York: Harper and Row, 1971); and Martin Benjamin, "Pacifism for Pragmatists," *Ethics* 83, no. 3 (1973): 196–213. George Weigel rejects just war pacifism as discussed in Weigel, "The Just War Tradition and the World after September 11," *Logos: A Journal of Catholic Thought and Culture*, Summer 2002, 13–44; and Weigel, "Moral Clarity in a Time of War," *First Things* 128 (January 2003). Also see James Turner Johnson, "Just War Tradition and the New War on Terrorism" (Pew Forum on Religion and Public Life Discussion, with Jean Bethke Elshtain and Stanley Hauerwas), at www.pewforum.org. The present work also relies on the following sources for discussions of just war and of pacifism: Walzer, *Just and Unjust Wars*; Rawls, *Law of Peoples*; Paul Ramsey, *The Just War* (New York: Charles Scribner's Sons, 1968); Jenny Teichman, *Pacifism and the Just War* (Oxford: Blackwell, 1986); Jonathan Glover, *Causing Death and Saving Lives* (New York: Penguin, 1977), chap. 19. For Walzer's recent critique of just war pacifism see *Arguing about War*, esp. chaps. 1 and 6. And for a discussion of the limits of just war theory as applied in Iraq see Johan Verstraeten, "From Just War to Ethics of Conflict Resolution: A Critique of Just-War Thinking in the Light of the War in Iraq," *Ethical Perspectives* 11, no. 2–3 (2004).

28. John Dewey, "Democratic Ends Require Democratic Methods for Their Realization," in *John Dewey: Later Works* (Carbondale: Southern Illinois University Press, 1981), 14:367–68.

29. Tom Rockmore, "Can War Transform Iraq into a Democracy?" *Theoria*, April 2004.

30. Lucas, "From Jus ad Bellum," 379.

31. Just war pacifism looks for moral necessity and not mere permissibility. Unlike the more standard interpretation of the just war theory, just war pacifists set up a more stringent standard for what is required. Just war pacifists will support war only when it would be wrong to avoid war. I take the notion of stringency from Samuel Scheffler, "Morality's Demands and Their Limits," *Journal of Philosophy* 83, no. 10 (1986): 531–36. On permissibility see David McCarthy, "Rights, Explanations, and Risks," *Ethics* 107, no. 2 (1997): 205–25. For further discussion in the context of just war theory see Laurie Calhoun, "Killing, Letting Die, and the Alleged Necessity of Military Intervention," *Peace and Conflict Studies* 8, no. 2 (November 2001).

32. This example is taken from Calhoun, "Killing."

33. Jervis, "Why the Bush Doctrine Cannot Be Sustained," 355.

Chapter Nine

Jus in Bello and the War in Iraq

When a country's right to war is questionable and uncertain, the constraints on the means it can use are all the more severe. Acts permissible in a war of legitimate self-defense, when these are necessary, may be flatly excluded in a more doubtful situation.

—John Rawls, *A Theory of Justice*[1]

The war in Iraq gives us good reason to be skeptical of arguments in favor of war. Although the debate about the war in Iraq is ongoing, one cannot deny that the initial rationale for the war turned out to be false: weapons of mass destruction (WMD) were not found in Iraq and even President Bush has admitted that the WMD argument presented a flawed basis for war. This gives us a reason to suspect that governments exaggerate threats, misrepresent data, and perhaps even deliberately lie in support of their war agendas. Similar problems have occurred in the past, for example in the notorious Gulf of Tonkin Resolution that led the United States into the Vietnam War. Thus it is reasonable to be skeptical of those who advocate going to war. This skepticism is further justified if we turn to the issue of *jus in bello*.

JUSTICE IN WAR AND DEMOCRATIC RESPONSIBILITY

The problem of thinking critically about the application of the principle of *jus in bello* is a perennial one. One can find this problem in Augustine's *Reply to Faustus the Manichaean*, where it is ultimately a question of obedience to God's will as executed by the sovereign. For Augustine, moral judgment rests on the sovereign, not the soldier: "For in some cases it is plainly the will of God that he should fight, and in others, where this is not so plain, it may be an unrighteous command on the part of the king, while the soldier is innocent, because his position makes obedience a duty."[2] For Augustine, the soldier's duty is obedience and in fulfilling this duty, the soldier remains innocent.

Another example can be found in Shakespeare's *Henry V*. Prior to the battle of Agincourt, Henry and his soldiers discuss the relationship between the justness of the cause and the responsibility of the soldiers who fight for the cause. This example is of interest because it expresses two rival views about responsibility in war. The first view—what I call *concentrated responsibility*—concentrates responsibility at the top of the chain of command, while the second—what I call *diffused responsibility*—diffuses responsibility downward through the military force.

The idea of *concentrated responsibility* is expressed by one of Henry's soldiers, Bates, who claims, "If his cause be wrong, our obedience to the King wipes the crime of it out of us." Another soldier, Williams, continues: "But if the cause be not good, the King himself hath a heavy reckoning to make." The idea here is that the commander in chief of a military force—that is, the one who makes the decision to go to war—is ultimately responsible for the death and destruction that are caused by the soldiers who fight under him. This idea is closely related to the "superior orders" defense that is often offered by those who are accused of war crimes. But it should be noted that since Nuremberg, this defense is acceptable only if the soldier believed that the superior order was a legally valid order and if he had no real moral choice in the matter. As the judgment at the Nuremberg trial puts it, "That a soldier was ordered to kill or torture in violation of the international law of war has never been recognised as a defence to such acts of brutality, though, as the Charter here provides, the order may be urged in mitigation of the punishment. The true test, which is found in varying degrees in the criminal law of most nations, is not the existence of the order, but whether moral choice was in fact possible."[3]

Ultimate responsibility for *ad bellum* judgments is concentrated at the top of the chain of command in the sovereign authority that is ultimately responsible for deciding whether the cause is just. Henry, it should be noted, does maintain that his "cause is just and his quarrel honorable." The difficulty is that it is not clearly so to his soldiers. In the current war in Iraq there is a similar sort of uncertainty about the issue of *jus ad bellum.* But military discipline requires that soldiers defer to the judgment of their superiors. And the principle of civilian control requires the military to obey the judgment of legitimate civilian leadership. Concentrated responsibility works well to describe the way that responsibility for the *ad bellum* decision rests with the sovereign. But concentrated responsibility is also useful for describing the problem of a military force that violates, as a matter of policy, principles of *jus in bello.* The judgment at Nuremberg recognized, for example, that hierarchies concentrate responsibility at the top. As Arendt points out in her discussion of this theme, "In general the degree of responsibility increases as we draw further away from the man who uses the fatal instrument with his own hands."[4]

The second view, diffused responsibility, is expressed by Henry in response to his men. Henry indicates that the purity of each soldier's soul is that soldier's own responsibility, even while admitting that soldiers have a duty to obey the king. He says, "Every subject's duty is the King's, but every subject's soul is his own." And indeed, Henry claims that the king cannot be held responsible for the misdeeds of his soldiers. He says, "There is no king, be his cause never so spotless, if it comes to the arbitrement of swords, can try it out with all unspotted soldiers." Even if an army fights in pursuit of a just cause, there will be corrupt soldiers who violate just war principles. The idea of diffused responsibility holds that the sovereign is not ultimately responsible for the misbehavior of such unjust warriors. This view diffuses responsibility downward through the chain of command. A similar view has been expressed by Bush administration officials who have claimed that the notorious incidents at Abu Ghraib were the result of a few sadistic soldiers. The idea of diffused responsibility makes sense from the perspective of the commander in chief, who does not have direct command over each and every soldier. Indeed, President Bush made use of the notion of diffused responsibility in his ultimatum to Saddam Hussein (March 17, 2003), where he stated that Iraqi soldiers have a duty to disobey immoral orders: "It will be no defense to say, 'I was just following orders.'" One would assume that the same idea should apply to American forces: soldiers have a moral duty that is greater than mere obedience.

For the most part, the idea of diffused responsibility works only with regard to the question of *jus in bello.* One should be careful, however, for if we take this idea seriously, then responsibility for war crimes is thought not to rest at the top of the chain of command—that is, unless the commander were to directly order such crimes. War crimes are in fact often ordered from the top down. This was true in Nazi Germany. And in the real battle of Agincourt, Henry ordered his soldiers to kill their French prisoners in violation of what Shakespeare calls the "disciplines of war." More recently, the Bush administration has flirted with torture and has created conditions in which torture would be more likely to occur.[5] Commanders are responsible for the misbehavior of their soldiers when the commanders directly order or indirectly create conditions that make war crimes possible.

As a general principle when thinking about responsibility in war, it is preferable to make all parties involved more aware of their responsibility. A synthetic view thus might be called *shared responsibility*. This is the idea that all parties are responsible, even though different sorts of responsibility are located at different levels in the chain of command. This idea is especially appropriate for modern democratic armies in which citizen-soldiers both serve in the military and vote for civilian leadership. Soldiers should obey their commanders within limits established by the principles of *jus in bello*, and commanders have a responsibility to create the discipline that leads to respect for these principles. In a democracy, civilian leadership has a similar sort of responsibility. And ordinary citizens have an obligation to ensure that our soldiers fight justly and fight only in just wars.

A great deal of responsibility remains concentrated in the commander in chief, who has the ultimate responsibility both for making judgments about *jus ad bellum* and for creating and maintaining a disciplinary structure in which principles of *jus in bello* are upheld. With regard to the U.S. war against Iraq, the decision to go to war is the responsibility of the president, and the president is responsible for appointing civilian and military leaders who in turn establish rules of engagement, training, and discipline. But in a democracy responsibility is also shared by the whole of the people. In a democracy where citizens authorize wars through the electoral process and through procedures of deliberative democracy, there is a shared responsibility that implicates the commander in chief, the soldiers who fight, *and* the citizens who authorize war. The decision to go to war in a democracy is supposed to be governed by democratic processes, and the representatives who make these decisions are supposed to be accountable to the people. Moreover, even though the military is a hierarchical and somewhat closed structure, in a democracy there is supposed to be civilian control of the military. With this control comes responsibility, including responsibility for how soldiers fight. Admittedly, this responsibility is indirect: citizens have no power to directly affect the rules of engagement. Nonetheless, citizens do have an obligation to ensure—through representatives who exercise civilian control—that those who fight in our names adhere to principles of *jus in bello.*

It is not surprising that those in power advocate the idea of diffused responsibility: it allows them to avoid the implications of a theory of concentrated responsibility that would place the blame for atrocities at the top. I maintain, however, that that responsibility for atrocity rests, at least in part, at the top of the chain of command. Those at the top establish both the goals and the appropriate means to obtain these goals. Moreover, training and discipline are the responsibility of those at the top of the chain of command. We must not, then, allow commanders to duck their responsibility. But we should also recognize that in a democracy responsibility also flows up the chain of command toward the sovereign power that rests in the hands of the people. Thus ordinary citizens have some responsibility to ensure that wars fought in our names are fought for just causes and that they are fought within limits prescribed by principles of *jus in bello.* And thus skeptical pacifism is a reasonable stance for citizens to adopt: we should be reluctant to authorize wars, unless we can be sure that they will be fought justly.

JUS IN BELLO, THE JUSTICE OF THE CAUSE, AND THE SLIDING SCALE

It might seem that the primary focus for ordinary citizens who wonder whether a war is just should be the principles of *jus ad bellum* because ordinary citizens are better able to judge the application of these principles than the applications of principles of *jus in bello.* Those who adopt this position might agree with Walzer that *in bello* and *ad bellum* principles are "logically independent."[6] According to this idea it is possible for a soldier to fight unjustly in pursuit of a just cause, and it is possible for a soldier to fight justly in pursuit of an unjust cause. We see this in the idea of concentrated responsibility expressed by Henry's soldiers. It seems that soldiers are ultimately not responsible for *ad bellum* decisions: questions about just cause are decided at the top of the military hierarchy. On the other hand, it is plausible that soldiers are always required to fight according to the principles of *jus in bello,* even if the justice of the cause is in doubt. This idea is closely related to the idea of diffused responsibility.

An additional argument separating the two sets of principles is George Weigel's idea that the principles of *jus in bello* are focused on "contingencies," which are not the proper object of moral judgment.[7] For Weigel, greater moral clarity is possible only when we focus on questions of *jus ad bellum*; questions of *jus in bello* are too difficult for us to answer due to the details and complicated nature of the information we would need in order to make sound judgments about this. Weigel uses this distinction to argue against just war pacifists who are "squeamish" about the means of war, especially the indiscriminate means of modern mechanized warfare. For Weigel, the question of means is secondary to the question of ends.

One could follow Weigel and claim that there is a division of labor in democracy with regard to who applies which part of the just war theory. One might argue that while the justice of the cause matters to all of us, it is only soldiers in the field who can answer the question of whether a war is being fought by just means, since it is these soldiers who are doing the fighting. In this sense, responsibility for evaluating *ad bellum* questions belongs to all of us, while responsibility for *in bello* questions is left to soldiers and the military hierarchy. The idea here is that ordinary citizens should simply trust the professionals to do what is necessary in warfare and to do it justly.

But the claim that ordinary citizens should ignore *in bello* questions is inadequate. In a democracy, each of us is responsible for the behavior of the soldiers who fight in our names. The idea of shared responsibility denies that we can simply leave war to the professionals. We ought not ignore the way our military fights and focus only on the outcome. Indeed, the idea of civilian control requires institutional safeguards and bureaucratic procedures for supervising the activities of the military. Citizen vigilance is an essential part of this, as it is the will of the citizens that will force the bureaucratic apparatus to take its supervisory responsibility seriously.

In a democracy, citizens ought to ask critical questions about how our forces fight. Such questions should have been asked when it became clear that Allied forces were bombing population centers in World War II. They should have been asked when it became clear that American forces were using napalm, Agent Orange, and other defoliants during the Vietnam War. And we should continue to ask these questions as our forces fight in Iraq and elsewhere in the war on terrorism. Citizens must continue to think critically about how wars are fought in our names because a democratic nation's military is ultimately responsible to the people. This is true for principled reasons that are tied to civilian control and democratic legitimacy: a democratic people's army is an army that exists to serve the interests and defend the values of the people. It is also true for pragmatic reasons: citizen vigilance will serve as a check on unbridled military force.

These claims about civilian control and democratic responsibility remain true whether the war was initially fought for a just or unjust cause. In a war fought for a just cause, citizen vigilance will ensure that the means remain morally acceptable. In wars fought for less obviously just causes, citizen vigilance is even more important. Having a just cause is not enough; ongoing critical evaluation of the means of fighting is essential. War is a complex human enterprise and our judgments about war should reflect this complexity. War crimes can be committed in pursuit of just causes, and heroism and valor can be exhibited in unjust conflicts. Once we have initiated a war (whether for just or unjust reasons), we have a responsibility both to fight justly and to focus on creating *post bellum* conditions for peace and the restoration of order.

An absolute pacifist may argue that fighting is always wrong and that the best solution is simply to stop fighting. Especially in a war fought for an unjust cause, the most plausible way to do right is for the unjust aggressor to stop fighting. The difficulty is that a simple retreat may produce more long-term harm. In Iraq, for example, the United States is no longer merely an aggressor: the United States is now an occupying force whose primary task is one of stabilization in preparation for *post bellum* peace. One might say that the cause for which we are fighting has now shifted. As Walzer recently put this, there is a "new argument" now that we are the occupying power.[8] Prior to the war the cause and the argument were about the removal of Saddam Hussein. Now the cause is stabilization. We have now shifted from *ad bellum* arguments to *post bellum* arguments. Tragically, the pursuit of *post bellum* justice may require continued fighting. Insurgent forces in Iraq are now targeting Iraqis. Iraqi police and military forces are unable to establish security and prevent the slide toward civil war. We have an obligation as the occupying power to create conditions for stability and peace. But as we fulfill this obligation, it is obvious that we must fight according to the principles of *jus in bello*. Indeed, these principles always apply regardless of the stage in the argument, *ad bellum* or *post bellum*.

Of course, continued occupation also antagonizes the insurgency. The question of when to withdraw from a conflict is a complex one requiring practical judgment. But the principle to be kept in mind is that the goal should be to reduce harm and establish order as quickly as possible while adhering to principles of *jus in bello.*

Although it seems obvious that once a war is launched, our focus necessarily shifts from *ad bellum* concerns to *in bello* principles, this does not mean that we can ignore the *ad bellum* question. Indeed the question of the initial justification of war points us toward the issue of who is ultimately responsible for damage done and who has the obligation to fix this damage and bear the cost of the fight for *post bellum* justice. Rawls gives us some guidance about this. He postulates a sort of sliding scale of justification that takes into account both *jus ad bellum* and *jus in bello.* He says in a passage that is quoted with approval by Walzer: "When a country's right to war is questionable and uncertain, the constraints on the means it can use are all the more severe. Acts permissible in a war of legitimate self-defense, when these are necessary, may be flatly excluded in a more doubtful situation."[9] The idea here is that if we are uncertain about our ends, we should be even more cautious about the means we employ in pursuit of these ends.

The difficulty of this sliding scale is that it can seem to be a simple sort of consequentialism: the better or more urgent our goal, then the more cavalier we can be about our means. This can lead to the subversion of just war limits in what Walzer and Rawls call "the supreme emergency": if our very way of life were at stake, we would be justified, according to Walzer and Rawls, in violating principles of *jus in bello.*[10] I am very skeptical of this idea.[11] The principles of *jus in bello* should be held as principles that are not contingent on the urgency of our ends. The obligation not to deliberately target innocent noncombatants is the key principle here.[12] If we give this principle up, then we head toward the slippery slope that culminates in consequentialist justifications of the use of terrorism in war. To see that this slope can indeed be slippery, consider the problem of what Jonathan Glover has called "military drift."[13] This occurs when military necessity—that is, the need to win—leads fighting forces to violate the principles of *jus in bello.* The slippery slope of this kind of consequentialism can be found, for example, in the Allied bombing campaigns in World War II: what may have begun as a battle of supreme emergency in the case of Britain in 1940 became a battle that employed terror tactics in pursuit of unconditional surrender.[14]

Once we move beyond the question of *jus ad bellum*, we must remain committed to the *in bello* principle that the innocent have a sacred immunity that cannot be deliberately violated no matter what end we are pursuing. The real thrust of any sort of pacifism and also, I think, the heart of the just war theory, is that we have an absolute duty to avoid harming the innocent. Indeed, we should reject attempts to finesse this point such as are found in Walzer's (and Rawls's) idea of the supreme emergency exemption, just as we should reject arguments that attempt to justify terror bombing or the use of other sorts of terrorism.[15]

The justification of terrorism is not, I should note, Rawls's intention. Indeed, the point of the sliding scale, as Rawls originally formulates it, is to put a limit on the sort of crass consequentialism that can lead to terrorism. Moreover, Rawls acknowledges that when there is doubt about the cause, we have even greater reason to be concerned about respect for *in bello* principles. In this sense, the *in bello* principles are indeed logically independent: they hold for everyone regardless of the justness of the cause. The point of a Rawlsian "sliding scale" should not be to justify atrocities as a response to supreme emergencies. Rather, it should be to remind us of the extreme diligence that is required in wars that are fought for dubious causes.

JUS IN BELLO IN THE CASE OF IRAQ

There are many difficulties for ordinary citizens who want to be able to assess whether wars are being fought within the limits of *jus in bello*. Most notably, we lack access and expertise. The question here is thus how we can judge whether a war is fought justly when we lack both access and expertise.

Judgments about the *in bello* principles of proportionality can be answered adequately only by those who understand the relative costs and benefits of certain actions in light of short- and long-term tactical and strategic goals. These are the "contingencies" that Weigel cites in order to downplay the import of *in bello* principles. Ordinary citizens lack access to tactical and strategic information, and even if we had the information, we would lack the relevant expertise to evaluate it. Similarly, discrimination requires that we not intentionally harm innocent noncombatants. But the standard just war theory allows that the deaths of some innocents can be justified by the principle of double effect. And the idea of discrimination assumes that it is a simple task to tell who is an innocent noncombatant. The problem is that, in the first case, ordinary citizens have no way of knowing whether and how the principle of double effect applies when innocent noncombatants are killed. Likewise, ordinary citizens have no way of knowing whether civilians who are reportedly killed are really innocent noncombatants.[16] These problems are exacerbated in conditions of urban warfare and in light of the way that insurgent forces deliberately muddle the combatant/noncombatant distinction.

A. The Noncombatant Body Count in Iraq

Ordinary citizens cannot simply acquiesce in light of these difficulties for judging what is happening in a war. Rather, we should do our best to formulate careful judgments, even while acknowledging methodological difficulties. Moreover, as I shall argue here, there are some obvious facts that should be acknowledged as we think critically about the way war is fought. The first and most obvious one is that a military force that is concerned with *in bello* principles should be self-critical. That is, a military force that is trying to be proportionate in its use of force and that is trying to discriminate between legitimate targets and innocent noncombatants should take care to assess and reassess its actions. And this critical self-assessment should be made open to the public so that the public can fulfill its obligation of citizen vigilance.

However, we have good reason to be skeptical of our military today because it has deliberately evaded this duty. Gen. Tommy Franks is widely reported as saying with regard to the war in Afghanistan that "we don't do body counts." And the same is true in Iraq. To my knowledge the U.S. military has not publicly estimated the number of civilian casualties. Ordinary citizens have no way of knowing whether classified casualty assessments exist. However, we can safely assume that they do because the military is interested in these numbers for a variety of reasons: tactical, strategic, technological, and moral. At any rate, a responsible military should be interested in this question and the cavalier attitude of General Franks is disturbing. The public has a right and an obligation to know the damage that is being caused in our names. By either ignoring the body count or keeping it secret, the military gives the unsavory appearance of callousness. Moreover, the suspicion is that there is indeed something to be hidden, as if the costs of this war in terms of noncombatant casualties cannot be justified.

This point is emphasized not to say that United States and coalition forces have in fact violated the principles of *jus in bello*. Rather, I aim only to show the difficulty confronted by ordinary citizens who want to be able to judge the war effort. At best we must admit that we have no good reason to trust the military on this question because they have not provided evidence that they are respecting the principles of *jus in bello*. In other words, the burden of proof rests on the military: they must show us that the war has been fought justly. In this regard I disagree with Jean Elshtain, who has written in defense of the war in Afghanistan that "it is very clear that every effort is being made to separate combatants from noncombatants, and that targeting civilians has been ruled out as an explicit war-fighting strategy."[17] I am not claiming that the United States is deliberately targeting noncombatants. Rather, my point is that we do not know whether or not this is true. Elshtain continues: "The United States must do everything it can to minimize civilian death—and it is doing so. The United States must express remorse for every civilian death in a way that is not simply rote—and it is doing so. The United States must investigate every incident in which civilians are killed—and it is doing so."[18] I hope that what she says is true. However, the U.S. military has not done a good job of proving that these claims are in fact true. And the military has an obligation to prove to the people that it is upholding these standards.

Despite the lack of information from military sources, there have been several reputable attempts to come up with an accurate body count. According to the Iraq Body Count project (www.iraqbodycount .net), as of October 2007, there have been over 80,000 civilian deaths in this war. A rival estimate by Roberts and Burnham published in November 2004 in the medical journal, the *Lancet*, puts the number of Iraqi deaths caused by the war at 100,000. And a more recent estimate using the same methodology puts civilians upward of 600,000. Regardless of how we assess the different methodologies used in these estimates, it is safe to say that a significant number of Iraqi noncombatants have died.[19]

Of course, these numbers tell us nothing by themselves about whether *in bello* principles have been violated. Some of these deaths may be caused by the insurgency. Others who have been killed may have themselves been part of the insurgency. But it is plausible that some of the deaths are the result of warfare aimed at the regular Iraqi army—early in the war—and now at insurgents. More troubling, however, is the fact that early in the war many of these deaths were the result of aerial bombing and artillery campaigns that employ cluster bombs, which are indiscriminate killers. Still we do not know how or whether the principle of double effect could be used to justify these deaths. A report by Human Rights Watch (HRW), however, points us toward a judgment. This report from the early days of the war (2003) emphasizes the problem of cluster bombs. These bombs spread damage beyond the immediate target; unexploded bomblets can remain on the scene and cause harm at a later time. Nonetheless, HRW reports that the U.S. Department of Defense was committed to carefully planning the aerial campaign. This careful planning included extensive "collateral damage estimates" before targets were approved: these estimates were intended to minimize civilian death. Indeed, HRW cites a *Washington Post* report that claimed that targets for which there was a collateral damage estimate of more than thirty civilian deaths had to be approved by Secretary of Defense Donald Rumsfeld himself. HRW thus admits that the U.S. military was aware of the need to minimize noncombatant death, that they had procedures in place that were designed to help them comply with this demand, and that this procedure concentrated responsibility up the chain of command. Nonetheless, HRW does claim that the United States failed to adequately protect noncombatants in several ways. Here are a few of the report's conclusions.

- Attacks on "leadership targets" were both ineffective and caused disproportional collateral damage.
- Attacks on electrical power facilities and media installations were difficult to justify.
- The use of cluster bombs should be more controlled, and there should have been a plan to deal with unexploded ordinance.
- Finally, the report laments the fact that, as yet, there has been no thorough investigation of collateral damage by the military itself.

The question remains: How can we (ordinary citizens) know what is going on? How can we adequately assess the question of whether principles of *jus in bello* are being upheld? There are some reasons to be skeptical here. The numbers provided by Iraq Body Count and by Roberts and Burnham support a skeptical stance. And the HRW report shows us that despite a good-faith effort on the part of the military, questions remain. Therefore, the burden of proof rests on the military.

We have good reason to be skeptical of whether this war is being fought within proper limits. And the same skeptical problems will arise in future wars because the military does not "do body counts" or at least, they do not make these public. We will return in a moment to the question of what we should do about this skepticism. Before turning to this question let us consider another aspect of *jus in bello*.

B. War Crimes in Iraq

Although the principles of proportionality and discrimination are among the most important of the principles of *jus in bello*, we should also consider other aspects of what Walzer calls "the war convention," which is the established set of norms that govern combatant behavior, as found in long-established customs of war, in military procedure, and in international law and conventions such as the Geneva Conventions. Several recent events beg us to consider these issues. First, we should consider the abuse and torture that occurred at the Abu Ghraib prison, at Guantánamo Bay, and elsewhere in the war on terrorism. Second, we should consider cases in which U.S. soldiers have shot and killed wounded Iraqis. One such incident was captured on video in November of 2004: a U.S. Marine killed a wounded insurgent in a mosque in Fallujah. Another one resulted in a U.S. Army sergeant pleading guilty in early December 2004 to a murder charge for killing a wounded Iraqi youth. And third, we should consider the recent case in which American soldiers are accused of raping and murdering an Iraqi girl and her family in Mahmudiya.

Torturing prisoners and killing wounded enemies are violations of the "war convention," that is, those conventions for warfare that focus primarily on the treatment of combatants (I am assuming for the sake of argument that the Iraqis involved were combatants). And rape is a war crime: an activity that is *mala in se* and so banned.

Before rushing to judgment here, however, we should acknowledge that it is possible to imagine arguments that would justify some of these atrocities. Soldiers could appeal to what might be called "military necessity": if the Abu Ghraib prisoners had important information about the growing insurgency, for example, then the abuse might be justified on consequentialist grounds if it was thought that these actions would force the prisoners to divulge information that could be used to quell the insurgency. Moreover, the torturers could appeal to the notion of concentrated responsibility and make the claim that they were "just following orders." Recall, however, that I argued previously that although responsibility is concentrated up the chain of command, this does not fully absolve soldiers of responsibility for misdeeds.

The argument about military necessity is easier to justify when it is directed at combatants who may in fact have operational knowledge and who are or may once have been a direct threat to the soldiers involved. The action of the marine who shot the wounded insurgent in the Fallujah mosque makes sense from the standpoint of military necessity if we recall that the victim was an insurgent who had been fighting against the marines and if we recall that the insurgents had employed the tactic (itself a war crime) of booby-trapping the bodies of dead and dying insurgents. Further justifications may be offered. In the murder case, the soldier claimed that he killed the youth to put him out of his misery.

But the rape and murder case in Mahmudiya cannot be justified on any such grounds. Rape is always a crime of war—there can be no justification for it. The deliberate killing of prisoners and neutralized combatants is a war crime. And although there has been ongoing debate about the use of torture in the war on terrorism, torture remains a crime. The U.S. military—to its credit—condemns and punishes such actions. The military should be commended for responding to these incidents with investigations and military trials. Thus, in fact, none of the attempts at justification discussed above will work. The U.S. Army's report on Abu Ghraib indicated, for example, two basic explanations of the Abu Ghraib abuses: (1) moral corruption on the part of a small group of sadistic soldiers, and (2) a lack of discipline on the part of leaders.[20] In other words, the army appeals to notions of both diffused and concentrated responsibility. These explanations are supplemented in this report by considering command and control problems, doctrinal ambiguity, poor training, and inexperience on the part of the soldiers involved. The same sorts of problems can be found in the case of other violations of the rules of engagement and war crimes.

My goal here is thus not to condemn the entire military force for these actions. The very fact that the military has investigated and condemned these incidents shows that our military is committed to the principles of the war convention and that they admit that rape and other atrocities remain crimes of war.

These cases remind us that war is a nasty business and that no army consists entirely of "unspotted soldiers." And this fact gives us—citizens who authorize war—further reason to be skeptical of it. One may try to evade this conclusion by claiming that the ultimate blame for much of the civilian casualties in Iraq rests, for example, on Saddam Hussein's regime since it placed military targets in civilian centers, using civilians as shields. The blame could be placed both on the former military and on the insurgents who deliberately removed their uniforms and insignia in an attempt to blend in with the civilian population. In the same way, the insurgency could be blamed for the death of the insurgent in the mosque in Fallujah, since it is the insurgency, after all, that has booby-trapped bodies and led to the conditions in which the U.S. Marines would have been suspicious of the wounded man. Moreover, the insurgency itself is guilty of war crimes both in its use of terrorism and in its use of decapitation as a method for dealing with hostages. It is obvious that some of the blame does rest on the insurgents.

But the much-publicized incidents discussed here remind us that even well-intentioned armies risk violating the standard principles of justice in war. Soldiers can be sadistic and fueled by rage. This can be exacerbated by poor discipline, poor training, or lack of clear rules of engagement. And the strategies of the insurgency make it clear that it will be quite difficult for soldiers—even soldiers committed to justice in war—to fight effectively while maintaining the distinction between combatants and noncombatants and while remaining committed to the rules of engagement. To put it bluntly: war is a chaotic business that inevitably leads to violations of the principles of justice in war. And a counterinsurgency war makes this even more likely. This is why citizens should be reluctant to authorize war to begin with: we cannot be sure that wars fought in our names will be fought within proper limits. Indeed, these cases (and others from wars fought in the twentieth century) remind us that we have good reason to suppose that wars fought in our names will result in violations of the war convention and of principles of *jus in bello*.

CONCLUSION

If we suspect that the means to some end will be immoral, then we should not pursue the end. It is possible that wars can be fought justly. But the case of Iraq reminds us that even well-trained armies violate principles of *jus in bello*. Soldiers will occasionally use more violence than is proportional; they will have a difficult time distinguishing between combatants and noncombatants; and some soldiers will engage in heinous crimes like torture and rape. The fact of the matter is that when we unleash the dogs of war, some of these dogs will run wild. We should recall that Henry V made this claim when he admitted that the king cannot assume that all of his soldiers will be "unspotted." But Henry made this claim to evade his responsibility. It is not enough to claim that we didn't intend for our soldiers to torture and rape or that we expected them to more fully discriminate between combatants and noncombatants. After all, we should have known that war—by its very nature—involves a flirtation with atrocity. We know in advance that atrocities will be committed.

Judgments about war must acknowledge that war—even wars fought by modern armies in pursuit of a just cause—creates conditions in which brutality and cruelty are likely. It is naive to assume that our soldiers will all be unspotted. And it is not sufficient merely to prosecute war crimes after the fact; we must anticipate that war crimes will be committed before we send our troops to war. This should make us more reluctant to authorize war to begin with, since we all share responsibility for the wars that are fought in our names. This alone is enough to lead one toward just war pacifism: war is to be avoided because we know that principles of *jus in bello* will be violated even by the best of armies.

The just war pacifist critique should be the default position for ordinary citizens. It is up to the military to prove to us that they will fight (and are fighting) within proper limits. This is even more important when there is dispute about the cause of the war, as Rawls indicates in his discussion of the sliding scale. We are always justified in demanding that our soldiers fight as scrupulously as possible, and in war that is not clearly just, we are even more justified in making this demand. For a military force to claim simply that "we don't do body counts" is not an appropriate response. Nor is it appropriate for responsibility for violations of the war convention to be diffused onto those at the lower levels of the chain of command. The public deserves a thorough accounting for suspected violations and the ascription of blame must focus on the top levels of the chain of command.

My goal here is not to condemn the many honorable men and women who are serving in the armed forces. Rather, I offer this argument in solidarity with them. They alone are not responsible for this conflict or how it is fought; we all are. The pacifist impulse to resist and question the justness of war remains an important part of democratic deliberation about war. And this skepticism about war may help to ensure that moral principles are adhered to when war does break out.

NOTES

1. John Rawls, *A Theory of Justice* (Cambridge, MA: Harvard University Press, 1971), 379.

2. Augustine, *Reply to Faustus the Manichean*, Book 22, para. 75 from New Advent Library of Church Fathers (www.newadvent.org/fathers/140622.htm).

3. *Judgment of the International Military Tribunal for the Trial of German Major War Criminals*, at www.yale.edu/lawweb/avalon/imt/proc/judlawch .htm. For discussion see Larry May, "Superior Orders, Duress, and Moral Perception," in *The Morality of War*, ed. Larry May, Eric Rovie, and Steve Viner (Upper Saddle River, NJ: Prentice Hall, 2006).

4. Hannah Arendt, *Eichmann in Jerusalem* (New York: Viking Penguin, 1963), 247.

5. For discussion of these crimes and conditions see Seymour M. Hersh, *Chain of Command* (New York: HarperCollins, 2004); and Mark Danner, "The Logic of Torture," *New York Review of Books* 51, no. 11 (June 24, 2004), and "The Truth about Torture," *New York Review of Books* 51, no. 10 (June 10, 2004). For a recent discussion see Derek Jeffreys, "Eliminating All Empathy: Personalism and the 'War on Terror,'" *Logos: A Journal of Catholic Thought and Culture* 9, no. 3 (2004): 16–44.

6. Michael Walzer, *Just and Unjust Wars* (New York: Basic Books, 1977), 21.

7. George Weigel, "The Just War Tradition and the World after September 11," *Logos: A Journal of Catholic Thought and Culture* 5, no. 3 (Summer 2002): 13–44. I criticize Weigel in Andrew Fiala, "Citizenship, Epistemology, and the Just War Theory," *Logos: A Journal of Catholic Thought and Culture* 7, no. 2 (2004). For further discussion of Weigel see John Hymers, "Regrounding the Just War's 'Presumption against Violence' in Light of George Weigel," *Ethical Perspectives* 11, no. 2–3 (2004).

8. Michael Walzer, *Arguing about War* (New Haven, CT: Yale University Press, 2004), 162.

9. John Rawls, *Theory of Justice*, 379; Walzer, *Just and Unjust Wars*, 229.

10. Walzer *Just and Unjust Wars*, chap. 16; John Rawls, *The Law of Peoples* (Cambridge, MA: Harvard University Press, 1999).

11. See Andrew Fiala, "Terrorism and the Philosophy of History: Liberalism, Realism and the Supreme Emergency Exemption," special issue, *Essays in Philosophy* 3 (April 2002), at sorrel.humboldt.edu/~essays/v3cline.html.

12. I hold this principle as an absolute limit, which leads to pacifism in practice. It is possible to imagine a war that is fought without violating this principle, which is why just war pacifism is not absolute pacifism. However, modern warfare—especially nuclear warfare—makes it more likely that this principle

will be violated than not. For a recent discussion of the combatant/noncombatant distinct see Michael W. Brough, "Combatant, Noncombatant, Criminal," *Ethical Perspectives* 11, no. 2–3 (2004): 176–88; and Brough, "Legitimate Combatancy, POW Status, and Terrorism" in *Philosophy 9/11: Thinking about the War on Terrorism*, ed. Timothy Shanahan (New York: Open Court, 2005).

13. Jonathan Glover, *Humanity: A Moral History of the 20th Century* (New Haven, CT: Yale University Press, 2000).

14. For further discussion of the problem of pursuing unconditional surrender see G. E. M. Anscombe, "War and Murder" and "Mr. Truman's Degree," both in *Ethics, Religion, and Politics* (Minneapolis: University of Minnesota Press, 1981).

15. See: F. M. Kamm,"Failures of Just War Theory: Terror, Harm, and Justice," *Ethics* 114 (July 2004): 650–92; Virginia Held, "Violence Terrorism, and Moral Inquiry," *Monist* 67, no. 4 (October 1984); and Kai Nielsen, "Against Moral Conservatism," *Ethics* 82, no. 3 (1972): 219–31.

16. For discussions of the difficulty of discrimination and the equally difficult notion of noncombatant "innocence" see Anscombe, "War and Murder"; George Mavrodes, "Conventions and the Morality of War," in May, Rovie, and Viner, *Morality of War*; and Thomas Nagel, "War and Massacre," in May, Rovie, and Viner, *Morality of War*.

17. Jean Bethke Elshtain, *Just War against Terror* (New York: Basic Books, 2003), 67.

18. Elshtain, *Just War*, 69.

19. We might debate the methodology of these reports. Iraq Body Count uses news reports to come up with its data—a death must be reported in two media sources to be registered in the count   and it attempts to report only noncombatant deaths. Roberts and Burnham used survey teams who conducted interviews at randomly selected spots throughout Iraq in the fall of 2004 and projected from these cluster surveys a nationwide casualty estimate. Roberts and Burnham, we should note, did not distinguish between combatants and noncombatants. It is not surprising that Roberts and Burnham came up with this higher number, as not every death is reported in the news and so not every death will make it into the Iraq Body Count tally.

20. The army's report is found on the *Washington Post*'s website: www.washingtonpost.com/wp-srv/nationi/documents/fay_report_8-25-04.pdf.

Part III

SKEPTICAL
DEMOCRATIC PACIFISM

Chapter Ten

The Myth of Pacifism

Very few wars are worth fighting.

—Bertrand Russell[1]

The arguments of the preceding chapters express skepticism about the myth of the just war. This should incline us toward a sort of pacifism. However, I do not intend to argue for an absolute form of pacifism that holds that war is always wrong. It is possible to imagine some sorts of warfare that meet just war requirements. Just wars are *possible*. Unless one assumes that human beings are *always* mistaken, vicious, or evil, it is possible that war can be just. But the mere possibility of a just war does not mean that any real war is actually just. Indeed, experience shows us that it is *probable* that most wars will be unjust. The previous chapters have shown some of the problems with real wars, especially the war on terrorism. Other philosophers have reached similar skeptical conclusions about war. James Sterba recently concluded from his analysis of recent wars: "In fact, most of the actual uses of belligerent means in warfare that have occurred turn out to be unjustified."[2] Such conclusions take the just war theory seriously and apply its principles to the sorts of wars that are actually fought.

The general conclusion of this book is a sort of practical pacifism. In order to clarify this sort of pacifism it is useful to contrast it with absolute pacifism. Absolute pacifism is mythological in the sense that it relies on certain assumptions that are not grounded in empirical reality. Absolute pacifism is usually connected to religious faith in some system of higher goods. Absolute pacifism usually promises some sort of redemption or compensation in which the evils that have been suffered in this world will be overcome. And it is often linked to a retreat from the world that disavows allegiance to states or nations. But practical pacifism does not rely on these sorts of mythic promises and other worldly commitments. The sort of pacifism I want to defend here is primarily an antiwar position. For this reason it might be called *just war pacifism*: it reaches a pacifist conclusion from a stringent application of the just war theory. Although there are implications for further topics ranging from the death penalty to vegetarianism, there is no straight line from antiwarism to a more extensive commitment to nonviolence. One could, for example, accept the idea of personal self-defense but still question whether war is actually justifiable.

One of the most common complaints against pacifism is that it requires meek submission to evil. But let me be clear that this sort of pacifism is the mythological variety. Here we might think of Tolstoy's understanding of the Christian gospel as requiring nonresistance. But even Gandhi admitted that personal self-defense is acceptable in some circumstances. When asked by his son what he should have done when Gandhi was attacked, Gandhi told him that "it was his duty to defend me even by using violence."[3]

Another complaint against pacifism is that it is a kind of cowardice, as if the pacifist were afraid to fight. But Martin Luther King Jr., Gandhi, and other adherents of nonviolence have shown that a commitment to nonviolence requires substantial courage: the courage to stand up against violence while knowing that violence will be used against you. Nonviolent resisters are willing to die for their beliefs. While soldiers are willing to die and to kill, pacifists are willing to die in order not to kill. It is easy to see that this sort of self-sacrificial pacifism makes the most sense within a religious framework that contains myths about immortality, final judgment, and an eternal reward for peace.

Not all forms of pacifism are based on religious faith. It is possible to use utilitarian or deontological arguments to reach pacifist conclusions. But generally, the more absolute and all-pervasive one's commitment to pacifism, the more likely it is to be tied to some sort of religious faith. Less absolutist forms of pacifism are more closely related to the just war theory, which aims to clarify when violence and war might be justifiable. Religious belief helps because it assures those committed to nonviolence that their suffering will be redeemed. This is why Gandhi and Martin Luther King Jr. held that suffering—especially undeserved suffering—could be redemptive. For Christians this view is ultimately linked to a conception of Jesus as the suffering and dying servant. The most robust forms of pacifism hold to some version of this saintly ideal: the hero of pacifism is the suffering saint.

This chapter will consider a variety of pacifisms and will argue in favor of a contingent commitment to a limited form of pacifism. This discussion will be organized by looking at various ways that pacifism might be understood.

ABSOLUTE AND CONTINGENT PACIFISM

There are different answers to the question of how obligated we are to reject war. *Absolute pacifism* is understood as a maximal and universal rejection of war. Absolutism in ethics (or moral absolutism) holds that moral principles are eternal and unchanging and that they admit no exceptions. So, absolute pacifism holds that war is always wrong.

Relativism is usually opposed to absolutism as the rejection of such absolute moral principles. Relativism can provide no reason to support pacifism. But there is a type of pacifism that is not absolute, known as *contingent pacifism*. While absolute pacifism admits no exceptions to the rejection of war, contingent pacifism is usually understood as a principled rejection of a particular war. A different version of contingent pacifism can also be understood to hold that pacifism is only an obligation for a particular group of individuals and not for everyone. Contingent pacifism can also be a principled rejection of a particular military system or set of military policies. Contingent pacifists may accept the permissibility or even necessity of war in some circumstances and reject it in others, while absolute pacifists will always and everywhere reject war.

Absolute pacifism is often connected with a divine command approach to ethics in which nonviolence is seen as a religious commandment. Thomas Merton explains that most absolute pacifists have a larger metaphysical view: "The fully consistent practice of nonviolence demands a solid metaphysical basis both in being and in God."[4] In the West, absolute pacifism is often derived from the Christian ideal of nonresistance to evil as required by Jesus's pronouncements about nonresistance in the Sermon on the Mount. In Indian traditions, the principle is grounded in the commitment to ahimsa, or nonviolence, that is derived from a larger metaphysical picture which emphasizes karmic interdependence, ascetic discipline, and compassion. The religious foundation of absolute pacifism is often tied to the idea that there is merit in suffering violence without retaliating. As Martin Luther King Jr. puts this, "Unearned suffering is redemptive."[5]

Absolute pacifism is a mythological ideal that is grounded in a larger eschatological construct. One source for this in the Christian tradition is Jesus's claim that his kingdom is not of this world. The key passage is from John 18:36. Jesus is confronted by Pilate, who asks whether he is king of the Jews. Jesus replies:

> My kingdom is not of this world: if my kingdom were of this world, then would my servants fight, that I should not be delivered to the Jews: but now is my kingdom not from hence.

For Christian pacifists, this means that a follower of Jesus should not employ force to maintain worldly kingdoms, for the true kingdom is beyond this world.[6] This leads Mennonites and others to advocate a clear separation between religious values and secular values. This separation can be grounded in biblical passages such as Acts 5:29: "We must obey God rather than men." For many Christians who follow in the Augustinian tradition, such passages conflict with the Pauline requirement of obedience to the sovereign and his power to use the sword, as derived from chapter 13 of Paul's letter to the Romans. For pacifists, Jesus's commands in the Gospels—to love the neighbor, turn the other cheek, and not return evil for evil—are more important than Paul's ideas about the sovereign's sword. At any rate, Christian pacifists such as Tolstoy, Yoder, Hoyt, Augsburger, and Hauerwas have repeatedly emphasized the fact that Christian pacifism cannot be divorced from Christian faith. It is ultimately faith in the kingdom of God that makes absolute pacifism possible.

Some versions of absolute pacifism go so far as to abjure the idea of personal self-defense. Other absolute pacifists may define pacifism merely as "antiwarism" and allow for personal self-defense while rejecting the impersonal and political violence of war. Almost every defender of absolute pacifism recognizes the difficulty of attaining the absolute idea. Gandhi writes the following in his autobiography: "Man cannot for a moment live without consciously or unconsciously committing outward himsa [violence]. . . . A votary of ahimsa [nonviolence] therefore remains true to this faith if the spring of all his actions is compassion, if he shuns to the best of his ability the destruction of the tiniest creature, tries to save it, and thus incessantly strives to be free from the deadly coil of himsa. He will be constantly growing in self-restraint and compassion, but he can never become entirely free from outward himsa."[7] The ideal of absolute nonviolence is nearly impossible to achieve because of the problem of personal self-defense. And this is made more difficult if nonviolence is supposed to be extended beyond killing humans. We must harm other beings in order to survive: we must kill in order to eat. But the biggest problem is that the world often presents us with difficult "kill or be killed" choices as in the question of self-defense or a war of self-defense. This is why absolute pacifism is mythological. It may be possible only for perfect beings inhabiting a perfect world. Or, as many Christians put it, it is possible only if you believe that the kingdom of God is here and now within you.[8]

Absolute pacifists may hold that it is better to be killed than to kill. As Augsburger puts it, "As Christians our answer to violence in the world is simply that we don't have to live; we can die."[9] Such a choice may be impossible without deep religious faith. But pacifists will also often argue that this way of describing a situation—as one where the choice is "kill or be killed" or "kill or die"—usually presents us with a false dilemma: often there are other nonviolent alternatives to either killing or being killed. But when presented with such a stark choice, absolute pacifism may require self-sacrifice.

Contingent, or conditional, pacifism qualifies such an uncompromising condemnation of violence and warfare. Contingent pacifism does not then rely on religious belief or the myths of immortality, and it allows for exceptions in extreme cases. It is thus easier to accept for those of us who are more sympathetic to humanism. And indeed, it has broad appeal for philosophers and scientists. Albert Einstein and Bertrand Russell, for example, were both supporters of the war against Nazi Germany, despite the fact that both of them considered themselves to be pacifists. Russell identifies his position as what he calls "relative political pacifism."[10] Russell uses the word "relative" to describe the contingent nature of the commitment to peace: one's commitment to pacifism depends on or is relative to the nature of the war. Relative pacifism means, for Russell, "that very few wars are worth fighting, and that the evils of war are almost always greater than they seem to excited populations at the moment when war breaks out."[11] Russell calls his position "political" because his emphasis is on war and political institutions, not on a personal commitment to nonviolence.

There are several varieties of contingent pacifism.

First, pacifism may not be required of all moral agents. Thus pacifism may be required only for members of particular professions. Pacifism is often thought to be a professional obligation of certain religious vocations. But such a vocation may be thought of as a choice of conscience that is not universally required. In this version of contingent pacifism, the prohibition against violence applies only to those who take a vow or make a pledge to renounce violence and war. Within this two-tiered approach, the vow of peacefulness might be considered a sort of supererogatory ideal that is not required of others. But it is also possible for the two-tiered approach to contain an implicit condemnation of those who do not take up the higher calling of pacifism.

A second sort of contingent pacifism holds that if a particular war or military policy is prudentially unwise it should be resisted. Such prudential pacifism is based on cost-benefit analyses focused on the facts of particular conflicts. A more principled sort of prudential pacifism can be based on the general claim that war usually causes more harm than good.

A third sort of contingent pacifism will appeal to the just war theory and claim that a given war is unjust according to this theory. As John Rawls says of what he calls "contingent pacifism," "The possibility of a just war is conceded but not under present circumstances."[12] This idea is closely related to "just war pacifism" as developed in the last couple of decades by critics of the just war tradition: just war pacifism maintains that modern wars are not fought according to the standards of the just war theory because, for example, they make use of aerial bombardment and other means that do not adequately discriminate between combatants and noncombatants. Such a claim may result in a nearly absolute proscription against war under present circumstances. And it may contain an absolute prohibition against certain sorts of war, such as nuclear war. Most so-called just war pacifists are contingent pacifists in this sense: they object to the way modern wars are fought. And they generally admit that just war principles are acceptable, even if they think that these principles lead to a general rejection of war.

With the just war theory in mind, contingent pacifism may focus on the basis for war (as in the just war idea of *jus ad bellum*), on the way that the war is fought (as in the just war idea of *jus in bello*), or on the expected outcome of the war (as in the idea of *jus post bellum*). With regard to *jus ad bellum*, contingent pacifists may reject the legitimacy of the authority who is fighting, they may claim that war is not being fought as a last resort, they may deny that the war is being fought for a just cause, or they may claim that war is being fought with malign intentions. With regard to *jus in bello*, contingent pacifists may worry that innocent noncombatants are being harmed or that soldiers are employing means *mala in se* (such as rape or torture). Finally, with regard to *jus post bellum*, contingent pacifists may object to wars that will undermine long-term peace, justice, and stability. In general, most contingent pacifists will claim that the wars they reject are disproportional responses to the harms they seek to prevent.

A fourth form of contingent pacifism might be called *political pacifism*. This approach adheres to pacifism as a strategic political commitment within an adversarial system. In political discourse, the so-called doves are usually not absolute pacifists. Rather, they define themselves in opposition to the so-called hawks who advocate war and funding for the war system. Political pacifists need not have an absolute commitment to nonviolence; nor need they have a principled commitment to the ideas of the just war theory. Rather, they can reject militaristic policies for strategic political purposes that have to do with budget priorities or other issues. Political pacifism may seem to be merely opportunistic, but opposition parties who offer critical perspectives on militarism are an important component of adversarial democracy. Moreover, political pacifists can end up forming useful coalitions with other more principled pacifists and absolute pacifists.

Finally, another version of contingent pacifism can be called, following Robert Holmes, *liberal-democratic pacifism* or simply *liberal pacifism*. Holmes argues that modern warfare runs counter to the values of liberal democracy. Thus those who are committed to liberal values should not support war. Essential for this claim is the idea that "no one has a right to command others to kill, and no one is justified in killing on command."[13] The sort of pacifism that is derived from this claim is contingent on the fact that modern warfare involves a hierarchically organized military system and mass conscription. It is possible that war could be fought without conscription or without military hierarchy, but Holmes argues that this is unlikely in the modern world. Moreover, this sort of pacifism is contingent on our social and political commitments. Those who are committed to other social and political ideologies may find that war and the war system are morally and politically acceptable.

Contingent pacifism is often based on empirical and historical judgments about the way wars are fought. In this way, contingent forms of pacifism attempt to avoid mythologizing the commitment to peace. Empirical judgments will vary depending on changing circumstances. And these judgments are also contingent on the availability of information about why and how wars are fought. It is possible, then, that contingent pacifists can admit that there may be conflicting judgments about the justice of a particular war. Unlike contingent pacifism, absolute pacifism rejects war in an a priori fashion: one of the first principles of absolute pacifism is that war (or violence more generally) is always wrong. Thus absolute pacifism will claim that any judgment that leads to the justification of war is wrong.

MAXIMAL AND MINIMAL PACIFISM

The difference between maximal (or broad) and minimal (or narrow) pacifism has to do with the extent of the commitment to nonviolence. This difference can be explained with reference to the questions of what sorts of violence are rejected, and who is the recipient or beneficiary of nonviolent concern. It is easy enough to say that pacifists reject war. But there is an open question about how war is defined and thus about what sorts of actions are rejected by pacifists. There is, of course, a continuum between maximal and minimal pacifism, with maximal pacifism rejecting all forms of war and violence. Minimal versions of pacifism fall away from this in various directions. Maximal pacifism is closely related to absolute and universal formulations of pacifism; minimal pacifism has more in common with contingent and particular versions of pacifism.

There are a variety of actions that can be described as "war": terrorism, insurgency and counterinsurgency, civil war, humanitarian intervention, full-fledged interstate conflict, and world war that includes the possible employment of nuclear weapons. Most pacifists will reject nuclear war and full-fledged interstate conflict. But there are differences about whether, for example, civil war or humanitarian intervention can be justified. For example, some who could be described as pacifists supported the use of military force during the American Civil War. At issue in thinking about these differences are questions about the importance of sovereignty and human rights, as well as the question of how best to create stability in the face of social unrest. One difficult issue for some pacifists is the question of using violence in defense of human rights or in opposition to tyranny. Maximal pacifists will reject all use of military force, even in defense against dictators or in response to egregious human rights violations.

Maximal versions of pacifism will condemn all taking of life. Pacifists may also extend their rejection of violence to include a rejection of the death penalty, meat eating, and abortion. More narrow versions of pacifism may take into account the distinction between the innocent and the guilty, holding only that the innocent may not be harmed. This distinction is important for thinking about the question of noncombatant immunity in war, with many pacifists arguing that war is wrong because it puts the innocent at risk. Some opponents of the death penalty will make a similar argument about the death penalty and the risk of executing the innocent. And opponents of abortion will also claim that the act harms the innocent.

The connection between war, the death penalty, and abortion is made in the Catholic "seamless garment" approach that aims to develop a "consistent ethic of life." This approach condemns all actions that harm innocent persons, and it is often extended to a rejection of all harm, without regard for the distinction between innocence and guilt. Such a view has been defended most famously by Pope John Paul II, who was skeptical of all sorts of violence including war, the death penalty, suicide, euthanasia, and abortion. Pacifists may also extend moral concern to include concern for all sentient beings, and thus pacifists may also condemn meat eating and animal cruelty. Gandhi, for example, extended ahimsa maximally to include avoiding harm to sentient beings.

More maximal versions of pacifism tend to be mythological. There are dozens of complicated questions that must be answered in order to weave a seamless antiviolence or pro-life garment. For example: Are animals sentient? Are fetuses persons? Are criminals deserving of respect? And how does suicide fit with our conception of autonomy? But maximal pacifists often simply assume a unified answer to such questions that is grounded in some deep metaphysical outlook. The Dalai Lama, for example, notes that the Tibetan Buddhist tradition grounds its maximal version of nonviolence in the idea of reincarnation:

> The Tibetan Buddhist tradition teaches us to view all sentient beings as our dear mothers and to show our gratitude by loving them all. For, according to Buddhist theory, we are born and reborn countless numbers of times, and it is conceivable that each being has been our parent at one time or another. In this way all beings in the universe share a family relationship.[14]

The Dalai Lama argues that one need not accept this myth in order to develop compassion and nonviolence. But the mythological construct certainly helps.

While I admire the idealism of maximal versions of pacifism, I find it hard to believe the mythological constructs that are used to support it. But this is not necessary for a minimal commitment to antiwar pacifism. The complications of figuring out whether we should avoid harming fetuses or fish or murderers are avoided in the minimalist antiwar position. For antiwar pacifism, the key point is that it is wrong to kill actual human beings who are innocent of any crime. But even if we accept that some humans can be killed—for example, soldiers who consent to serve—a minimal version of antiwar pacifism can be derived from the idea that it is wrong to harm those innocent humans who end up being killed as collateral damage.

UNIVERSAL AND PARTICULAR PACIFISM

This distinction has to do with the issue of whether everyone is required to be a pacifist or whether pacifism can be a moral choice of some particular individuals. This is related to the question of whether pacifism is a duty for all or whether it is supererogatory. This distinction recognizes different answers to the question of who is obligated to be a pacifist. Universalism in thinking about pacifism will hold that if war is wrong, it is wrong for everyone and thus that soldiers who fight are wrong, as are those who support the war system that encourages them to fight. Particular pacifists articulate their position as merely personal and do not condemn the war system or soldiers who choose to fight. Universal pacifism is closely connected with absolute and maximal versions of pacifism; particular pacifism is related to contingent and minimal pacifisms.

One way that this distinction between universal and particular pacifism has been enacted in history is through the idea of vocational pacifism. Vocational pacifism holds that pacifism is a special obligation of a particular vocational service, but that it is not required of all. In this sense, pacifism is supererogatory. Religious clerics may thus be required to renounce violence, while ordinary members of their congregations may not be so obliged. Particular pacifism is thus connected to contingent pacifism: the moral demand of pacifism may be contingent on one's social position. This sort of vocational pacifism can be extended to explain how members of some religious communities— Quakers, Mennonites, the Amish, and so on—might opt out of military service.

This distinction can be understood by considering whether pacifism is morally necessary or whether it is merely morally permitted. The universalist answer to this question is: if war and violence are wrong, then pacifism is morally necessary and those who fight are wrong. But some pacifists appear to hold that it is not wrong to fight (or that some persons are permitted to fight), even though the pacifist herself may choose (or is obliged by some vocational commitment) not to fight. A conscientious objector may thus choose not to fight while not condemning those who do. Conscientious objection is often articulated as a personal belief about pacifism that does not apply to others. This is why pacifists who opt out of war as conscientious objectors are usually not viewed as traitors: their conscientious objection is not viewed as having universal significance. Eric Reitan has recently argued that one may adopt a sort of "personal pacifism" that need not be universally applied. One way of understanding this is to connect it with the idea of tolerance. A personal pacifist may believe that pacifism is the right choice, but she may choose to tolerate others who do not make the same choice. A personal pacifist may also espouse a sort of relativism that holds that a commitment to pacifism is merely a personal commitment that cannot be used to condemn others who make different commitments.

This idea of particular pacifism is a subtle one and it often becomes mythological. Christian pacifists will explain their community's difference in terms that point toward a distinction between those who serve Caesar and those who serve God. Critics will argue that this sort of particularism is incoherent, especially if it is understood as a sort of relativism. Those patriots who claim that conscientious objectors are traitors may argue that pacifism cannot be a particular or personal choice. Critics of pacifism will argue that pacifism is morally wrong because they think that patriotism or justice requires fighting or at least supporting the war effort. This objection would hold that if a war is justified, then conscientious objectors are wrong to reject it. Particularists will reply by claiming that their rejection of war is a personal choice or a matter of faith. It seems to me, however, that there must be a universal answer to the question of whether war is wrong. The risk of relativism is too great here.

SKEPTICAL AND PRIMA FACIE PACIFISM

Arguments in defense of pacifism are usually based on a negative claim about the immorality of violence and war. Thus pacifism is usually derived by negation. Pacifism tells us primarily what not to do. As Cheyney Ryan has argued, pacifism is a "skeptical position." Ryan puts it this way: "Its general claim is that the proponent of killing cannot produce a single compelling argument for why killing another person is permissible."[15] One of the skeptical problems that Ryan addresses is the problem that occurs in killing in self-defense. When a Victim kills an Aggressor in self-defense, this killing occurs before the Aggressor has actualized his malicious intention. In this case, killing in self-defense is out of proportion to the harm done, since the Victim who kills in self-defense was not himself killed. A skeptical version of pacifism can thus develop from the worry that when we choose to kill in self-defense, we never know whether this killing is in fact justifiable.

This sort of skeptical position can be linked to the just war tradition's concern with the question of "last resort" in thinking about *jus ad bellum*. Skeptical pacifists wonder how we would know that we ever reach the stage of last resort, when violence becomes necessary. One way that pacifists articulate this concern is to focus on the variety of nonviolent measures that could be employed before it becomes necessary to resort to force. Indeed, it may be argued that to resort to violence is to admit to a failure of imagination and to give up hope that more humane forms of problem solving and conflict resolution can be effective. Moreover, pacifists will note that it is not sufficient to try nonviolent methods once and then disregard them. Rather, one must engage in a variety of nonviolent actions, and one must try these nonviolent alternatives more than once.

This sort of skepticism can itself become mythological. The demand for absolute certainty is unrealistic. In ordinary life, we almost always act on less-than-perfect certainty. Pure skepticism would leave us immobilized with doubt. It should be obvious, as well, that the last-resort criterion of just war theory cannot be read so as to always preclude resort to war. In some cases—say, when enemy troops cross the border— it is obvious that nonviolent means have failed. But skeptical pacifism can avoid the myth of absolute certainty, if skepticism is merely used to clarify the burden of proof. Mythological skepticism denies that the war can ever be justified. Pragmatic skepticism clarifies the burden of proof and demands that the proponent of war prove to a reasonable extent that war is a justifiable last resort.

A somewhat different version of skeptical pacifism can be found in critiques of militarism and the ideology and propaganda that lead people to support war. This skeptical stance is what I have called in this book (and elsewhere) *practical pacifism*. This skepticism produces a practical political pacifism that is based on the fact that citizens have no good reason to trust that their governments are telling them the truth about war and its justification. And it claims that wars usually fail to live up to the standards of the just war theory.

This skepticism is derived from historical judgments about the tendency of governments to manipulate information in order to provoke the citizenry toward war. In light of such skepticism, the burden of proof for the justification of war is placed on the government, which must prove that the dangerous and presumptively immoral activity of war can in fact be justified.

This sort of skepticism might also be called *prima facie pacifism*; this is the idea that war is usually wrong except in certain extraordinary circumstances when it is compellingly shown that the evil of war is a sort of lesser evil that is necessary for some greater good. Prima facie pacifism presumes that war is wrong but allows for exceptions. It avoids the mythological demand for absolute certainty by clarifying the burden of proof that the proponent of war has to bear: it is up to the proponent of war to prove, in a given circumstance, that war is in fact morally necessary.

CONCLUSION

With these distinctions in place, let me conclude by arguing that the most plausible position is a contingent form of minimal pacifism that is both universal and moderately skeptical. This has the following implications.

First, we should avoid the absolutist claim that all wars are wrong. It would be quite difficult to establish that everything that is called "war" is always wrong. At best, we can make contingent or conditional judgments based on the particulars of a given situation. The just war theory provides us with criteria that can be used to judge the rightness or wrongness of war. But our presumption should be that war is wrong based on a stringent and restrictive reading of the just war principles.

It is easy enough to see the limits of absolute pacifism if we imagine the justification of a limited use of arms against an evil enemy. For example, if a terrorist group were intent on using weapons of mass destruction to kill millions, and if the battle against this group of terrorists would occur in an unpopulated area where noncombatant casualties would be minimal, then it seems pretty clear that such a military action would be justifiable. Thus, for example, some use of force against al-Qaeda could have been justified after September 11, especially if the use of force were constrained in such a way as to avoid collateral damage. Nonetheless, we should remain cautious about this permission for war. When we see how the war in Afghanistan has proceeded, we have good reason to be skeptical of this conflict as well. In Afghanistan, there have been several thousand civilian casualties (although there is no clear number here, the range is somewhere between five thousand and ten thousand). The war has gone on for nearly six years and there is still much instability in Afghanistan. Moreover, al-Qaeda and the Taliban have not been defeated. Thus it is not clear that in this case, war was the right decision.

Second, this commitment to pacifism is easiest to defend when pacifism is understood in a minimal sense as directed only against war. It is fairly obvious that mass killing is morally problematic, and the more people involved in a conflict, the greater the moral problem. There are different arguments to be made about the death penalty, abortion, suicide, or meat eating. I am sympathetic to some of these arguments, but they require much further reflection. The easiest argument is directed against mass killing of human beings, especially wars that harm innocent noncombatants.

Third, the conclusion of this approach is supposed to have a universal implication. There is something odd about those who claim that pacifism is a personal opinion or something confined to the vows of a religious vocation. The question of whether war can be justified must have an answer that is true (or false) for everyone.

Fourth, this argument is skeptical. It is ultimately about disenchanting the myths of war, especially the myth of the just war. Its focus is negative and critical. At best, it aims to clarify the burden of proof.

Finally, this point of view aims to be free of the religious basis of other forms of pacifism. It does not need to be grounded in God's commands or in religious eschatology. Nor does it need the support of ideas such as karma or redemptive suffering. And it does not rely on myths about reincarnation or immortality. Rather, it is grounded in a pragmatic synthesis of Kantian and utilitarian concerns. The Kantian (or deontological) basis is that war harms persons, especially innocent persons who do not deserve to be harmed. The utilitarian concern is that wars produce chaos, instability, and unhappiness for large numbers of people.

For these reasons, wars are usually presumed to be wrong. And it remains up to the proponent of a given war to prove that the war in question will be just.

NOTES

1. Bertrand Russell, "The Future of Pacifism," *American Scholar* 13 (1943): 8.
2. James Sterba, "The Most Morally Defensible Pacifism," in *Pazifismus: Ideengeschichte, Theorie und Praxis*, ed. Barbara Bleisch and Jean-Daniel Strub (Bern: Haupt Verlag, 2006), 202. For a different approach that also stringently rules out most wars as unjust see Murray Rothbard, "Just War," at www.lewrockwell.com/rothbard/rothbard20.html.
3. Gandhi, "Doctrine of the Sword," quoted in Sterba, "Most Morally Defensible Pacifism."
4. Thomas Merton, *Thomas Merton on Peace* (New York: McCall, 1971), 209.
5. Martin Luther King Jr., *A Testament of Hope: The Essential Writings of Martin Luther King Jr.*, ed. James Melvin Washington (San Francisco: Harper and Row, 1986), 18.
6. See Herman A. Hoyt, "Nonresistance," in *War: Four Christian Views*, ed. Robert G Clouse (Downers Grove, IL: Intervarsity, 1981).
7. Mohandas K. Gandhi, *Autobiography: The Story of My Experiments with Truth* (Boston: Beacon Press, 1993), 439.
8. Cf. Matthew 3:2; Luke 17:20. For a detailed discussion see Leo Tolstoy's book, *The Kingdom of God Is within You* (New York: Dover, 2006).
9. Myron S. Augsburger, "Christian Pacifism," in Hoyt, *War: Four Christian Views*, 92; an updated version of this essay was published soon after September 11, 2001, on the Intervarsity website, at www.intervarsity.org/news/christian-pacifism.
10. Russell, "Future of Pacifism."
11. Russell, "Future of Pacifism," 8.
12. John Rawls, *A Theory of Justice* (Cambridge, MA: Harvard University Press, 1971), 382.
13. Robert Holmes, "Pacifism for Nonpacifists," *Journal of Social Philosophy* 30, no. 3: 398.
14. Dalai Lama, "A Human Approach to World Peace," at www.dalailama.com/page.62.htm.
15. Cheyney C. Ryan, "Self-Defense, Pacifism and Rights," *Ethics* 93 (1983): 509.

Chapter Eleven

Citizenship, Responsibility, and Peace

Liberal peoples have nothing to go to war about.

—John Rawls, The Law of Peoples[1]

When one begins to see through the myths of war, the next question is how to put this new insight into practice. One response is to retreat from the world in order to find a kind of separate peace. But such a retreat solves nothing. And those who take this path might indeed be called cowards and free riders. The real challenge is to creatively engage the world with eyes wide open to the myths and rhetorical challenges of political life. The key to this creative engagement is the process and practice of what is called *deliberative democracy*. We need more and better deliberation and debate. The hopeful conclusion is that the myths of war will fade away when more people participate in democratic deliberation and when this deliberation is more rational and more open to diverse viewpoints.

Democratic deliberation is no panacea. The idea of democracy ca become mythological, when it is viewed as a final solution to the pro lem of war. Since Plato, there has been a sustained critique of demo racy. And parts of that critique continue to hold: democratic societ are often driven by a lack of wisdom, and democratic peoples can easily tricked by demagogues who use the myths of war and politic lead democratic peoples to make unwise and unjust decisions. While note this caveat, however, democracy remains the best hope we h We live in a second-best world. Human beings are not perfect. Pe

are ignorant, lazy, and self-interested. But since these same human beings are those who presume to act as leaders, the same problems will be
found in any other form of government.

The best hope for progress beyond the myths of war is found in what
is called the *democratic peace theory*. This theory holds that the solution to war is the spread of democracy. This ideal can become mythological—as if the mere institution of democracy were enough to solve
the problem of war. In addition to democratic institutions, we need more
and better education about the myths of war, and a stronger sense of the
responsibilities of citizenship. The hope is that as this need is fulfilled,
people will be more cautious about supporting war; wars will thus be
fewer; and the wars that are fought will be fought more justly.

THE PROMISE OF THE DEMOCRATIC PEACE

The great hope of democratic peace theory is that as democracy
spreads, there will be fewer wars because liberal peoples have no reason to go to war with one another. Indeed, Doyle and others argue that
this is an empirical fact of history.[2] The basic idea is that since democracies do not fight one another, the spread of democracy will mean that
there will be fewer wars. It is, of course, important to note that democracies do fight against nondemocracies. This is why the democratic
peace is a peace among democracies.

If democracy is the solution we might think that a war to spread democracy is necessary as a step on the way to creating the democratic
peace. Some such idea was proposed by Rousseau in his critique of the
Abbé de Saint-Pierre's *Plan for Perpetual Peace*. It was found in the
idea that World War I would be a war to end all wars and a war to make
the world safe for democracy. This idea inspired a number of other wars
in the twentieth century. And it continues to inspire those who defend
the Bush Doctrine in American foreign policy and the American adventures in Afghanistan and Iraq. Democratic peace theory becomes
mythological when it is used to support aggressive democratizing wars.

Tied to the ideal of the democratic peace is the idea that when democracies fight, they fight wars that have a just cause—according to principles of *jus ad bellum*—and they fight these wars justly—according to
the principles of *jus in bello*. Although this just war analysis is not the
primary focus of the democratic peace theory, it is clearly linked to it.
The just war theory aims to reduce both the severity and frequency of

war, and it aims to produce just outcomes. Such just outcomes would appear to include democratic structures of government, especially if these structures tend to promote justice and peace. In general, the concept of "democracy" invoked here is one that includes the idea that human rights are respected. Perhaps the term *liberal-democracy* makes this clearer, but most of the democratic peace theorists use the word *democracy* in a way that is also supposed to include the liberal protection of human rights and a division of powers. Thus democracies are presumed to be, by definition, just. And if democracies are, according to this definition, devoted to protecting human rights, then they should also be committed to defending human rights within war, which is the basic idea behind the principles of *jus in bello*.

There is an ongoing dispute, however, about the causal story that explains the fact of the democratic peace. Kant—whom most consider as the source of the democratic peace idea—explains that the process of public deliberation and public consent will act as a brake on war. If citizens were asked whether they want to fight wars that will require them to sacrifice their lives and their money, citizens would be extremely cautious about approving war. Ideas like this are dear to the heart of those who defend deliberative democracy. Other explanations of the democratic peace are, of course, possible. Perhaps democracies are also capitalistic and so they find trade more profitable than war. Or perhaps the division of powers in democracies creates a check on the power of the executive and the armed forces. Or maybe democratic peoples develop a psychological aversion to war along with trust in the process of negotiation and compromise. Much of this can be tied together in the claim, defended recently by Spencer Weart, that the democratic peace is explained by the entirety of what he calls "republican" political culture.

But this does not explain the zeal for war that can be found in democracies. The Iraq war seems to show us a case in which a democracy— the United States—launched an aggressive war, even though that democracy was not itself directly attacked. The notion of preemptive war can be used to explain this (as discussed in chapter 6). And Iraq might also be a case of a war to spread democracy. But what is interesting is the zealousness for war among Americans during the run-up to the war. One reason for this was that Americans were misinformed about the war. Many thought that Iraq had something to do with the 9/11 attacks. Many thought that Iraq posed a direct terrorist threat to the safety of the United States. And many thought that it would be easy to establish a stable democracy in Iraq. These ideas were, of course, all false. But they show us that democracy is no guarantee of wise judgment about war. Democratic peoples are susceptible to the myths of war, and they can be manipulated by demagogues to have a mythological faith in the power of democratizing wars.

One key issue for the democratic peace theory is the question of what exactly counts as a democracy. A significant terminological problem is that most defenders of the "democratic" peace theory actually focus on the importance of "republican" politics. Kant's ideal was a liberal constitutional republic and not a direct democracy. Weart's ideas are similar. Weart defines a well-established republic as follows:

> A well-established republic is a regime that not only has formal republican institutions to allow for public contestation among equals, but also a political culture among the leadership such that governance actually uses and relies upon those institutions. In short, we can only call a regime a well-established republic if the leaders customarily tolerate full public contestation among citizens.[3]

The idea of the republican system is similar to the idea of deliberative democracy, where the guiding principle is that there should be free, open, and public deliberation about public policy. Cohen explains the ideal of deliberative democracy as follows: "Citizens in such an order share a commitment to the resolution of problems of collective choice through public reasoning, and regard their basic institutions as legitimate in so far as they establish the framework for free public deliberation."[4] It is easy to see that this idea is grounded on a nonviolent ideal. As Rummel says, "Democracy is a method of nonviolence."[5] Stable democracies are supposed to have found viable nonviolent ways to resolve social problems. The hope of liberal thinkers from Kant to Rawls is that the public use of reason will lead toward peace and justice. When wars must be defended in a public forum, the hope is that there will be fewer wars, these wars will be fought for just reasons, and they will be fought more justly. But again, the case of Iraq gives us reason to doubt the myth that reason and justice always prevail in a democracy.

The hopeful thesis of those who defend the democratic peace idea rests on an assumption about the power of democratic citizenship. The assumption is that citizens of democracies have the power to ensure that wars are fought for just causes and that they are fought justly. This power is supposed to be exercised through institutional means (i.e., elections) and through public deliberation (the media, public discussions, local conversations, etc.). Related to these assumptions about the power of democratic citizenship is a normative claim: citizens ought to think critically about the ethics of war and they ought to demand public justification of war. The promise of democratic peace will be achieved when citizens fulfill this obligation.

Despite the hope of democratic peace theory, there is no guarantee that democracies will be peaceful or that when they fight they will fight justly. As David Spiro put this, "Liberal regimes can incite their populace to foolish wars just as easily as illiberal regimes."[6] More recently, Amy Gutmann and Dennis Thompson have reminded us—with a special focus on failures of democratic deliberation that led to the war in Iraq—that deliberative democracy is only a procedural safeguard, not a final answer to political problems: "Deliberative democrats do not claim that deliberation is a panacea, that it can turn bad outcomes into good ones, only that it is better than its alternatives."[7] We must admit that the invasion of Iraq represented a sort of failure of democratic deliberation. This failure reminds us how important it is to develop better deliberation and to further empower democratic citizenship.

We should also admit that the invasion of Iraq is *not* a counterexample to the claim that democracies do not go to war against other *democracies*. However, it is a reminder of the limits of the democratic peace theory, and of one of the risks of that idea. The limit of the theory is the relationship between democracies and nondemocracies, or as Rawls puts it, the relationship between well-ordered states and states that are not well ordered (outlaw states and those that are burdened with unfavorable conditions). The risk of the idea is the very idea of a crusade for democracy, which continues to guide our thinking about the war in Iraq. Rawls suggests that the most peaceful way to deal with outlaw regimes is to establish a truce or modus vivendi. But a more obvious way for a stable democracy to deal with a rogue state is to intervene and force a transformation toward democracy.

Two problems for the deliberative democratic hope can be mapped onto the *ad bellum/in bello* distinction. First, since it requires substantial wisdom, information, and expertise to correctly apply principles of *jus ad bellum*, it is not clear that ordinary citizens are capable of making good judgments about *jus ad bellum*. But such judgments are essential so long as democratic peace theory recognizes that democracies can wage just wars against aggressive nations and in defense of human rights; that is, so long as democracies are not supposed to be entirely pacific. Just wars can be fought according to principles of justice that democratic peoples hold dear: the ideas of state sovereignty and human rights. In some cases it will be clear to citizens when there is a just cause for war (for example, in the face of outright aggression). But decisions about going to war also involve judgments about whether war is a last resort and whether war is a proportional response to provocations. To make good judgments about just cause, last resort, and proportionality, citizens need information and expertise. The difficulty is that ordinary citizens lack experience and expertise in thinking about such questions. This is exacerbated by the fact that there are good reasons to keep strategic information secret. Thus citizens also lack access to information that would allow them to make good judgments. And, what is worse, leaders lie, deceive, and manipulate information. For democratic deliberation to be effective, citizens need good education and free and open access to true information.

The second problem is that even in wars that are waged for just causes, citizens lack the capacity to judge the rules of engagement and other aspects of *jus in bello*. Moreover, the very responsiveness of democratic government to the will of the people makes it easy for political pressure to lead beyond the limits of principles of *jus in bello*. Democratic peoples—like any people that fights a war—want victory. And public deliberation once war has commenced can lead democratic peoples to demand a quick end to war. This sort of political pressure can lead to violations of the principles of *jus in bello* in the name of efficiency. It can also lead to a failure to complete the mission and obtain conditions of *jus post bellum*, such that after war we have only chaos and disorder.

The solution to these problems is more and better public deliberation about just war principles, about the need to resort to war, and about the methods employed in fighting. This solution is not easily implemented, however, because of the secretive and bureaucratic nature of decisions about warfare and war strategizing and because of the interest that democratic peoples have in efficiency and utility. Moreover, democratic deliberation is especially fragile in wartime: it can easily be hijacked by demagoguery that pushes democratic citizens to support wars that are immoral and to support strategies that violate just war principles.

Democratic deliberation is thus no panacea that can prevent a polity from fighting unjust wars. Although Kant and other defenders of democratic peace theory think that public deliberation would produce better judgments about going to war, critics of democracy—such as Plato—remind us that democratic peoples can be easily manipulated by demagogues. Although Plato proposes the philosopher-king as a solution to this problem, this solution comes with its own risks—that is, despotism. The best solution is thus not to give up on democracy, but to increase the level of honesty, openness, and rationality in public discourse and to help citizens develop virtues of democratic citizenship.

Citizens thus need to better understand the importance of their shared responsibility for war. In a democracy each citizen bears some responsibility for decisions that are made about war. The hope is that when citizens take this responsibility seriously, the polity as a whole will make better decisions. It is easy for a people to be swept away by "war fever." But citizens who understand their shared responsibility for wars that are fought in their names will resist the pressures of war fever by demanding justifications of war and of the means employed in fighting.

This is the hope. However, there are severe obstacles to be overcome in order to actualize this hope. The history of American militarism in the last century shows us the problems mentioned above. The United States has violated principles of *jus in bello* and *jus ad bellum* in its recent wars. These are failures of deliberative democracy. Seeing these failures will help us imagine the solution, which is increased citizen responsibility and a more robust sort of deliberative democracy. Indeed, this is the only solution that is acceptable for those of us committed to the democratic ideal.

THE AMERICAN EXAMPLE

If we look at the United States as an example of deliberative democracy, it is clear that democracies fight many wars. In the last hundred years, the United States has fought several major wars in Europe and Asia, and now in the Middle East. Democratic peace theorists will explain such wars as wars against nondemocracies. According to this interpretation, the United States does not go to war against other democracies; it only fights against nations that are not democratic, that violate their citizens' rights, and that are aggressive. And more recently, the guiding idea of U.S. foreign policy has been an active, forward-leaning attempt to spread democracy.

Some may question whether the United States is a deliberative democracy. One might focus such a critique on some of the undemocratic aspects of the American system: the control of the two major parties, the role of money in American politics, or the nature of the federal system and the electoral college. While these institutional conditions do tend to undermine democracy, American politics is still organized according to the idea that policy decisions must be made through a public process in which parties make arguments and are willing to abide by the decisions of reasonable deliberative bodies. Public deliberation does occur in American politics. It occurs in the Senate, in presidential speeches, on the Op-Ed pages, and on television news programs. American policy is formulated and defended by public arguments that appeal to publicly available reasons. It is true that American politics is not an ideal deliberative democracy. In light of some of the problems mentioned above, it is clear that there is vast room for improvement in the quality of public reason in the United States. However, policy decisions are not made in the United States without some form of public deliberation.

American public discourse about war also appeals to the ideals of the just war theory. Despite this, the evidence shows that the United States in general violates just war principles. The United States has fought wars in which the cause was not clearly just, and the United States has used tactics that violate the principles of *jus in bello*. I will consider three examples here: World War II, the Vietnam War, and the more recent Iraq war. I will attempt to generalize from these examples and come up with a list of problems that democracies must confront. I will derive a couple of problems from each war, but I believe that these problems generally apply to all of these wars.

WORLD WAR II

Most Americans consider World War II the paradigm of a just war. Indeed, this war can be understood as a classic example of a war in which democratic regimes fought against nondemocratic regimes. The memory of this war provides the model for most subsequent wars against an evil enemy. Carl Lesnor has argued that all of our subsequent enemies have been modeled after Hitler.[8] Just war thinkers such as Michael Walzer have a fondness for the World War II paradigm. And President Bush has repeatedly invoked World War II as a model for his aggressive war against what he calls "Islamo-fascism." This paradigm focuses primarily on the question of just cause. The fight to oppose Japanese imperialism, Nazi fascism, and genocide is held to be a good fight. And the fight itself aimed at establishing a more lasting peace by helping to sow the seeds of democracy in Germany and Japan. Even outspoken pacifists such as Bertrand Russell and Albert Einstein made an exception for the fight against fascism. However, this memory of the "good war" overlooks the fact that the Allied forces violated principles of *jus in bello* during this war.

It is instructive then to remember Elizabeth Anscombe's protests against President Harry Truman's decision to use atomic bombs to destroy Hiroshima and Nagasaki. Anscombe—who was not a pacifist— claimed that Truman was a kind of murderer and war criminal. Anscombe objected to tactics that deliberately target noncombatants: carpet or area bombing, and the use of incendiary bombs and atomic weapons. The American use of these indiscriminate weapons of mass destruction reminds us that although the cause of the "good war" may have been just, the means employed in this war were not.

Anscombe reminds us that one of the chief problems of the Allied approach to World War II was the demand for unconditional surrender. According to Anscombe's analysis of the atomic bomb attacks against Japan, such attacks would not have been necessary if the United States had been more willing to negotiate.

There are many complicated historical facts that must be considered when trying to understand what happened toward the end of World War II. One obvious fact is that the United States and its allies demanded unconditional surrender so that they could extirpate the fascist ideology that gave rise to the war in the first place. This was a sort of crusade for democracy, and the only acceptable outcome of this crusade was the total surrender of the enemy. It was the demand for unconditional surrender that itself led to the excesses of Hiroshima and Nagasaki. Another important point is the fact of "military drift": through the course of the war, military necessity came to be the primary rationale for decision making (cf. Glover). This was closely linked to Truman's explicit rationale for dropping the bombs, which was a utilitarian concern for saving the lives of American soldiers. In an interview in 1955 Truman explained his reasoning as follows:

> They never would have surrendered otherwise. I don't believe in speculating on the mental feeling and as far as the bomb is concerned I ordered its use for a military reason—for no other cause—and it saved the lives of a great many of our soldiers. That is all I had in mind.[9]

This utilitarian calculation reminds us of the problem confronted by democratic politicians who lead a nation into war. Noble principles such as those of *jus in bello* are not strong enough to withstand the political pressure to save the lives of one's own soldiers. A democratically elected commander in chief must operate on the basis of national interest and be responsive to the public demand for reducing casualties. Truman's decision can be understood as being necessitated by the demands of democratic politics. To see this imagine a counterfactual scenario. If Truman had not used the atomic bombs and had instead launched an invasion of Japan and ended up losing tens or hundreds of thousands of American soldiers in the process, and if the American people had found out later that the atomic bomb had been available, it is easy to imagine that Truman would have been accused of failing to fulfill his duty to preserve the lives of American soldiers. So the reality of democratic politics produced a situation in which it was relatively easy for Truman to make the decision to kill two hundred thousand people, most of whom were noncombatants.

Let me indicate, then, two dangers that we find in the case of World War II.

1. Democratic nations that fight wars for good democratic reasons can end up violating the principles of *jus in bello* as they fight.
2. Democratic nations will violate these principles because democratic politics requires quick victories at low cost to the nation.

THE VIETNAM WAR

The injustice of the war in Vietnam is well known. Not only was the war a continuation of colonialism but it was sold to the American people on the basis of the discredited "attacks" in the Gulf of Tonkin. The war continued for more than a decade. And American forces violated principles of *jus in bello* in this war. These violations include atrocities such as the My Lai massacre, in which innocent noncombatants were deliberately killed. We might also recall the systematic use of incendiary devices (including napalm) and the use of defoliants such as Agent Orange. These weapons are illegitimate because of the nature of the injuries they cause, because of the indiscriminate nature of the harm they cause, and because of the long-term negative effects of these weapons on people and the environment.

Walzer reminds us that the war in Vietnam was unjust to begin with and that it was fought unjustly. With regard to colonial wars that must contend with popular guerrilla forces, Walzer concludes:

The war cannot be won, and it should not be won. It cannot be won, because the only available strategy involves a war against civilians; and it should not be won, because the degree of civilian support that rules out alternative strategies also makes the guerrillas the legitimate rulers of the country. The struggle against them is an unjust struggle as well as one that can only be carried on unjustly.[10]

Vietnam appears to give us a reason to believe that deliberative democracy can have an effect in controlling war. Eventually, the will of the American people turned against this war—in part because citizens became aware of both the injustice of the cause and the atrocious nature of the means that were being employed. Walzer's conclusion is that antiwar protesters were in the right and the American people in general had a responsibility to rise up in protest against the war. I will turn to this in more detail in a moment. However, we must remember that protests against the Vietnam War were painful events for the American polity. More importantly, it took many long years for the protests against the war in Vietnam to have the effect of ending the war. Long before Vietnam, Anscombe worried about the ineffectual nature of citizenship in her essay, "Mr. Truman's Degree." She says that "protests by people who have not power are a waste of time." This is why she claims that she must speak out as an intellectual who has some power to shape public opinion. Despite this warning, the Vietnam era provides a hopeful example of how mass protests by the people can produce change. Nonetheless, it is true that by the time these protests became effective, significant damage had already been done; nearly sixty thousand Americans had died, and millions of Vietnamese had been killed.

The case of Vietnam leads us to two other conclusions.

3. The protests of the people can be instrumental in ending a war, and these protests can be based on principled objections to war that make use of the just war theory.
4. These protests will, however, take a long time to be effective, and their effect will come too late to avoid significant harm.

THE IRAQ WAR

All four of the above conclusions can be found in the case of the American invasion and occupation of Iraq. But I want to focus on an even more important point that comes to the fore in considering the war in Iraq: the slippery nature of the just cause for war. The war in Iraq was justified in public as a response to a just cause according to the standards of the just war theory. The primary rationale—about Iraq's weapons of mass destruction—appealed to the idea of preemptive war that is found in the just war tradition. Although the American policy of preemptive war expands the traditional notion in light of the nature of the terrorist threat, it is important to remember that just war theory (and international law) does allow for preemption as discussed in chapter 6. The secondary rationale for the war—the removal of a tyrant and the pursuit of democracy—also fits with the just war idea of humanitarian intervention. And indeed, it coheres well with the values of democratic politics, as discussed in chapter 8.

The debacle in Iraq shows us that the idea of a just cause can be manipulated by politicians. We saw this also in Vietnam. But more significantly, the Iraq war reminds us that serious and honest people can disagree about whether there is a just cause for war (see, for example, the prowar ideas of Elshtain, Weigel, Johnson, and other defenders of the just war tradition). One of the main reasons for this is that we lack information and expertise that can help us evaluate threats. Indeed, the Iraq war reminds us that intelligence experts themselves disagree about the nature of threats. It also shows us how intelligence can be manipulated for political purposes. Moreover, when it comes to making decisions about some of the other principles of *jus ad bellum*, it seems that there is no way to guarantee reasoned consensus. For example, the question of whether war is a last resort is disputable: some will claim that all reasonable nonviolent methods of resolving a conflict have been employed and that war is unavoidable; others will counsel patience and advocate more and better use of nonviolent methods. Another example has to do with the question of proportionality. Judgments about whether war is a proportional response to a threat require significant knowledge and expertise. And even the experts disagree, in part, because judgments about proportionality are based on speculation about present threats and future outcomes.

When we connect all of this with political reality and the use of propaganda and rhetoric, it becomes apparent that it is quite difficult for ordinary citizens to make good judgments about war. When President Bush issued his claims about the need for war, Americans trusted him and his judgment. Americans wanted to believe that the war in Iraq was a way of taking the war on terrorism to the enemy: a way of fighting them there so we wouldn't have to fight them here, as President Bush has been fond of saying. But as we have learned, this trust in the president was misplaced and the president's judgment was poor. The Iraq war leaves us with two other conclusions.

5. The people lack adequate information and expertise to make good judgments about the just cause of war.
6. The people are also often misinformed and manipulated by rhetoric, propaganda, and the mistaken judgments of their leaders.

This brief discussion of the recent history of American war making should leave us with a conclusion that is skeptical of the assumptions of the myth of the democratic peace theory. Let me bring my conclusions together here:

1. Democratic nations that fight wars for good democratic reasons can end up violating the principles of *jus in bello* as they fight.
2. Democratic nations will violate these principles because democratic politics requires quick victories at low cost to the nation.
3. The protests of the people can be instrumental in ending a war, and these protests can be based on principled objections to war that make use of the just war theory.
4. These protests will, however, take a long time to be effective, and their effect will come too late to avoid significant harm.
5. The people lack adequate information and expertise to make good judgments about the just cause of war.
6. The people are also often misinformed and manipulated by rhetoric, propaganda, and the mistaken judgments of their leaders.

These conclusions should make us skeptical of an unduly hopeful interpretation of the democratic peace theory. However, we cannot despair and simply give up on democracy. Rather, the only justifiable solution to this problem is more and better democracy. Democracy must be combined with serious and sustained criticism of the myths of political life including the myth of the just war. Other solutions to the problem of war rely on more authoritarian forms of government such as were envisioned by Plato, and these alternative solutions come with their own sets of problems.

DEMOCRACY AND SHARED RESPONSIBILITY

There are a variety of ways to improve the nature and effectiveness of democratic deliberation. One important idea is to increase citizens' sense of their *shared responsibility*. All citizens of a democracy bear some responsibility for wars that are fought in their names, even though there are different degrees of responsibility based on the social division of labor. Shared responsibility implicates citizens who support the war effort either explicitly or implicitly through the electoral process. This notion of shared responsibility can be distinguished from a more traditional and authoritarian idea of what might be called *concentrated responsibility*, which concentrates responsibility at the top of the chain of command. This view can also be distinguished from a notion of *diffused responsibility*, through which those who authorize war divorce themselves from responsibility for the misdeeds of the soldiers who fight in their names. These ideas are introduced in chapter 9. My thesis here is that if we increased our sense of shared responsibility, the hope of democratic citizenship would be made more effective.

Concentrated responsibility holds that those at the top of the chain of command are ultimately responsible for decisions about war. This idea fits better with authoritarian regimes in which power and responsibility are concentrated at the top. While power and responsibility are inevitably concentrated in the hands of some members of a democratic polity—in the president, for example—democratic politics assumes that those sites of concentrated power are still accountable to the people. It is true that the president of the United States is the commander in chief (and "the buck stops" there). But the president is elected by the people. And he remains accountable to the people. This accountability occurs through formal processes such as elections and, in extreme cases, impeachment. But it also occurs through less formal deliberative procedures. As a member of a democratic polity, the president must provide public justification for his decisions and he must respond to public criticism. Thus, even though some power and responsibility are concentrated at the top, in a democracy there is also shared responsibility for decisions that are made at the top.

Diffused responsibility holds that war making is done by those functionaries who are hired for that purpose. This idea fits best with a mercenary army or perhaps with Plato's idea of a timocratic regime. With regard to a mercenary force, the polity hires an army and gives the army the power to accomplish its tasks (i.e., it "leaves it up to the professionals"). Those who focus on diffused responsibility may claim that "we" (the people) have no control over the army, especially once the army is set off on some task. However, it is impossible to completely free the polity of responsibility for the misdeeds of its army. In fact, in a democracy, the army is usually made up of citizen-soldiers and it is regulated by laws that have democratic legitimacy. Generally, democracies will assert civilian control over the military.[11] In other words, the army remains accountable to the people, and elected civilian authorities are supposed to have the final authority over military decisions. Thus a democratic nation's army "fights in our names." Moreover, in a democracy, professional soldiers remain for the most part co-citizens who themselves retain the capacity to vote on and deliberate about military decisions.

So we should understand war fighting in a democracy by using the idea of shared responsibility. This idea has much in common with Michael Walzer's discussion of collective responsibility in *Just and Unjust Wars* (chapter 18). Walzer discusses various ways in which we might ascribe blame for unjust wars. For example, in light of some of the decisions at the Nuremberg tribunals, Walzer recognizes that blame can be located at the top of the chain of command. But he also acknowledges that responsibility permeates a polity, especially in a democracy. At the very least, citizens have a shared sense of their collective responsibility that can be found in the shame that citizens might feel with regard to the actions of their nation. At a more extreme level, citizens can feel a sort of metaphysical guilt in which we blame ourselves (and all of our co-citizens) for immoral wars.

Walzer indicates that in general each member of a democracy shares some burden of guilt and responsibility for wars that are fought in our names. Those who vote in favor of war policies and who actively support the war effort have more responsibility. But those who attempt to stay neutral and avoid the subject also have a kind of responsibility. It seems that only those who actively fight against an unjust war can be excused. The danger is, however, that this can require significant risks: the risks of conscientious objection, civil disobedience, and in exceptional cases the risk that comes from betraying one's country. Walzer concludes by accentuating the moral demand placed on each citizen when his nation fights an unjust war: "He must do all he can short of accepting frightening risks, to prevent or stop the war."[12]

This is quite a demanding position. If one is not actively fighting against an unjust war, then one shares a kind of responsibility, shame, and guilt for the war. While it is true that ordinary citizens should not be punished for complicity in an unjust war, they should at least suffer from pangs of conscience.

With this in mind, let me conclude this section by turning directly to a proposal for how shared responsibility should work. We should each take seriously our nation's warring activities. This means that we should actively and publicly question and deliberate. And when it is apparent that a war is unjust, we must speak out. We do this not only because it is an abstract duty of citizenship. We do it also because of solidarity with those who have a more substantial burden, especially the soldiers who fight in our names. These soldiers are our friends, relatives, and co-citizens. We want to be sure that when we authorize them to kill and be killed, we do so for just reasons.

If democratic citizens took this ideal of shared responsibility seriously, there would be more and better deliberation about military decisions. It is easy to hide sloth, self-interest, and ignorance behind the claim that responsibility is concentrated in the hands of the politicians or behind the claim that responsibility ultimately rests only on those who fight. But in a democracy, we each have a say in the decisions of the whole. We each share this responsibility equally. Deliberative democracy will be improved when we are more serious about what is at stake for each of us according to this ideal of shared responsibility.

CONCLUSION

Let us return for a moment to the discussion of Truman's decision to drop the bombs on Japan. As mentioned, there was political pressure that led to this decision. One wonders, however, if a better-educated and more virtuous polity would be able to avoid this sort of pressure. If citizens understood their shared responsibility for war and if they better understood the principles of morality in war, perhaps they would demand that their leaders make more just decisions about warfare. The case of Vietnam can be looked at to see that engaged citizenship informed by just war principles can be effective. But Vietnam also reminds us that this sort of process takes a long while to be effective. Moreover, the risk remains—as we saw in the case of Iraq—that just war principles and the information that is needed to apply them can be manipulated for political purposes.

While there are reasons for pessimism about the democratic peace theory, the hope is that there would be fewer wars and that wars would be fought more justly if citizens took their responsibility seriously and if institutions of deliberative democracy allowed for citizens to assert their responsibility. This ideal is contrasted with the present state of affairs in which citizens often abdicate their responsibility for wars fought in their names. This occurs because citizens are not properly educated about the responsibilities of citizenship and because citizens easily succumb to political myths such as the just war myth. In mass societies it is easy for citizens simply to give up and give in to the decisions of authorities. Sometimes this happens when authorities encourage blind obedience and patriotism. But acquiescence is a failure of citizenship. We must not give up our responsibility.

Citizens need better education about the responsibilities of citizenship. This holds true for all of the decisions that a deliberative democracy must make. But decisions about war are among the most momentous decisions that a polity can make. Thus it is even more important to remember the obligations and virtues of democratic citizenship during wartime. The virtues of citizenship include honesty, modesty, charity, tolerance, and integrity.[13] During wartime there is great pressure for citizens to give up these virtues. During wartime some appear to think that the virtues of deliberative citizenship should be replaced by other virtues such as obedience, conformity, and respect for authority. But we have seen that democracies can end up violating just war principles. Thus there is no good reason for democratic citizens to acquiesce to authority and give up on the deliberative project. There is no good reason for citizens not to cultivate the virtues of citizenship and to question the myths and lies that are used to lead us into immoral actions.

Of course, there is no single solution to the problem of war. I strongly support, for example, developing international institutions that can make wars more infrequent. But these institutions will be fruitless unless nations develop more vigorous institutions of deliberative democracy and unless citizens develop the sorts of virtues mentioned here while also vigorously taking up the obligations of citizenship. Deliberative democracy does not promise an end to war or even an end to unjust war. Human beings are fallible and there is no final solution to the problem of war. However, the deliberative model provides the best hope for progress toward justice and peace. The obligation to develop more and better democracy rests heavily on the United States, the de facto global hegemon. Moreover, citizens of the United States have a similarly unique obligation to assume the burden of shared responsibility, to develop virtues of citizenship, to educate themselves about the just war myth, and to work to ensure that war remains within moral limits.

NOTES

1. John Rawls, *The Law of Peoples* (Cambridge: Harvard University Press, 1999), 47.
2. See Michael Doyle, *Ways of War and Peace* (New York: Norton, 1997); Rawls, *Law of Peoples*; R. J. Rummel, *Power Kills: Democracy as a Method of Nonviolence* (New Brunswick, NJ: Transaction, 1997); or Spencer R. Weart, *Never at War: Why Democracies Will Not Fight One Another* (New Haven, CT: Yale University Press, 1998).
3. Weart, *Never at War*, 19.
4. Joshua Cohen, "Deliberation and Democratic Legitimacy," in *Contemporary Political Philosophy*, 2nd ed., ed. Robert E. Goodin and Philip Pettit (Malden, MA: Blackwell, 2006), 161.
5. Rummel, *Power Kills*, 101.
6. David E. Spiro, "The Insignificance of the Liberal Peace," *International Security* 19, no. 2 (Fall 1994): 80.
7. Amy Gutmann and Dennis Thompson, *Why Deliberative Democracy?* (Princeton, NJ: Princeton University Press, 2004), 41.
8 Carl Lesnor, "The Good War," *Philosophical Forum* 36, no. 1 (Spring 2005).
9. Robert H. Ferrell, ed., *Truman and the Bomb*, chap. 19. Harry Truman Online Library, at www.trumanlibrary.org/whistlestop/study_collections/bomb/ferrell_book/ferrell_book_chap19.htm.
10. Michael Walzer, *Just and Unjust Wars* (New York: Basic Books, 1977), 195–96.
11. See Samuel P. Huntington, *The Soldier and the State* (Cambridge, MA: Harvard University Press, 1959).
12. Walzer, *Just and Unjust Wars*, 301.
13. Cf. Robert Talisse, *Democracy After Liberalism: Pragmatism and Deliberative Democracy* (New York: Routledge, 2005), 112–13.

Works Cited

Ajami, Fouad. "The Autumn of the Autocrats." *Foreign Affairs*, May/June 2005.

Allhoff, Fritz. "Terrorism and Torture." In Shanahan, *Philosophy 9/11 Thinking about the War on Terrorism*.

Anderson, Benedict. *Imagined Communities*. London: Verso, 1983.

Anscombe, G. E. M. *Ethics, Religion, and Politics*. Minneapolis: University of Minnesota Press, 1981.

Aquinas, Thomas. *Summa Theologica*. In May, Rovie, and Viner, *The Morality of War*.

Arend, Anthony Clark. "International Law and the Preemptive Use of Military Force." *Washington Quarterly* 26, no. 2 (Spring 2003): 89–103.

Arendt, Hannah. *Eichmann in Jerusalem*. New York: Viking Penguin, 1963.

Armstrong, Karen. *Holy War*. New York: Anchor Books, 2001.

Augsburger, Myron S. "Christian Pacifism." In Clouse, *War: Four Christian Views*.

Augustine. *Reply to Faustus the Manichaean*. At www.newadvent.org/fathers/1406.htm.

Averroes, "Jihad." In May, Rovie, and Viner, *The Morality of War*.

Bacevich, Andrew. *American Empire: The Realities and Consequences of U.S. Diplomacy*. Cambridge, MA: Harvard University Press, 2002.

Bass, Gary J. "Jus Post Bellum." *Philosophy and Public Affairs* 32, no. 4 (October 2004): 384–412.

Baur, Michael. "What Is Distinctive about Terrorism, and What Are the Philosophical Implications?" In Shanahan, *Philosophy 9/11: Thinking about the War on Terrorism*.

Bell, Daniel M., Jr. "Just War Engaged: Review Essay of Walzer and O'Donovan." *Modern Theology* 22, no. 2 (April 2006).

Bell, David A. *The First Total War: Napoleon's Europe and the Birth of Warfare as We Know It.* New York: Houghton Mifflin, 2007.

Bellamy, Alex J. "Supreme Emergencies and the Protection of Non-Combatants in War." *International Affairs* 80, no. 5 (2004): 829–50.

Benhabib, Seyla. "Toward a Deliberative Model of Democratic Legitimacy." In *Democracy and Difference: Contesting the Boundaries of the Political,* edited by Seyla Benhabib. Princeton, NJ: Princeton University Press, 1996.

Benjamin, Martin. "Pacifism for Pragmatists." *Ethics* 83, no. 3 (1973): 196–213.

Berdyaev, Nikolai. *Slavery and Freedom.* New York: Scribner's, 1944.

Berman, Paul. *Terror and Liberalism.* New York: Norton, 2003.

Bernard of Clairvaux. "Holy War." In Holmes, *War and Christian Ethics.*

Bess, Michael. *Choices under Fire.* New York: Knopf, 2006.

Boggs, Carl. *Imperial Delusions: American Militarism and Endless War.* Lanham, MD: Rowman & Littlefield, 2005.

Boot, Max. "The Bush Doctrine Lives." *Weekly Standard,* February 16, 2004.

Brandt, Richard. "Utilitarianism and the Rules of War." In May, Rovie, and Viner, *The Morality of War.*

Brough, Michael W. "Combatant, Noncombatant, Criminal." *Ethical Perspectives* 11, no. 2–3 (2004): 176–88.

——. "Legitimate Combatancy, POW Status, and Terrorism." In Shanahan, *Philosophy 9/11: Thinking about the War on Terrorism.*

Bush, George W. Speeches and policy statements. At www.whitehouse.gov.

Cady, Duane L. *From Warism to Pacifism.* Philadelphia: Temple University Press, 1989.

Cady, Duane L., and Robert Phillips, *Humanitarian Intervention.* Lanham, MD: Rowman & Littlefield, 1996.

Calhoun, Laurie. "Killing, Letting Die, and the Alleged Necessity of Military Intervention." *Peace and Conflict Studies* 8, no. 2 (November 2001).

Calvin, John. "Civil Authority and the Use of Force," from *Institutes of the Christian Religion.* In Holmes, *War and Christian Ethics.*

Casebeer, William. "Torture Interrogation of Terrorists: A Theory of Exceptions (with Notes, Cautions, and Warnings)." In Shanahan, *Philosophy 9/11: Thinking about the War on Terrorism.*

Charles, J. Daryl. *Between Pacifism and Jihad.* Downer's Grove, IL: Intervarsity, 2005.

Chomsky, Noam. *Hegemony of Survival: America's Quest for Global Dominance.* New York: Henry Holt, 2004.

Clausewitz, Carl von. "On the Art of War." In May, Rovie, and Viner, *The Morality of War.* Clouse, Robert G., ed., *War: Four Christian Views.* Downers Grove, IL: Intervarsity, 1981.

Cohen, Joshua. "Deliberation and Democratic Legitimacy." In *Contemporary Political Philosophy.* 2nd ed., edited by Robert E. Goodin and Philip Pettit. Malden, MA: Blackwell, 2006.

Cole, Darrell. "Good Wars." *First Things* 116 (October 2001): 27–31.

———. *When God Says War Is Right: The Christian's Perspective on When and How to Fight.* Colorado Springs, CO: Waterbrook Press, 2002.

Dalai Lama. "A Human Approach to World Peace." At www.dalailama.com/page.62.htm.

Danner, Mark. "The Logic of Torture." *New York Review of Books* 51, no. 11 (June 24, 2004).

———. "The Truth about Torture." *New York Review of Books* 51, no. 10 (June 10, 2004).

Dawkins, Richard. *The Selfish Gene.* Oxford: Oxford University Press, 1989.

de Wijze, Stephen. "Tragic-Remorse—the Anguish of Dirty Hands." *Ethical Theory and Moral Practice* 7 (2004).

Dershowitz, Alan. *Shouting Fire: Civil Liberties in a Turbulent Age.* New York: Little, Brown, 2002.

Dewey, John. "Democratic Ends Require Democratic Methods for Their Realization." In *John Dewey: Later Works*, vol. 14. Carbondale: Southern Illinois University Press, 1981.

Dombrowski, Daniel A. "Rawls and War." *International Journal of Applied Philosophy* 16, no. 2 (Fall 2002).

Doyle, Michael. *Ways of War and Peace.* New York: Norton, 1997.

Elshtain, Jean Bethke. *Just War against Terror.* New York: Basic Books, 2003.

Ferrell, Robert H., ed., *Truman and the Bomb.* Harry Truman Online Library. At www.trumanlibrary.org/whistlestop/study_collections/bomb/ferrell_book/ferrell_book_chap19.htm.

Fiala, Andrew. "Citizenship, Epistemology, and the Just War Theory." *Logos: A Journal of Catholic Thought and Culture* 7, no. 2 (April 2004).

———. "Defusing Fear: A Critical Response to the War on Terrorism." In Shanahan, *Philosophy 9/11: Thinking about the War on Terrorism.*

———. "Pacifism." In *Stanford Encyclopedia of Philosophy.* 2006. At plato.stanford.edu/entries/pacifism/.

———. *The Philosopher's Voice.* Albany: SUNY Press, 2002.

———. *Practical Pacifism.* New York: Algora Press, 2004.

———. "Practical Pacifism after the War in Iraq." *Journal for the Study of Peace and Conflict* (Wisconsin Peace and Conflict Studies), 2004–2005.

———. "Terrorism and the Philosophy of History: Liberalism, Realism, and the Supreme Emergency Exemption." Special issue, *Essays in Philosophy* 3 (April 2002). At www.sorrel.humboldt.edu/~essays/fiala.html.

———. "The Vanity of Temporal Things: Hegel and the Ethics of War." *Studies in the History of Ethics*, February 2006.

———. *What Would Jesus Really Do?* Lanham, MD: Rowman & Littlefield, 2007.

Fischer, John Martin, Mark Ravizza, and David Copp, "Quinn on Double Effect: The Problem of 'Closeness.'" *Ethics* 103, no. 4 (1993).

Foot, Philippa. "The Problem of Abortion and the Doctrine of the Double Effect." *Oxford Review* 5 (1967). Reprinted in Foot, *Virtues and Vices and Other Essays in Moral Philosophy*. Berkeley: University of California Press, 1978.

Foucault, Michel. *Society Must be Defended: Lectures at the Collège de France, 1975–76*. New York: Picador, 2003.

Fukuyama, Francis. *America at the Crossroads: Democracy, Power, and the Neoconservative Legacy*. New Haven, CT: Yale University Press, 2006.

———. *The End of History and the Last Man*. New York: Free Press, 1991.

———. "The Neoconservative Moment." *National Interest*, Summer 2004.

Fullinwider, Robert K. "Terrorism, Innocence, and War." In *War after September 11*, edited by Verna V. Gehring. Lanham, MD: Rowman & Littlefield, 2003.

Gaddis, John Lewis. "A Grand Strategy of Transformation." *Foreign Policy*, November/December 2002.

Gandhi, Mohandas K. *Autobiography: The Story of My Experiments with Truth*. Boston: Beacon Press, 1993.

Gehring, Verna V., ed., *War after September 11*. Lanham, MD: Rowman & Littlefield, 2003.

Glover, Jonathan. *Causing Death and Saving Lives*. New York: Penguin, 1977.

———. *Humanity: A Moral History of the 20th Century*. New Haven, CT: Yale University Press, 2000.

Gracian, Baltasar. *The Art of Worldly Wisdom*. London: Macmillan, 1892.

Greenwood, Christopher. "International Law and the Pre-emptive Use of Force: Afghanistan, Al-Qaeda, and Iraq." *San Diego International Law Journal* 4 (2003): 7–37.

Grotius, Hugo. *The Law of War and Peace*. Indianapolis: Bobbs-Merrill, 1925. Selections reprinted in May, Rovie, and Viner, *The Morality of War*.

Gutmann, Amy, and Dennis Thompson. *Why Deliberative Democracy?* Princeton, NJ: Princeton University Press, 2004.

Hammond, John L. "The Bush Doctrine, Preventive War, and International Law." *Philosophical Forum* 36, no. 1 (March 2005): 97–112.

Hauerwas, Stanley. *The Peaceable Kingdom*. Notre Dame, IN: Notre Dame University Press, 1983.

———. *Performing the Faith: Bonhoeffer and the Practice of Nonviolence*. Grand Rapids, MI: Brazos, 2004.

———. *Should War Be Eliminated?* Milwaukee, WI: Marquette University Press, 1984.

Hedges, Chris. *War Is a Force That Gives Us Meaning*. New York: Public Affairs, 2002.

Hegel, G. W. F. *Phenomenology of Spirit*. Oxford: Oxford University Press, 1977.

———. *Philosophy of Right*. Cambridge: Cambridge University Press, 1991.

Heisbourg, François. "A Work in Progress: The Bush Doctrine and Its Consequences." *Washington Quarterly* 26, no. 2 (Spring 2003): 75–88.

Held, Virginia. "Violence, Terrorism, and Moral Inquiry." *Monist* 67, no. 4 (October 1984).

Hersh, Seymour M. *Chain of Command: The Road from 9/11 to Abu Ghraib.* New York: HarperCollins, 2004.

Holmes, Arthur F., ed. *War and Christian Ethics.* 2nd ed. Grand Rapids, MI: Baker Academic, 2005.

Holmes, Robert. "Pacifism for Nonpacifists." *Journal of Social Philosophy* 30, no. 3 (Winter 1999): 387–400.

Holmes, Robert. *On War and Morality.* Princeton, NJ: Princeton University Press, 1989.

Hooker, Brad. "Ross-Style Pluralism versus Rule-Consequentialism." *Mind*, n.s., 105, no. 420 (1996): 531–52.

Hoyt, Herman A. "Nonresistance." In Clouse, *War: Four Christian Views.*

Human Rights Watch. "Off Target." 2003. At www.hrw.org/reports/2003/usa1203/.

Huntington, Samuel P. *The Soldier and the State.* Cambridge, MA: Harvard University Press, 1959.

Hymers, John. "Regrounding the Just War's 'Presumption against Violence' in Light of George Weigel." *Ethical Perspectives* 11, no. 2–3 (2004).

Ignatieff, Michael. "The Burden." *New York Times Magazine*, January 5, 2003.

———. *The Lesser Evil.* Princeton, NJ: Princeton University Press, 2004.

Jeffreys, Derek. "Eliminating All Empathy: Personalism and the 'War on Terror.'" *Logos: A Journal of Catholic Thought and Culture* 9, no. 3 (2004): 16–44.

Jervis, Robert. "Understanding the Bush Doctrine." *Political Science Quarterly* 118, no. 3 (2003): 365–88.

———. "Why the Bush Doctrine Cannot Be Sustained." *Political Science Quarterly* 120, no. 3 (2005): 351–77.

John Paul II, Pope. "World Peace Day Address" (January 1, 2004). At www.vatican.va/holy_father/john_paul_ii/messages/peace/documents/hf_jp-ii_mes_20031216_xxxvii-world-day-for-peace_en.html.

Johnson, Chalmers. "Republic or Empire." *Harper's Magazine*, January 2007.

———. *The Sorrows of Empire.* New York: Henry Holt, 2004.

Johnson, James Turner. *Just War Tradition and the Restraint of War.* Princeton, NJ: Princeton University Press, 1981.

———. *The War to Oust Saddam Hussein: Just War and the New Face of Conflict.* Lanham, MD: Rowman & Littlefield, 2005.

Johnson, James Turner, Jean Bethke Elshtain, and Stanley Hauerwas. "Just War Tradition and the New War on Terrorism." Pew Forum on Religion and Public Life Discussion, 2001. At www.pewforum.org.

Judgment of the International Military Tribunal for the Trial of German Major War Criminals. At www.yale.edu/lawweb/avalon/imt/proc/judlawch.htm.

Kamm, F. M. "Failures of Just War Theory: Terror, Harm, and Justice." *Ethics* 114 (July 2004): 650–92.

Kant, Immanuel. *Perpetual Peace*. In *Kant: Political Writings*. Cambridge: Cambridge University Press, 1991. Also in May, Rovie, and Viner, *The Morality of War*.

Kekes, John. *Against Liberalism*. Ithaca, NY: Cornell University Press, 1997.

———. *A Case for Conservatism*. Ithaca, NY: Cornell University Press, 1998.

King, Martin Luther, Jr. *A Testament of Hope: The Essential Writings of Martin Luther King Jr.* Edited by James Melvin Washington. San Francisco: Harper and Row, 1986.

Kohn, Richard H. "The Erosion of Civilian Control of the Military in the United States Today." *Naval War College Review* 15, no. 3 (Summer 2002). At www.nwc.navy.mil/press/Review/2002/summer/pdf/art1-su2.pdf.

———. "How Democracies Control the Military." *Journal of Democracy* 8, no. 4 (1997).

Krauthammer, Charles. "Democratic Realism: An American Foreign Policy for a Unipolar World" Irving Kristol Lecture at the American Enterprise Institute, 2004.

———. "The Neoconservative Convergence." *Commentary* 120, no. 1 (July–August 2005).

Kraynak, Robert. *Christian Faith and Modern Democracy*. Notre Dame, IN: Notre Dame University Press, 2001.

Kristol, Irving. "The Neoconservative Persuasion." *Weekly Standard* 8, no. 47 (August 25, 2003).

Lesnor, Carl. "The 'Good' War." *Philosophical Forum* 36, no.1 (Spring 2005).

Locke, John. *A Letter Concerning Toleration*. In *Classics of Modern Political Theory*, edited by Steven M. Cahn. Oxford: Oxford University Press, 1997.

Luban, David. "Preventive War." *Philosophy and Public Affairs* 32, no. 3 (July 2004): 207–48.

———. "The Romance of the Nation-State." In May, Rovie, and Viner, *The Morality of War*.

Lucas, George. "From Jus ad bellum to Jus ad pacem." In May, Rovie, and Viner, *The Morality of War*.

Mavrodes, George. "Conventions and the Morality of War." In May, Rovie, and Viner, *The Morality of War*.

May, Larry. "Superior Orders, Duress, and Moral Perception." In May, Rovie, and Viner, *The Morality of War*.

May, Larry, Eric Rovie, and Steve Viner, eds. *The Morality of War*. Upper Saddle River, NJ: Prentice Hall, 2006.

McCarthy, David. "Rights, Explanations, and Risks." *Ethics* 107, no. 2 (1997): 205–25.

McIntyre, Alison. "Doing Away with Double Effect." *Ethics* 111 (2001).

McMahan, Jeff. "The Ethics of Killing in War." *Ethics* 114 (2004): 693–733.

Mead, Walter Russell. *Power, Terror, Peace, and War: America's Grand Strategy in a World at Risk.* New York: Vintage/Random House, 2005.

Merry, Robert W. *Sands of Empire: Missionary Zeal, American Foreign Policy, and the Hazards of Global Ambition.* New York: Simon & Schuster, 2005.

Merton, Thomas. *Thomas Merton on Peace.* New York: McCall, 1971.

Miller, Richard B. *Interpretations of Conflict.* Chicago: University of Chicago Press, 1991.

Monten, Jonathan. "The Roots of the Bush Doctrine: Power, Nationalism, and Democratic Promotion in U.S. Strategy." *International Security* 29, no. 4 (2005): 112–56.

Montesquieu, Baron Charles de. *The Spirit of the Laws.* Cambridge: Cambridge University Press, 1989.

Nagel, Thomas. "War and Massacre." In May, Rovie, and Viner, *The Morality of War.*

Narveson, Jan. "Is Pacifism Consistent?" *Ethics* 78, no. 2 (1968): 148–50.

———. "Pacifism: A Philosophical Analysis." *Ethics* 75, no. 4 (1965): 259–71.

———. "Terrorism and Pacifism: Why We Should Condemn Both." *International Journal of Applied Ethics* 17, no. 2 (2003): 157–72.

Nielsen, "Against Moral Conservatism." *Ethics* 82, no. 3 (1972): 219–31.

Northcutt, Michael S. *An Angel Directs the Storm.* London: I. B. Tauris, 2004.

Norvin, Richard. "Double Effect and Moral Character." *Mind*, n.s., 93, no. 371 (1984): 381–97.

Nye, Joseph S. *The Paradox of American Power: Why the World's Only Superpower Can't Go It Alone.* Oxford: Oxford University Press, 2002.

O'Donovan, Oliver. *The Just War Revisited.* Cambridge: Cambridge University Press, 2003.

Orend, Brian *Human Rights: Concept and Context.* Orchard Park, NY: Broadview Press, 2002.

———. "Jus Post Bellum." *Journal of Social Philosophy* 31, no. 1 (Spring 2000): 117–37.

———. "War." In *Stanford Encyclopedia of Philosophy.* At plato.stanford.edu/entries/war.

Pavlischek, Keith. "Just and Unjust War in the Terrorist Age." *Intercollegiate Review*, Spring 2002.

Popper, Karl. *The Open Society and Its Enemies.* Princeton, NJ: Princeton University Press, 1971.

Quinn, Warren S. "Actions, Intentions, and Consequences: The Doctrine of Double Effect." *Philosophy and Public Affairs* 18, no. 4 (Fall 1989): 334–51.

Ramsey, Paul. *The Just War.* New York: Charles Scribner's Sons, 1968.

———. *War and the Christian Conscience.* Raleigh, NC: Duke University Press, 1961.

Rawls, John. "Fifty Years after Hiroshima." In *Collected Papers.* Cambridge, MA: Harvard University Press, 1999.

———. *The Law of Peoples*. Cambridge, MA: Harvard University Press, 1999.

———. *A Theory of Justice*. Cambridge, MA: Harvard University Press, 1971.

Rice, Condoleezza. "Dr. Condoleeza Rice Discusses President's National Security Strategy." October 1, 2002. At www.whitehouse.gov/newsreleases/2002/10/20021001-6.html.

Roberts, L., and G. Burnham. "Mortality before and after the 2003 Invasion of Iraq: Cluster Sample Survey." *Lancet* 364 (November 20, 2004): 1857–64.

Rockmore, Tom. "Can War Transform Iraq into a Democracy?" *Theoria* 103 (April 2004).

Ross, W. D. *The Right and the Good*. Oxford: Clarendon Press, 1930.

Rothbard, Murray. "Just War." At www.lewrockwell.com/rothbard/rothbard20.html.

Rousseau, Jean-Jacques. *The Social Contract*. In *The Social Contract and Discourse on the Origin of Inequality*. New York: Washington Square Press, 1967.

Rule, James B. "'Above All, Do No Harm': The War in Iraq and Dissent." *Dissent*, Summer 2005.

Rummel, R. J. *Power Kills: Democracy as a Method of Nonviolence*. New Brunswick, NJ: Transaction, 1997.

Russell, Bertrand. "The Ethics of War." *International Journal of Ethics* 25, no. 2 (January 1915).

———. "The Future of Pacifism." *American Scholar* 13 (Winter 1943): 7–13.

Ryan, Cheyney C. "Self-Defense, Pacifism and Rights." *Ethics* 93 (1983).

Sapiro, Miriam. "Iraq: The Shifting Sands of Preemptive Self-Defense." *American Journal of International Law* 97, no. 3 (July 2003): 599–607.

Sauer, Tom. "The Pre-Emptive and Preventive Use of Force: To Be Legitimized or to Be De-Legitimized?" *Ethical Perspectives* 11, no. 2–3 (2004): 130–43.

Scalia, Antonin. "God's Justice and Ours." *First Things* 123 (May 2002): 17–21.

Scheffler, Samuel. "Morality's Demands and Their Limits." *Journal of Philosophy* 83, no. 10 (1986): 531–36.

Schroeder, Paul W. "Iraq: The Case Against Preemptive War." *American Conservative*, October 21, 2002.

Schultz, George P. "Hot Preemption." *Hoover Digest*, no. 3 (2002).

Shanahan, Timothy, ed. *Philosophy 9/11: Thinking about the War on Terrorism*. New York: Open Court, 2005.

Sharlet, Jeff. "Through a Glass, Darkly: How the Christian Right is Reimagining American History." *Harper's Magazine*, December 2006.

Shue, Henry. "Torture." *Philosophy and Public Affairs* 7, no. 2 (1978).

Spencer R. Weart. *Never at War: Why Democracies Will Not Fight One Another*. New Haven, CT: Yale University Press, 1998.

Spiro, David E. "The Insignificance of the Liberal Peace." *International Security* 19, no. 2 (Fall 1994): 50–86.

Sterba, James. *Justice for Here and Now.* Cambridge: Cambridge University Press, 1998.

———. "The Most Morally Defensible Pacifism." In *Pazifismus: Ideengeschichte, Theorie und Praxis*, edited by Barbara Bleisch and Jean-Daniel Strub. Bern: Haupt Verlag, 2006.

———, ed. *Terrorism and International Justice.* Oxford: Oxford University Press, 2003.

———. *The Triumph of Practice over Theory in Ethics.* Oxford: Oxford University Press, 2005.

Suarez, Francisco. "On War." In May, Rovie, and Viner, *The Morality of War.*

Taft, William H., IV. "The Legal Basis for Preemption." Council on Foreign Relations Roundtable. At www.cfr.org/publication.php?id=5250#.

Talisse, Robert. *Democracy after Liberalism: Pragmatism and Deliberative Democracy.* London: Routledge, 2005.

Taylor, Mark Lewis. *Religion, Politics, and the Christian Right.* Minneapolis: Augsburg Fortress Press, 2005.

Taylor, Terence. "The End of Imminence?" *Washington Quarterly* 27, no. 4 (Autumn 2004): 57–72.

Teichman, Jenny. *Pacifism and the Just War.* Oxford: Blackwell, 1986.

Teson, Fernando. "The Liberal Case for Humanitarian Intervention." In May, Rovie, and Viner, *The Morality of War.*

Thoreau, Henry David. "On the Duty of Civil Disobedience." In May, Rovie, and Viner, *The Morality of War.*

Thucydides. *History of the Peloponnesian War.* New York: Penguin, 1954.

Tolstoy, Leo. *The Kingdom of God Is Within You* (New York: Dover, 2006).

U.S. Catholic Bishops. "The Challenge of Peace: God's Promise and Our Response." Pastoral letter, 1983.

Verstraeten, Johan. "From Just War to Ethics of Conflict Resolution: A Critique of Just-War Thinking in the Light of the War in Iraq." *Ethical Perspectives* 11, no. 2–3 (2004).

Vitoria, Francisco de. "On the Law of War." In May, Rovie, and Viner, *The Morality of War.*

Waldron, Jeremy. "Locke: Toleration and the Rationality of Persecution." In *John Locke: A Letter Concerning Toleration in Focus*, edited by John Horton and Susan Mendus. London: Routledge, 1991.

Walzer, Michael. "Political Action: The Problem of Dirty Hands." *Philosophy and Public Affairs* 2, no. 2 (Winter 1973): 160–80.

Walzer, Michael. *Arguing about War.* New Haven, CT: Yale University Press, 2004.

———. *Just and Unjust Wars.* New York: Basic Books, 1977.

———. "No Strikes." *New Republic*, September 30, 2002.

———. "Terrorism: A Critique of Excuses." In *Social Ideals and Policies*, edited by Steven Luper. Toronto: Mayfield Press, 1999.

Wasserstrom, Richard. "On the Morality of War." *Stanford Law Review* 21:1627–56. Reprinted in *Moral Problems*, edited by James Rachels. New York: Harper and Row, 1971.

Webster, Daniel. Letter to Lord Ashburton, July 27, 1842. At www.danorr.com/webstet/webster_july27_1842.htm.

Weigel, "The Just War Tradition and the World after September 11." *Logos: A Journal of Catholic Thought and Culture* 5, no. 3 (Summer 2002): 13–44.

———. "Moral Clarity in a Time of War." *First Things* 128 (January 2003): 20–27.

———. *Tranquillitas Ordinis.* Oxford: Oxford University Press, 1989.

Wilkins, Burleigh. "Humanitarian Intervention: Some Doubts." May, Rovie, and Viner, *The Morality of War.*

Wilson, Woodrow. "President Woodrow Wilson's War Message." In *War Messages*, 3–8. 65th Cong., 1st sess. Senate Doc. No. 5, Serial No. 7264. Washington, DC, 1917. At net.lib.byu.edu/~rdh7/wwi/1917/wilswarm.html.

Wolfowitz, Paul. Speech at the International Institute for Strategic Studies, December 2, 2002. At www.iiss.org.

Wrangham, Richard, and Dale Peterson. *Demonic Males: Apes and Origins of Human Violence.* New York: Houghton Mifflin, 1996.

Yoder, John Howard. *The Original Revolution.* Scottdale, PA: Herald Press, 2003.

Yoo, John. "International Law and the War in Iraq." *American Journal of International Law* 97, no. 3 (July 2003): 563–76.

Young, Iris Marion. *Inclusion and Democracy.* Oxford: Oxford University Press, 2000.

Index

Weart, Spencer, 179, 180
Webster, Daniel, 82, 92
Weigel, George, 24, 45, 50; on in
  bello principles, 146, 149
Weil, Simone, 56
Wijze, Stephen de, 115
Wilson, Woodrow, 59, 61, 68
Winthrop, John, 59, 61
Wolfowitz, Paul, 82
World War I, 5, 59, 178

World War II, 5, 6, 19, 23, 57; and
  American Exceptionalism, 60–63,
  71; and supreme emergency,
  104–105, 148; and
  neoconservatism, 132; and citizen
  vigilance, 146; and American just
  war violations, 184–86

Yoder, John Howard, 33, 51
Yugoslavia, 57

About the Author

Andrew Fiala is associate professor of philosophy at California State University, Fresno, and director of the Ethics Center at Fresno State. He is the author of *The Philosopher's Voice, Practical Pacifism , Tolerance and the Ethical Life, and What Would Jesus Really Do?* Fiala is also co-editor of the journal, *Philosophy in the Contemporary World.* For more information: www.andrewfiala.com.